BROOKLYN'S PROMISED LAND

Brooklyn's Promised Land

The Free Black Community of Weeksville, New York

Judith Wellman

NEW YORK UNIVERSITY PRESS
New York and London

NEW YORK UNIVERSITY PRESS
New York and London
www.nyupress.org

References to Internet websites (URLs) were accurate at the time of writing.
Neither the author nor New York University Press is responsible for URLs that
may have expired or changed since the manuscript was prepared.

Library of Congress Cataloging-in-Publication Data
Wellman, Judith.
Brooklyn's promised land : the free black community of Weeksville, New York /
Judith Wellman.
pages cm   Includes bibliographical references and index.
ISBN 978-0-8147-2415-6 (cl : alk. paper)
1. Weeksville (New York, N.Y.)—History. 2. Brooklyn (New York, N.Y.)—History.
3. New York (N.Y.)—History. 4. African Americans—New York (State)—
New York—History. I. Title.
F128.68.W43W45 2014
974.7'23--dc23   2014020829

New York University Press books are printed on acid-free paper,
and their binding materials are chosen for strength and durability.
We strive to use environmentally responsible suppliers and materials
to the greatest extent possible in publishing our books.

Manufactured in the United States of America

10 9 8 7 6 5 4 3 2 1

Also available as an ebook

To the people of Weeksville

past,
present, and
future;

to Joan Maynard, whose light still shines;

and to all those who carry on the dream
of independence, freedom, and respect
for African Americans
and all people everywhere.

CONTENTS

Maps appear as an insert following page 136.

LIST OF ILLUSTRATIONS

MAPS (AS AN INSERT FOLLOWING PAGE 136)

ACKNOWLEDGMENTS

No book emerges like Athena from the head of Zeus, without precedent, prologue, or help from many people. Thanks first and always to all the libraries and archives whose collections made this research possible, including the Dickinson College House Divided Project, Kings County Clerk's Office, Brooklyn Historical Society, Brooklyn Public Library, LaGuardia Community College, National Archives and Records Administration, National Portrait Gallery, New-York Historical Society, New York Public Library (especially the Schomburg Center for Research in Black Culture and the Lionel Pincus and Princess Firyal Map Division), New York State Library, Queens Historical Society, Syracuse Public Library, Syracuse University (Bird Library and Department of Art), and the Weeksville Heritage Center. I am deeply grateful for the help of librarians, archivists, and technicians at each of these institutions, without which this research would not have been possible.

Key online newspaper sources were also essential. These include but are not limited to the African American newspaper collection of Accessible Archives, the *Brooklyn Eagle* online through the Brooklyn Public Library, the *New York Times* online, Fultonhistory.com, Genealogy Bank, and Ancestry.com.

This project originated as a National Register nomination, funded by Save America's Treasures, for the houses now owned by the Weeksville Heritage Center. The Weeksville research team helped complete this nomination in record time, and I think we were all amazed at what we found. Thanks to Cynthia Copeland for helping to plan and carry out the research, Liz Atack for working on the bibliography of maps and deed searches, Lee French for photograph and deed searches, Victoria Huver for searching through microfilm of the *New York Age* and *New York Globe*, Barbara Lindo for finding manuscript censuses, Mark Malo-Wellman for his expertise in Adobe Photoshop, Theresa Ventura for putting census records into Excel databases, quickly and accurately (even when the handwriting seemed almost impossible to read), and Patrick Schroeder for finding pension records in the National Archives.

Thanks also to Douglas Deal, Mike Devonshire, Joan Geismar, Ann Grady, Bernard Herman, Kate Johnson, Claudia Kavanaugh, Kathleen LaFrank, Neil Larson, Harry Bradshaw Matthews, Mark Peckham, Bruce Popkin, Gretchen Sorin, and Myron Stachiw for their timely and helpful advice. Thanks to my friend Stephanie Dyer for first introducing me to Joan Maynard and the Weeksville houses in the late 1970s. Thanks also to Michael Boston, Pam Green, James Hurley, and Jennifer Scott for their careful reading of drafts of this book.

As always, my family has provided sustaining support. I remain forever grateful to my husband, Paul Malo (1930–2008), who created a world of beauty and love for all of us, filled with music, art, gardens, and a love for old buildings. My children, Mark and Amaliya, bring joy and hope for the future. And my mom, Marguerite Matteson, remains an inspiration.

Most especially, thanks to the staff and Board at the Weeksville Heritage Center, whose constant and cheerful support made this project in every way a pleasure to work on. Thank you, Pam Green, Jennifer Scott, Judith Burgess-Abiodun, Rex Curry, Megan Goins Diouf, Anna French, Radiah Harper, Clement Scantleberry, and especially Joan Maynard, whose guiding spirit shines over all.

Introduction

Brooklyn's Promised Land, Weeksville, 1835–1910

"A Model for Places of Much Greater Pretensions"

In 1910, fifty-nine-year-old Alfred W. Cornish, born in New York State and a plasterer by trade, and forty-five-year-old Frances Cornish, his wife, born in Washington, D.C., were renting a house at 1698 Bergen Street, Brooklyn, New York.[1] Alfred Cornish had lived in this general neighborhood, off and on, since at least 1870, when he returned from Civil War service in the Fifty-Fourth Massachusetts Regiment.

Little did Frances and Alfred Cornish know that in the late 1960s a coalition of students, Boy Scouts, and local citizens would rediscover and identify their home as one of four nineteenth-century houses on Hunterfly Road, part of a once-thriving African American community called Weeksville. Part of this rediscovery included a salvage operation in houses about to be demolished between Troy Avenue, Pacific Street, Schenectady Avenue, and Dean Street (now the site of Weeksville Gardens). There, behind a mantelpiece, young searchers found a tintype of what people began to call the "Weeksville Lady." This unknown woman became the image and inspiration for a major effort to preserve and restore the Hunterfly Road houses as the centerpiece of the Weeksville Heritage Center. As tangible remains of a lost world, these houses and the Weeksville Lady form a powerful physical link between past and present. This is the story of these buildings, the people who built them, and the community they represent.

By their own actions, Weeksville's residents defined what was important to them—physical safety, education, economic self-sufficiency, and political self-determination. But, as they made personal choices, the Cornish family and their Weeksville neighbors also reflected major changes in the lives of all African Americans in the nineteenth century. Weeksville's story reflects in a microcosm the story of African Americans throughout Brooklyn, the state of New York, and the nation as a whole.

In 1860, on the eve of the Civil War, almost four million African Americans lived in the United States. Close to half a million (488,070) of them lived as free people.[2] Of these free people of color, 226,152 or 46.3 percent lived in the North. In theory at least, northern free people had choices about where to live. In 1860, the majority (55.7 percent) lived in mixed-race neighborhoods in large cities (defined as places with a population of more than 10,000). Of the 44.3 percent who lived in rural areas, many lived as single families or small groups in neighborhoods dominated by European Americans. Some African Americans chose another option—to move outside the United States to Liberia, Canada, or Haiti. And a very few enterprising pioneers made yet another decision: they formed independent free black communities—a hundred or more throughout the United States. Weeksville was one of these.

While reformers such as Frederick Douglass worked for racial integration within the dominant European American culture, Weeksville's founders intentionally created in the 1830s a race-based geographically separate community, advertising land "for sale to colored people." Nestled among steep hills and valleys of the Bedford Hills in eastern Brooklyn, Weeksville was figuratively (and parts of it were literally) a city upon a hill. Whereas many Long Island communities were made up of Dutch, English, and African American families who had known each other for generations, Weeksville's population was primarily African American. Many of its residents were new to the region, coming from all over the United States (including the South), the Caribbean, Western Europe, and Africa. By the 1850s, national leaders such as Henry Highland Garnet, Rufus L. Perry, and Martin Delany consciously attempted to make Weeksville part of what Wilson Jeremiah Moses called the "golden age" of black nationalism.[3]

By almost any measure, Weeksville was a success. It was one of the two largest independent free black communities in the United States. In 1850, 366 African Americans lived in Weeksville. By 1855, its African American population had grown to 521. People generally lived in safety, supported themselves financially, educated their children (in Colored

Weeksville Lady, a tintype of an unknown woman, taken ca. 1880, discovered in 1968 during the initial archaeological dig at Weeksville. Courtesy Weeksville Heritage Center.

School No. 2, which became Public Schools 68, 83, and 243), and set up their own churches (Bethel African Methodist Episcopal, Berean Baptist, and later St. Philip's Episcopal). Many of them also took an active part in local, state, and national politics. They enjoyed an exceptional rate of property ownership (10.4 percent of the total population owned property in 1850, a far larger proportion than that of any other known African American urban community).[4]

Weeksville residents also established at least two newspapers (*Freedom's Torchlight*, the *National Monitor*, and perhaps also the *People's Journal*). They formed the Citizens' Union Cemetery, supported the Abyssinian Benevolent Daughters of Esther Association, and created a baseball team, appropriately named the Weeksville Unknowns. In 1864, Weeksville became home to the African Civilization Society, which first promoted efforts to establish a colony in Liberia and then supported work among freed people of color in the South. Howard Orphan Asylum and the Zion Home for the Aged, both located in Weeksville, served the larger African American community in Brooklyn, Long Island, and New York City. After the Civil War, Weeksville residents spearheaded a successful effort to integrate Brooklyn's public schools. P.S. 83, the direct descendent of Colored School No. 2, became the first school nationally to integrate its teaching staff along with its student body. Weeksville's orphanage, home for the aged, and school all offered professional employment opportunities for women and led the way toward the vocal leadership of African American women in the Progressive movement.

Whereas most independent black communities were rural, Weeksville was suburban, tied economically to the city of Brooklyn, with a wide variety of occupations and a relatively large proportion of skilled workers, business owners, and professionals—both women and men. Between 1865 and 1910, Germans and native-born European Americans (with a scattering of Irish, Canadian, West Indian, and Chinese immigrants) joined African Americans in Weeksville, poised at the beginning of the great migration of African Americans from the South in the nineteen teens.

Weeksville nurtured exceptional African American leaders. Junius C. Morel, principal of Colored School No. 2, was a nationally known journalist, educator, promoter of the black convention movement, and activist. Morel was born in South Carolina and lived in Weeksville from 1847 until his death in 1874. He wrote prolifically for more than thirty years for the *Colored American, North Star, Frederick Douglass' Paper,* and *Christian Recorder* (the national African Methodist Episcopal newspaper), espousing both African American independence and racial and gender integration in public schools. Susan Smith McKinney-Steward, daughter of Sylvanus Smith, an early Weeksville landowner, became one of the nation's first African American woman doctors and a contributor to Zion Home for the Aged. Her sister, Sarah Smith Tompkins Garnet, Brooklyn's first female school principal, married Henry Highland Garnet. Garnet, a nationally important African American minister, abolitionist, and activist, helped establish the headquarters of the African Civilization Society (organized first to Christianize Africa and then to send African American teachers to Freedman's schools) in Weeksville before he emigrated to Liberia. T. McCants Stewart, lawyer, Brooklyn

School Board member, and A.M.E. pastor in Weeksville, promoted the integration of Weeksville's school and also emigrated to Liberia, where he revised Liberia's legal code. Maritcha Lyons developed her career as a teacher of teachers in Weeksville's integrated school. With McKinney-Steward and Sarah Smith Garnet, Lyons became one of Brooklyn's most important female leaders, advocating equal rights for both women and African Americans.

Many scholars have written recent histories of African Americans in Manhattan and Brooklyn, but few have included references to Weeksville. Manhattan studies include Thelma Willis Foote, *Black and White Manhattan: The History of Racial Formation in Colonial New York City*; Graham Hodges, *David Ruggles: A Radical Black Abolitionist and the Underground Railroad in New York City*; Shane White, *"Somewhat More Independent": The End of Slavery in New York City, 1770–1810*; Leslie Harris, *In the Shadow of Slavery: African Americans in New York City, 1626–1863*; Leslie M. Alexander, *African or American? Black Identity and Political Activism in New York City, 1784–1861*; and Ira Berlin and Leslie Harris, *Slavery in New York*. Carla Peterson, *Black Gotham: A Family History of African Americans in Nineteenth-Century New York City*, presented a detective story that uncovers the history of her family, which includes key African American leaders in both New York and Brooklyn.[5]

A few historians have written about the history of African Americans in Brooklyn. Craig Wilder, *A Covenant with Color: Race and Social Power in Brooklyn*, covered three centuries of race relations in Brooklyn. Robert Furman incorporated a focus on slavery and abolition in *Brooklyn Heights: The Rise, Fall, and Rise of America's First Suburb*. In 2012, Prithi Kanakamedala completed a study of abolitionism and African American life in Brooklyn, *In Pursuit of Freedom*, for the National Endowment for the Humanities project of the same name, sponsored by the Brooklyn Historical Society, the Weeksville Heritage Center, and the Irondale Ensemble.[6]

Scholars who have focused on Weeksville itself found few secondary references. When James Hurley, Dolores Jackson McCullough, and Robert Swan began their research in the late 1960s and early 1970s, only two historians, both of these in the twentieth century, had mentioned Weeksville in print. In 1912, Eugene Armbruster noted that

Malboneville, Carrsville, and Weeksville were "neighborhoods in Bed-ford." In 1928, he described Weeksville and Carrsville, with some details about its institutions, as lying between Crow Hill and the Long Island Railroad. In a church bulletin published about 1930, Mardita Hardy also noted the existence of the Weeksville community. In 1977, Robert Swan published a summary of his meticulous and detailed research, based on his extensive unpublished research papers, in Charlene Claye Van Derzee, *An Introduction to the Black Contribution to the Development of Brooklyn*. James Hurley prepared an exceptional annotated bibliogra-phy in 1978. About the same time, Dolores Jackson McCullough wrote an extensive student paper on Weeksville for her degree program at the City University of New York. David Ment and Mary Donovan dealt briefly with Weeksville in 1980 in *The People of Brooklyn: A History of Two Neighborhoods*. In 1988 Joan Maynard and Gwen Cottman pub-lished *Weeksville Then & Now*, a concise summary, with photographs, of the historic village and its twentieth-century rediscovery. Archae-ologists and architectural historians (including William Cary, William Askins, Roselle Henn, Edward Chappell, Joan Geismar, Neil Larson, and others) studied the Hunterfly Road houses themselves in depth. Archaeologist Joan Geismar's work over many years deserves special mention. This book builds on this legacy of caring and careful research.[7]

If Weeksville is so important, why was its history virtually lost? The answer relates to two phenomena: First, Weeksville's physical existence was, literally, almost wiped out after the Civil War. Between 1865 and 1890, Brooklyn's exploding population and the expansion of its grid sys-tem obliterated much of the historic village of Weeksville. Developers rebuilt Weeksville, leveling its uneven terrain, straightening its streets, moving or destroying many of its houses, and bulldozing its archaeo-logical evidence. The Kingsborough public housing project in 1941 and urban renewal in the late 1960s destroyed still more of Weeksville's his-toric fabric. Except for extensive archaeological work around the Hunt-erfly Road houses, almost nothing has so far been discovered of the foundations, privies, middens, and gardens that Weeksville residents created before the Civil War.[8]

Second, manuscript sources for Weeksville were relatively few. Before the Civil War, with few exceptions, Weeksville's residents created almost no written documents. Adults in Weeksville placed a high value on education, and they sent a high proportion of their children to the local school. But many of the first generation of Weeksville's adults were themselves unable to read or write. Except for the prolific journalism of educator and journalist Junius C. Morel and scattered works by ministers, Weeksville residents produced very few written sources before the Civil War.[9]

Instead of private manuscripts, this study relies heavily on public sources: newspapers, census records, deeds, assessments, wills, city directories, and Civil War pension records. Huge advances in online access to much of this material have aided this research immensely.

Newspapers deserve special mention. Before the Civil War, newspaper coverage of Weeksville was slim, primarily because Weeksville's separatism and independence made few blips on the radar of even vocal and powerful abolitionist presses. The *Brooklyn Eagle, New York Times*, and African American newspapers (such as Frederick Douglass's *North Star, Frederick Douglass' Paper*, and the *Christian Recorder*) carried only a few references to Weeksville. Of the two (and perhaps three) newspapers published in Weeksville itself, only one issue of one of them has ever been discovered.

After the Civil War, newspapers covered Weeksville more extensively. European American presses reflected three main perspectives: (1) developers and city planners worked to expand the grid system to Brooklyn's hills; (2) public school reformers (including Junius Morel, principal of Weeksville's Colored School No. 2; T. McCants Stewart, Weeksville resident and school board member; and Rufus L. Perry, Baptist minister and editor) debated how best to incorporate Weeksville's school into the larger Brooklyn school system; and (3) social reformers, both European American and African American, dealt with problems such as poverty, family disruption, old age, and crime, forming the local roots of the national Progressive reform movement. Police reports formed a fourth perspective, reporting on crime throughout Brooklyn, including Weeksville. Unless they dealt specifically with individuals who appeared elsewhere in the Weeksville story, I have not used these crime reports, and I have made no attempt to quantify them.

Newspaper articles demand critical analysis. Mainstream reporters generally reflected the view of people in the dominant European American culture. Much of the coverage in Weeksville in the *Brooklyn*

Eagle, for example, reflected the paper's Democratic politics, decidedly unsympathetic to African American independence. Some of the *Eagle's* coverage, however, particularly after the Civil War, was relatively straightforward, covering African American events and issues much as it reported activities of other Brooklyn citizens. African American newspapers such as the *Christian Recorder* and T. Thomas Fortune's *Globe* and *New York Age* provided particularly useful details.

Weeksville's virtual disappearance changed in 1966, when James Hurley, Joseph Haynes, and students at Pratt Institute rediscovered four frame houses on the old Hunterfly Road. (One, 1706–08 Hunterfly Road, burned in the 1970s and was reconstructed in 1990–91.) When the Model Cities Redevelopment Program project decided to demolish houses near the corner of Dean Street and Troy Avenue as part of a project to beautify Bedford-Stuyvesant, Jim Hurley, local residents (including William T. Harley), students from P.S. 243, participants in a government program called Youth in Action, and Boy Scouts from Troop 342 received permission to retrieve objects from the houses and yards around them. Out of this grew Project Weeksville and the Society for the Preservation of Weeksville and Bedford-Stuyvesant History, a community-based effort to discover and preserve Weeksville's history.[10]

Through Pratt Institute and the New York City Community College, Project Weeksville worked with Barbara Jackson and students in P.S. 243, promoted archaeological work, and supported Robert Swan's historical research. In 1970, student testimony, aided by Loren McMillan, director of Historic Richmond Town on Staten Island, convinced the city of New York to save these buildings from demolition and designate Weeksville a city landmark. Students from P.S. 243 raised the first eight hundred dollars toward the purchase of these houses.[11]

The legendary Joan Maynard, executive director of the Society for the Preservation of Weeksville and Bedford-Stuyvesant History, created a remarkable grassroots effort that brought Weeksville to national attention. Under her direction, what seemed like the impossible task of preserving and restoring the Weeksville buildings became a reality. In 2003, Pam Green became Weeksville's second executive director. With Green's leadership, the renamed Weeksville Heritage Center extensively restored the houses on Hunterfly Road, opened them with furnished interiors in 2005, enhanced Weeksville's community service role (with a farmers' market, concerts, and programs), and developed plans for a seven-million-dollar visitor center, completed in 2014.

As part of this immense process of preserving, restoring, and interpreting Weeksville's historic fabric, Pam Green received a Save America's Treasures grant to nominate the houses on Hunterfly Road to the National Register of Historic Places at the national level of significance. As a result of that work, the Weeksville houses are now listed on the National Register as the Hunterfly Road Historic District in New York, Kings County. This book began with extensive research for that National Register nomination, and its origins have shaped its current form. It focuses in part on the buildings of Weeksville, especially the remaining houses on Hunterfly Road. These houses are virtually intact examples of homes of free people of color in the urban North, continuously inhabited both by African Americans and European Americans from their construction until their acquisition by the Society for the Preservation of Weeksville and Bedford-Stuyvesant History in 1968.

But, as Ned Kaufman argued, places without people and story lose their meaning. To understand the historic meaning of these buildings, this book is a social history, highlighting the stories of people who created this community. These houses help tell the stories of families who represent the development of Weeksville from a thriving pre–Civil War African American community (1835–65) to its gradual absorption after the Civil War into the city of Brooklyn.[12]

The significance of these houses depends on when, where, and by whom they were built. If they were built before the Civil War, they represent Weeksville when it was predominantly an African American community. African Americans formed 82 percent of Weeksville's population in both 1840 and 1850. By 1865, however, African Americans formed only 33 percent of Weeksville's population. So if these houses were built after the Civil War, they were most likely constructed as rental housing in a predominately European American community.

Determining construction dates for these houses is not easy. On the one hand, architectural evidence strongly suggests a construction date before the Civil War. The basic style of these houses (with their gables parallel to the street), together with some of the physical details (including heavy timber framing, hand-wrought nails as well as cut nails, central chimneys, and interior fireplaces) indicate a construction date before 1850. To complicate matters, each house is different in form, supporting the idea that they were constructed by different people from different cultural hearths (including New England, South Carolina, and the Chesapeake) at different times. Interestingly, none echoes the predominant Dutch cultural forms of houses in the surrounding area. But each shares features common to the others (beaded molding, for example) suggesting that the houses were related to each other "by finish, framing, or form" and constructed, as architectural historian Edward Chappell hypothesized, "in a single era."[13]

In contrast to architectural evidence, archaeological materials, maps, and assessment records suggest that no houses were located on this site before the 1860s. The earliest artifact recovered from archaeological digs was a bottle manufactured between 1857 and 1870 under the cellar of 1698 Bergen Street, so that no house could have been located earlier on that site. Most artifacts date to the 1870s and later. The 1869 map by Matthew Dripps supports this hypothesis.[14]

There is also a third hypothesis, one that reconciles the conflict between architectural and archaeological evidence. In fact, these houses were built before 1860 but moved to their current location after the Civil War. Two written sources support this conclusion. First, the Brooklyn Eagle published a list of property sold in 1863 by the estate of real estate investor Samuel Bouton. This list described the property purchased by Frederick Volckening on the current Hunterfly Road site only as "lots" without houses. Second, Volckening's tax assessment included only empty lots on this site until 1874. All three extant Hunterfly Road houses were, in fact, almost certainly built by and for African Americans before 1860 and moved to their current location by German-born carpenter Frederick Volckening in the early 1870s. Moving buildings was common in the nineteenth century, and we know that extensive earthmoving took place in Weeksville after the Civil War, as developers filled in a local pond, built sewers and sidewalks, and leveled out the rugged terrain.[15]

As they struggled to build a community and assert their rights as free Americans, Weeksville's citizens created and constantly re-created a positive African American identity. They participated in every major national effort against slavery and for equal rights for free people of color, including the black convention movement, voting rights campaigns, the Underground Railroad, the Civil War, resistance to the draft riots in New York City, and Freedman's schools. After the Civil War, they developed an African American professional class and helped promote a variety of social service activities. They also created a remarkable school—one that whites as well as blacks attended. As a separate independent African American community, Weeksville also showed a persistent connection with emigration, especially emigration to Liberia.

This book is organized both chronologically and topically. Chapter 1 outlines issues of slavery, freedom, and economic development in the Brooklyn area between the American Revolution and Weeksville's origins in the 1830s. Chapter 2 outlines Weeksville's development before 1860, the high point of its existence as an independent black community. Chapter 3 traces specific events during the 1850s and 1860s, as Weeksville residents were caught up in increasingly dramatic debates over slavery, emigration, and Civil War. Chapter 4 outlines debates over Weeksville's school, the emergence of an orphanage and home for the aged, and the growing importance of women as leaders, as Weeksville merged into a multiethnic neighborhood, forming local roots of the emerging state and national Progressive movement. Chapters 5 and 6 discuss physical changes in Weeksville, as Brooklyn's grid gradually absorbed the old landscape. Chapter 7 discusses twentieth-century changes in Weeksville's built environment, as well as the rediscovery of the historic community in the 1960s. Each chapter includes brief biographies of one or more of Weeksville's families including the Weeks, Morel, Graham-LeGrant, and Bundick families, with vignettes of many of Weeksville's most famous national figures. And each chapter also focuses on the changing neighborhood of the houses on Hunterfly Road.

Today, the Weeksville Heritage Center and the small houses along the old Hunterfly Road bear witness to a community whose founders believed that African Americans, as Americans, are created equal. The dominant European American culture had guaranteed to every citizen the "inalienable right" to "life, liberty, and the pursuit of happiness." Yet, ironically, in order to assert their rights as American citizens, people in Weeksville had to set up their own community—not in Liberia, Canada, or Haiti—but on the outskirts of Brooklyn, in the margins of a space created by European Americans.

Weeksville's founders saw themselves as American citizens, and they wanted homes on American soil. From the beginning, they viewed this community as a base for physical safety, economic prosperity, education, and political power in America. Only by withdrawing from dominant-culture communities could they live out what many would call the American dream. Only by creating a separate space could they explore the full meaning of freedom.

1

"Here Will We Take Our Stand"

Weeksville's Origins, from Slavery to Freedom, 1770–1840

In 1835, only eight years after the end of slavery in New York State, the United States was in the middle of a frenzy of land speculation.[1] African Americans were not immune. In July, Henry C. Thompson ("a Colored Man," noted the deed), a leader of Brooklyn's African American community, purchased thirty-two lots of land—once part of John Lefferts's large farm—near the corner of Troy Avenue and Dean Street, on block 1335, just south of the new Long Island Railroad between Bedford and East New York. On March 26, 1838, in the middle of a terrible depression, James Weeks, forty-four-year-old stevedore, purchased two of these lots (279 and 280). In 1839, the *Brooklyn Directory* listed "James Weeks, Weeksville, Bedford." This is the first known reference to Weeksville as a distinct place. James Weeks purchased at least four more properties, one on November 1, 1839, a second on January 14, 1845, a third on May 8, 1849, and a fourth in May 1853. Cesar Weeks, probably James's brother, also purchased property nearby.[2]

Neither Weeks nor Thompson was the first African American to purchase land in Brooklyn's Ninth Ward. As Robert Swan has shown, William Thomas, a chimney sweep born in New York City, earned that honor, purchasing thirty acres along Hunterfly Road near the Flatbush line in 1832. Samuel Anderson, from Brooklyn, bought seven more acres a year later. Like Thompson, both Thomas and Anderson subdivided their land for sale to others.[3]

Other investors followed. At noon on Friday, June 7, 1839, more than a year after Weeks first bought his land, Francis P. Graham, a free person of color from Charleston, South Carolina, attended an auction held by W. R. Dean at 14 Fulton Street, in downtown Brooklyn. There he purchased part of a large farm and woodlands (parcels 19 and 20 and much of block 1350), south and east of James Weeks's land, sold by the estate of Samuel Garrittsen, Lefferts's son-in-law. Part of Graham's land bordered Hunterfly Road, which would become Weeksville's eastern boundary. Other African American land investors—Paul Pontou, Gabriel Boyer, and Henry Letate—also purchased parts of Garrittsen's farm.[4]

Henry Thompson, Samuel Anderson, and Francis P. Graham represent both the diversity and unity of early Weeksville land investors. All were united in their desire to create a free and independent African American community, a place of safety, educational and economic opportunity, and political power. But they differed from each other in many ways. They came from different parts of the country. They had different occupations. Some of them had been recently enslaved, and some were free people of color.

Samuel Anderson represents people once enslaved by local Dutch farmers who found freedom in Weeksville. In 1898, the *Brooklyn Eagle* did a lengthy story on Anderson. He had been born in slavery in Flatbush in 1810 and lived for many years at the corner of Church Avenue and Hunterfly Road. Very few African Americans lived in this area between 1820 and 1830. Samuel Anderson was most likely one of them.[5]

In 1898, Anderson lived in a small two-story white cottage set back on a narrow lane, about a mile east of Flatbush Avenue. The house was old, with a roof that needed repair and "weather beaten clapboards." But the house and yard were well kept, "spick and span" inside, with "bright old-fashioned flowers in the front yard" and a "thrifty garden" in the rear. Anderson had joined a Methodist Church in 1829 and worked as a preacher for much of his life. His aunt, Ruth Anderson Parrish, had been born nearby in 1784 and lived at least until she was 102 years old.[6]

Henry Thompson represents free people of color in Brooklyn who were both businessmen and activists. An entrepreneur and manufacturer of blacking (polish for boots and shoes), Thompson was a prominent leader of Brooklyn's African American community. He was a powerful and outspoken advocate of economic and educational opportunities. He served as president of the African Woolman Benevolent Society and ardently opposed efforts of the American Colonization Society to send African Americans to Liberia. The 1840 census listed

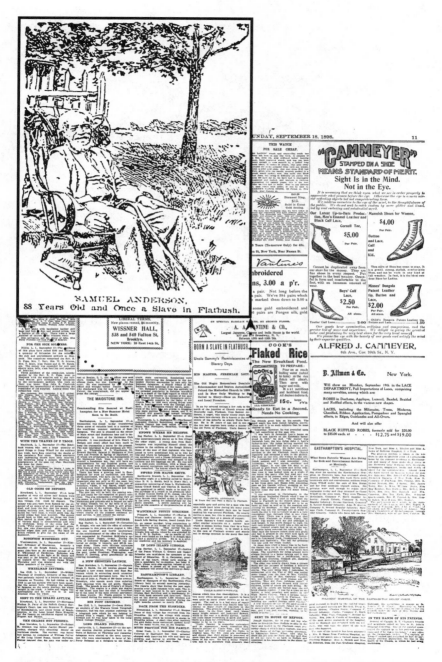

Samuel Anderson, *Brooklyn Eagle*, September 18, 1898. Courtesy Brooklyn Public Library, Brooklyn Collection.

"Uncle Sammy's Cottage," *Brooklyn Eagle*, September 18, 1898. Courtesy Brooklyn Public Library, Brooklyn Collection.

him as between the ages of thirty-six and fifty-four, head of a household of eight free people of color.[7]

Francis Prince Graham represents free people of color who settled in Weeksville from southern states. Graham was born in South Carolina about 1800. (The name Prince Graham is still common in South Carolina.) By 1822, Graham was living in Charleston, associated with an African church (most likely the new African Methodist Episcopal Church), and married to a woman named Sarah, with whom he had two children. In 1822, Francis Prince Graham, drayman, was arrested in connection with the Charleston slave rebellion associated with Denmark Vesey. On June 16, 1822, Vesey, an African American carpenter, launched a major uprising, designed to free people from slavery. Sixty-seven African Americans were convicted of "an Insurrection amongst the Blacks against the Whites." Thirty-seven of these were hanged. Graham escaped to New York but returned to Charleston for his trial, insisting, "As I was a free man, and could have stayed in New York if I pleased, I certainly would not have been such a fool as to run myself into such danger if I was in any way engaged in the plot." Convicted in spite of his protestations, Graham was judged guilty on July 21 and banished from South Carolina, on pain of death. At his own request, Graham boarded the *Dolphin*, sailing from Charleston harbor to Liberia.

His wife and children remained in Charleston. Sailing with him was a man named Butler. For the rest of his life, Graham took responsibility for a young man named Edward Butler, perhaps related to this shipmate.[8]

By 1829, Graham had moved back to New York City. He appeared in the city directory for 1829–30 as a shoemaker, living at 61 Mott Street. In 1832, he was ordained a deacon in the African Methodist Episcopal Church, working with elder Jacob Matthews in Asbury Church, New York City. In 1834, the New York Conference ordained him as an elder. His wife Sarah refused to leave Charleston, but Graham married at least twice more. On May 15, 1838, he married Judah Jackson from New York City, listing his own address as South Carolina. She died in childbirth in August 1839 at only twenty-five years old, and Graham acquired a large amount of property from Judah and her brother. Most likely, he invested at least part of this inheritance on property in Weeksville.[9]

By 1839–40, Graham had moved to 153 Orange Street, where the census listed him as head of a household of three free people of color, including one male aged twenty-four to thirty-five, one male aged thirty-six to fifty-four (perhaps Graham himself), and one female aged fifty-five to ninety-nine (perhaps Graham's sister Phebe LeGrant). Two people in this household worked in "manufacturing and trade," most likely Graham and one helper in the shoemaking business.[10]

In January 1839, Francis P. Graham served as secretary of a "Great Anti-Colonization Meeting" in New York City. The meeting protested strongly against colonization, as "anti-republican, anti-christian and anti-humane." A few months later, Graham bought land in Weeksville, twenty-four lots on Hunterfly Road, twenty-six lots near Albany and Troy Streets, and five acres farther south. He also owned a building at 371 Broadway in New York City and a church on Third Street, where he preached. By 1844, he had moved to Weeksville, where he lived on Hunterfly Road near the corner of Rochester Avenue and Bergen Street, set up a shoemaking business, and sold lots along Hunterfly Road and farther west, near the home of James Weeks, to African Americans from Virginia, Maryland, Pennsylvania, Washington, D.C., South Carolina, and Africa. As a pastor, shoemaker, real estate developer, community builder, activist, and husband, Graham earned a reputation as a man of "many eccentricities," noted the *New York Times*.[11]

Geography

Geographically, the emerging village of Weeksville was located in Brooklyn's Ninth Ward, about three and a half miles east of downtown Brooklyn. The main settlement stretched three-quarters of a mile wide by half a mile long, from Hudson (Kingston) Street on the west to Hunterfly Road on the east, Atlantic Avenue on the north to Park (Baltic) Avenue on the south.

Officially part of the city of Brooklyn, Weeksville actually formed an independent, almost totally African American enclave. It was set on a glacial moraine, commonly called Crow Hill (later morphed into Crown Heights), named for the large numbers of crows that flew over it every day on their way to Jamaica Bay. After 1850, these crows may have been attracted by the dead carcasses of animals brought to Crow Hill to make fertilizer. Boiling bones of dead animals rendered fat, and grinding them resulted in fertilizer.[12]

Crow Hill was one of the Bedford Hills, sandy glacial moraines that ran northeasterly from Brooklyn toward East New York and Jamaica. These hills were originally covered with thick woods. During the Revolution, however, the British denuded much of this forest, chopping down trees for firewood.

One of the Bedford Hills. "The Battle Pass in Prospect Park, Brooklyn, From a Sketch by G.L. Burdette, Taken in 1792." Henry Reed Stiles, *A History of the City of Brooklyn*, 3 vols. (Brooklyn, 1867–70; repr., Bowie, Md.: Heritage Books, 1993), 1:260.

Garrittsen tide mill, built 1636, demolished 1936. Photo by Robert L. Stillson. Edmund Drew Fisher, *Flatbush: Past and Present* (Flatbush Trust Company, 1901; repr., Whitefish, Mont.: Kessinger, n.d.).

Here and there, Indian trails crossed over the hills toward the south. Three of these roads were most important in the Weeksville area. One went through the Flatbush Pass, "Battle Pass," now in Prospect Park. A second, Bedford Pass, ran south from Bedford Corners, the nearest village east of downtown Brooklyn. Clove Road followed Bedford Pass, intersecting with the road to Jamaica (at the corner of what is now Atlantic Avenue and Franklin Avenue), cutting southwest through a deep valley toward Flatbush.

A mile east of Clove Road, a third trail called Hunterfly Road crossed Crow Hill south toward Jamaica meadows. Hunterfly Road marked the eastern edge of Weeksville. Its name was an anglicized version of the Dutch "Aander Vly," meaning "over to the creek" or "over to the meadow." This road was especially important for Dutch settlers, since it led directly to the salt meadows on Jamaica bay, past Vanderveer mill on Fresh Kill or creek and near the Garrittsen tide mill, powered by the rise and fall of tides. These salt meadows, like the nearby woods, were allotted to various Brooklyn settlers and became known as the Brooklyn meadows. Farmers cut this salt hay in September and used it as winter food for cattle.[13]

North of Crow Hill, both Clove Road and Hunterfly Road intersected the Brooklyn and Jamaica Turnpike, which paralleled what is now Fulton Street. East of Hunterfly Road, the Dutch purchased land in 1670 for use as woodlots, held in common until they were divided into narrow strips and given to individual families in 1693. These remained mostly undeveloped into the nineteenth century.[14]

The area around Weeksville was part of land once occupied by the Canarsee Indians. By the early eighteenth century, however, all of Kings County was officially in Dutch hands. Its original Indian settlers moved farther east on Long Island or west to the Delaware Valley. Beginning in the mid-seventeenth century, the Dutch granted patents to the Lefferts, Bergen, Remsen, Suydam, and other families. Dutch families, Dutch traditions, and Dutch language dominated the area, and remnants of these early Dutch families remained until the early twentieth century.[15]

In 1776, four generations after the original Lefferts family came to Bedford, the British invaded Brooklyn with thirty-one thousand Hessian soldiers. Sentiment was mixed between Tory and Patriot on Long Island, and local Dutch families fought on both sides. Lambert Suydam of Bedford commanded the Kings County Cavalry. Pieter Lefferts of Flatbush served as a lieutenant in the Continental Army. George Washington's own headquarters was in Brooklyn.

From August 26 to August 31, 1776, the British under generals Clinton and Cornwallis marched along Clove Road to Flatbush and Bedford and north along Hunterfly Road near the area that would become Weeksville. They set up a defensive line along the Jamaica Road (now Atlantic Avenue). Local Patriot families fled to safety farther east on Long Island. One young girl remembered the day the British landed as "one of the loveliest we had that summer. The sky was so clear and bright that you could scarcely think of it as a day that was to bring so much sorrow." Her family escaped with the help of Betty, a Canarsee Indian woman, who reported on British troop movements. Caesar, enslaved by the family, took his grandson Cato and drove the cattle into the woods,

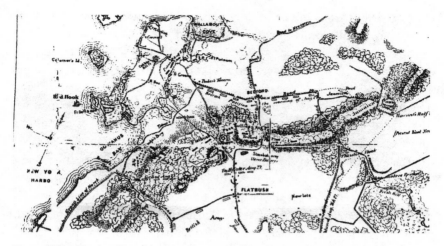

Henry Stiles, "Battle of Brooklyn, August 27, 1776." By the 1830s, Weeksville was located where Hunterfly Road ran north and south across the glacial moraine that ran east and west, toward the top right of this map. Clove Road went through the valley just west of Hunterfly Road, connecting Bedford on the north with Flatbush on the south. Henry Reed Stiles, *A History of the City of Brooklyn*, 3 vols. (Brooklyn, 1867–70; repr., Bowie, Md.: Heritage Books, 1993), 1:250–51.

while Mink, Caesar's son, stood guard over the house. The family saved a few cherished household goods—the "great Dutch Bible" with its little stand and the old Dutch clock. But the British burned their house and grain, in spite of Caesar's efforts to save it. In 1968, students digging in Weeksville would find a Revolutionary War cannonball, evidence of Weeksville's military importance.[16]

Although Washington successfully escaped across the river to Manhattan from Brooklyn Heights, the British held both New York City and Long Island for the rest of the war. Sympathetic though many Dutch families were to the Americans, they were often forced to take oaths of allegiance to the British, and their houses were commandeered to house both British and Hessian troops, as many as four hundred of them. Hendrick Suydam, who lived on New Bush Lane (connecting the Jamaica Turnpike with Newtown east of Weeksville) remembered how disruptive his family found the Hessians to be. They also brought fever, killing many of the local population. Gertrude Lefferts Vanderbilt reported that horses were taken, tools were stolen or burned, and farm laborers were almost nonexistent.[17]

American troops burned the Lefferts homestead in Flatbush to prevent it from falling into British hands. But the Lefferts home in Bedford was left standing and served as headquarters for British General
Gray, from which he ordered confiscation of crops from local farms.
To feed and warm British troops for another seven years, the British
needed huge amounts of food and wood. As part of their occupation,
they cut down trees for fuel, denuding much of Long Island, including
most likely much of the area that would become Weeksville.[18]

The British occupation affected everyone, but none more than Long
Island's enslaved labor force. Many enslaved people chose freedom
behind British lines over slavery in Dutch households. When the British
finally left New York City in 1783, Washington reluctantly concluded,
"The Slaves which have absconded from their Masters will never be
returned to them." About three thousand formerly enslaved Africans—
men, women, and children—sailed with British troops. Half were from
the South. About six hundred were from New York or New Jersey. They
settled in Nova Scotia, Sierra Leone, or elsewhere under British rule. In
1771, African Americans formed 13 percent of New York's population.
New York City was second only to Charleston, South Carolina, as the
city with the most concentrated black population in the United States.
Fifteen years later, in 1786, only 8.5 percent of New York State's population was African American (18,889 people), a testimony to the large
numbers of enslaved people who left their homes in New York City and
Long Island for freedom.[19]

By 1783, Pieter Lefferts built a new house on the old foundation of his
parents' home, near the corner of Flatbush Avenue and Maple Street.
Lefferts became one of the wealthiest and most influential men in Kings
County. He owned more than 240 acres of land and headed a household of eight family members and twelve enslaved people. As a judge,
Pieter served in 1788 as a member of New York State's convention to
ratify the new U.S. Constitution.[20]

Pieter Lefferts's cousin, Judge Leffert Lefferts, was born in the Bedford homestead in 1774, attended Columbia College in 1794, and
became, in 1823, the first judge of Kings County and the first president
of Long Island Bank. As a Federalist, Judge Leffert Lefferts ran twice for
Congress but lost both times.[21]

Lefferts House, built about 1783. Once located at 563 Flatbush Avenue, moved to Prospect Park in 1918. Photograph by Eugene L. Armbruster. Various members of the Lefferts family owned much of the land that became Weeksville. Collection of the New-York Historical Society.

Unlike his cousin, Pieter Lefferts's son John Lefferts was a Democrat. In 1813, he successfully ran against his cousin Leffert Lefferts for a seat in the U.S. House of Representatives (1813–15). He also served in the U.S. Senate (1820–25) and was a delegate to the New York State Constitutional Convention of 1821. After John Lefferts died in 1829, Sarah Lefferts, one of his eight heirs, sold part of the farm in 1834. It was this land that Henry C. Thompson purchased in 1835 and sold to Simon Van Curen in 1837. Van Curen sold it in 1838 to James Weeks, who gave his name to the new settlement.[22]

Until long after the Revolution, Kings County fields, including those of the Lefferts family, as Gertrude Lefferts Vanderbilt recalled, "waved with the graceful growth of grain": wheat, corn, oats, barley, and rye. After the opening of the Erie Canal in 1825, farmers shifted to market gardens, producing cabbages, turnips, potatoes, and other vegetables for New York City markets. Throughout the nineteenth century, Kings County was the second largest producer of garden vegetables in the United States, rivaled only by Queens County.[23]

With its rich farmlands, Kings County needed a large agricultural labor force. Much of the labor used on these farms was African American. Lefferts family members certainly held people in slavery. In 1698, Lefferts Pieterse owned three people in slavery. In 1766, a graveyard for African Americans stood near the four corners at Bedford, a physical reminder that many people of color lived and died in the area.[24]

In the early nineteenth century, John Lefferts of Flatbush, part of whose farm encompassed what would become Weeksville, continued to own people in slavery. In 1810, five people lived in slavery with the seven family members of his household. In 1820, the number of enslaved people in John Lefferts's household had increased to eight, along with one free man of color. In contrast, Leffert Lefferts of Bedford had no African Americans—free or enslaved—living in his household in 1820. But in 1830, three free people of color lived with four Dutch American members of his family.[25]

African American farmhand, Vanderveer farm, Flatbush, 1880s. Edmund Drew Fisher, *Flatbush: Past and Present* (Flatbush Trust Company, 1901; repr., Whitefish, Mont.: Kessinger, n.d.), 27.

Section from "Guy's Brooklyn Snow Scene, 1820," showing Brooklyn four years after its incorporation as a village. Stiles's key to this painting identified the young man pulling the rope for the pump as Samuel Foster, African American. The man standing two figures to the left of the horse at the pump is "Abiel Titus's negro servant 'Jeff.'" Henry Reed Stiles, *A History of the City of Brooklyn*, 3 vols. (Brooklyn, 1867–70; repr., Bowie, Md.: Heritage Books, 1993), 2:88.

Dutch farmers in Kings County, as well as settlers in Weeksville, relied on a symbiotic relationship with the city of Brooklyn. Downtown Brooklyn, with its East River docks, warehouses, and ferries, lay between three and four miles west of Weeksville, a ride of only a few minutes on the Long Island Railway. Brooklyn became a village in 1816 and a city in 1834. By 1840, with 36,233 people, it was the second largest city in New York State (after New York City). North of Brooklyn, the village of Williamsburgh was incorporated in 1827 as a port city, connected to upper New York City in 1840 by two ferryboat lines. In 1854, it was annexed to the city of Brooklyn.[26]

Brooklyn was closely tied both economically and socially to New York City. In 1860, John H. French noted in his *Gazetteer* that "all of the business of the co.—manufacturing, commercial, and agricultural—are so intimately connected with the interests of New York that the co. may be considered as a suburb of the great city." By 1860, eleven steam ferries connected Brooklyn to New York City.[27]

Brooklyn docks, "among the most extensive and commodious in the country," connected the city to ports elsewhere in the United States—including the American South—and Europe. "The whole water front of the city is occupied by ferries, piers, slips, and boat and ship yards," noted French, and these connected the city to national and international markets. The Brooklyn Navy Yard, as well as private piers and warehouses, employed many people in Brooklyn, including those who traveled to work from rural areas. Cotton merchants stored raw cotton in Brooklyn warehouses, awaiting shipment to British markets. Shipyards, lumberyards, distilleries, breweries, plaster mills, foundries, tobacco factories, and machine shops dominated manufacturing.[28]

Brooklyn's port linked it to national and international shipping. But Brooklyn was also part of an integrated system of land transportation. Kings County farmers provided most of the vegetables sold in New York City, and farm laborers, including African Americans, took their carts daily to early morning markets. Long into the nineteenth century, African Americans relied on sales of garden produce—from either their own gardens or those of their employers—in downtown Brooklyn and New York City for their livelihood. In 1892, Evelina Hicks Clark remembered that "one of the old colored servants, originally slaves in the family, daily took vegetables and fruits from her father's farm."

Brooklyn after it became a city. Note both steamboats and sailboats in the harbor. John Barber and Henry W. Howe, *Historical Collections of the State of New York* (New York: S. Tuttle, 1842; repr., Bowie, Md.: Heritage Books, 1999).

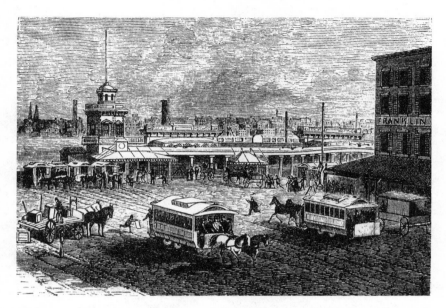

In 1840, Jason Davis, born enslaved, owned a horse-drawn omnibus like one of these. *Colored American*, May 16, 1840. Henry Reed Stiles, *A History of the City of Brooklyn*, 3 vols. (Brooklyn, 1867–70; repr., Bowie, Md.: Heritage Books, 1993), 3:550.

Roads also connected Brooklyn's port with villages and bays on Long Island, closely linked by water to Connecticut.[29]

After Robert Fulton invented the steam engine, he established the Fulton Ferry landing in 1814, revolutionizing access from New York City to Brooklyn. When they reached Brooklyn, eastbound passengers on the Fulton Ferry from New York could follow Fulton Street to Bedford, Jamaica, and eastern Long Island. Rail lines radiated from end points of ferry lines, so people could travel quickly and cheaply from almost any part of Brooklyn. And the fare was cheap. In 1850, the Union Ferry Company reduced the fare to one cent.[30]

From the South Ferry at the end of Atlantic Street, the Brooklyn & Jamaica Railroad ran east along Atlantic Avenue, just south of Fulton Street and just north of Weeksville. The Long Island Railroad took over this line in 1836, running both horse-drawn streetcars and steam trains directly from the ferry landing to what is now 158th Street in Jamaica. Today, it is the oldest railroad in the United States still operating under its original charter.

Many of the Dutch families in Kings County remained in their family homesteads until the late nineteenth and early twentieth centuries. The Suydam family homestead, owned by Lambert Suydam of Revolutionary War cavalry fame and his wife Mary Lefferts Suydam (and later by descendents Moses Suydam, Phebe Suydam, and Ann Suydam), stood into the late nineteenth century on Suydam Place, just south of Atlantic Avenue, on the northeast border of Weeksville. In 1909, Gertrude Lefferts Vanderbilt, descendent of John and Maria Lefferts, memorialized the life of Dutch farm families, including her own, in *The Social History of Flatbush and Manners and Customs of the Dutch Settlers in Kings County*.[31]

Members of the Lefferts family continued to own vast acreages along Clove Road, between Bedford and Flatbush. When Judge Leffert Lefferts died in 1847, he was one of the largest landowners in Brooklyn. His house at Bedford was replaced in 1881 by a new and much larger mansion for his daughter and son-in-law. But in 1889, the Lefferts property remained, noted the *Brooklyn Eagle*, "probably the largest tract of land now within the City of Brooklyn."[32]

Beginning in 1887, the John Lefferts family sold much of their land in Flatbush for residential development. Nevertheless, Lefferts family members continued to live in the house built by Pieter Lefferts in Flatbush, whose descendents owned the land that would become Weeksville, until 1918, when the house was moved to Prospect Park. It was opened to the public, operated by the Prospect Park Alliance and the Historic House Trust of New York City, and visitors learned about the history of Dutch families, Native Americans, and African Americans in Kings County.[33]

In the context of rapid economic growth and expanding transportation systems in the 1830s, African Americans as well as European Americans had opportunities to make money through land investment. It would have been surprising had people of color not taken advantage of this economic boom, simply as entrepreneurs. But they also worked in a larger context. They viewed land acquisition as a powerful tool in the transition from slavery to freedom. It was no coincidence that people such as Henry Thompson looked east toward woodlands and hills along the new railroad line.

Thompson and his compatriots had a model, of sorts. In 1825, African Americans had purchased land between Seventh and Eighth

Avenues and between Eighty-First and Eighty-Ninth Streets in Manhattan. There they established the community of Seneca Village. By the 1850s, at least 264 people (and maybe more) lived there, one-third of them Irish. Half of the African American families owned property. Their homes were surrounded by gardens, interspersed with three churches, two schools, and two cemeteries. This thriving community disappeared altogether in 1857, however, swallowed up under the new Central Park. Leslie Alexander argued that "Seneca Village represented and embodied a series of ideas: African pride and racial consciousness, the creation of lasting Black institutions, and the potential attainment of political power." Weeksville, too, became the physical crystallization of these ideals.[34]

When John Lefferts died in 1829, he left behind eight heirs, who divided up the land and offered much of it for sale. Division of John Lefferts family lands opened possibilities for new purchases. So did the sale in 1839 of another part of the Lefferts's estate, owned by son-in-law Samuel Garrittsen until his death in 1799 and most likely controlled by widow Mary Lefferts Garrittsen.

African American land investors saw their chance. According to Robert Swan, African Americans began buying land in the Ninth Ward of Brooklyn in 1832, the same year that the railroad was first chartered along Atlantic Avenue. William Thomas was the first. Samuel Anderson and others followed shortly.[35]

Land speculation across the country reached new heights in 1834–35, and eastern Brooklyn attracted entrepreneurs. In 1834, William Thomas sold nine acres of his land to Sylvanus Smith, a hog drover from Brooklyn; twelve acres to Daniel Collins; and six acres to Richard Thompson, from New York. Thompson and Anderson subdivided their land into lots of about one hundred by twenty-five feet and began selling them to African Americans who lived in Brooklyn and New York City.[36]

In 1834, five European Americans bought a major part of John Lefferts's farm. One of these was Edward Copeland, Brooklyn grocer, graduate of Columbia College, supporter of revolutions in Greece and Poland in the 1820s, and Whig mayor of Brooklyn in 1833. Copeland in turn sold 426 lots at auction in July 1835. Henry C. Thompson bought thirty-two of these lots located near what is now the corner of Troy and Dean Streets. In 1838, James Weeks purchased two of them.[37]

Motivated both by a desire to create a haven for African Americans and to make money as land speculators, Thompson and other African American real estate investors were successful on both counts. By the late 1830s, a distinct African American community had emerged just east of Bedford Corners. It grew up around Crow Hill, between Clove Road and Hunterfly Road. Steep hills, deep valleys, and woodlands traversed this area. "Nature has kindly done her best to make the place picturesque," noted the *Brooklyn Eagle* in 1873. "It is all hills and hollows. The hills are the highest, and the hollows the deepest of any in the city."

A large pond called Suydam's Pond, named after the local Dutch farm family whose farmhouse overlooked its east end, filled in a deep hollow between Crow Hill and Atlantic Avenue. Weeksville's residents built their houses west, south, and east of this pond. James Weeks settled in an area between Atlantic Avenue on the north and Crow Hill on the south, between what are now Troy and Schenectady Avenues, just west of this pond. After his initial purchase of lots 279 and 280 on March 28, 1838, he bought several more lots contiguous to these. By 1839, people began to call this new community Weeksville, after James Weeks. This area became the core of the community, with the largest concentration of settlers.[38]

Several families also lived on Crow Hill itself, south of Suydam's Pond. Others (including Francis P. Graham) created a neighborhood along Hunterfly Road, east of the pond and south of the old Suydam house. Still others, such as Samuel Anderson, settled south of Crow Hill, in an area noted for its large pig farms.

The result was less a coherent village than a scattered collection of small neighborhoods. Eventually, local people gave them nicknames: Fort Sumter was first established as a rude earthworks to protect people who fled from the draft riots in Manhattan in 1863. Castle Thunder was a two-and-a-half-story building at the corner of Bergen Street and Rochester Avenue, a gathering place for "nightly frolics." Bannon's Barracks (or Bannon's Row) encompassed "half a dozen frame houses on Butler Street," between Rochester and Buffalo Avenues, and its residents "derived their chief support from housebreaking," noted the *Brooklyn Eagle*. Other neighborhoods included Chicago Row (on the north side of Atlantic Avenue between Schenectady and Utica, where eight families were crowded together in each house) and the Canal Boat. These enclaves were separated by wide spaces of wild land. As late as 1883, the *Brooklyn Eagle* reported, "for blocks and blocks there were no sidewalks, no street lamps, no pavements and no houses."[39]

Land Sales in Weeksville

In contrast to parochial Dutch farmers, Weeksville's settlers were a cosmopolitan group. People came to Weeksville from both rural and urban areas of Brooklyn and New York, as well as parts of New England, Pennsylvania, New Jersey; the coastal areas of Maryland, Virginia, and the Carolinas; and Africa and the Caribbean. Weeksville's new settlers also stood apart from local people in another way: they were all people of color.

Weeksville's African American land investors consciously marketed their land to African Americans across the country. Above all, they were community builders. They focused not simply on selling land or making money. Their purpose was to sell land at a reasonable cost—"cheap, and free of any bond or mortgage"—for immediate development not of farms but of homes. They specifically targeted African Americans as home buyers. They advertised directly in African American newspapers, or if they advertised in the general press, they directed their ads toward African American readers.

A search through the Accessible Archives database of nineteenth-century African American newspapers (which includes *Freedom's Journal, Colored American*, 1837–41, *North Star*, 1848–51, *Frederick Douglass's Paper, National Era*, and *Christian Recorder*) revealed a total of six advertisements for Weeksville land. No comparable advertisements for real estate specifically targeted to African American buyers appeared for any other place in the country. Five Weeksville ads appeared in the *Colored American* between April 4, 1840, and August 7, 1841. One advertisement, reprinted four times, was for "75 lots of land situated in the 9th ward of the city of Brooklyn, near the Jamaica Railroad, clear of bonds and mortgage. For sale low, to suit purchasers. For further particulars, inquire of J. OSBORN & J.H. DIXON, 217 Centre St."[40]

Another advertisement appeared only once, on May 22, 1841, when African American real estate developer Paul Pontou (also known as Ponto) advertised,

LAND FOR SALE.

THE PUBLIC are most respectfully informed that 190 lots, varying
    from 25 by 100 to 140 feet deep, will be sold cheap, and free of
    any bond or mortgage. Said lots are situated in Bedford, in the
    vicinity of Brooklyn. For particulars, apply to
Paul Pontou, 294 Second st.
OSBORN & DIXON, 217 Centre st.
New York, May 22, 1841.[41]

A sixth ad appeared in the *North Star* on January 25, 1850: "TWENTY BUILDING LOTS, in the Ninth Ward of the City of Brooklyn, a few minutes' walk from the railroad, and ten minutes travel to the East River Ferries. Title indisputable. Persons wishing to purchase and improve immediately, will be accommodated on easy terms. Said lots front on Thompson Street and Morell's Lane, and adjoin Ward School No. 2."[42] In addition to these six advertisements in African American newspapers, Sylvanus Smith placed a real estate ad in the *New York Times* in 1855 for Weeksville land: "FOR SALE TO COLORED PEOPLE. Beautiful building lots at Weeksville in the IXth Ward of Brooklyn. Prices $130 to $200 terms cash. Buildings will be put up ready for May day at a rent of $200 [?] and over. Inquire of S.W. Smith, corner of Lafayette av. and Cumberland st. Brooklyn."[43]

Early references to African American settlements in the Ninth Ward sometimes referred to two communities: Weeksville and Carrsville. The 1841 tax roll for Brooklyn, for example, listed assessments for the "colored people" of Carrsville and the "colored people of Weeksville." In 1851, a Brooklyn correspondent for the *North Star* described a celebration of West Indian emancipation held at a picnic "between the villages of Weeksville and Corsville [*sic*], both colored settlements, about four miles from this place [downtown Brooklyn]." In 1853, however, J. W. Colton's *Map of the Country Thirty-Three Miles around the City of New York* showed only "Weeksville." In 1869, the *Eagle* referred to Carrsville generally as "the wild district" beyond Weeksville, east of Hunterfly Road.[44]

Some sources distinguished between Weeksville and Crow Hill, west and south of the main concentration of settlement. J. C. Sidney's *Map of 12 Miles around New York* (Philadelphia, 1849), the first map to identify Weeksville, showed "Weeksville" and "Crow Hill" as two separate places. In 1888, the *Eagle* similarly described Crow Hill as the area west of Schenectady Avenue. Weeksville was the territory from Schenectady to Buffalo Avenue, and Carrsville lay from Hunterfly Road to East New York. In 1889, the *Eagle* gave the name Crow Hill to much of the Twenty-Fourth Ward, noting that people often associated it with the "grim and gray building which looks like a fortress and is known as the King's County Penitentiary," standing at the highest point of the whole Crow Hill country. In 1919, Miss C. T. Davis remembered growing up at the corner of Schenectady Avenue and Wyckoff Street (St. Mark's), with Weeksville to the north and Carrsville to the south. The *Eagle*'s conclusion in 1888 probably best summed up the location of Weeksville and Carrsville: "It is only possible to give these divisions in a general way, as the 'oldest inhabitants' do not agree in laying out the boundaries, and it is a question if the lines were ever very decidedly fixed."[45]

Census listings in 1840 confirm the indistinct boundaries among Carrsville, Weeksville, and Crow Hill. In 1840, twenty-seven of the thirty-two independent African American households listed in the census for the Ninth Ward of Brooklyn lived in a section that included the families of James and Cesar Weeks. Only three European American families lived in this area. Only five African American families—those of Frederick Haight, Peter Holms, Isaac Johnson, Charles Lawrence, and Samuel Van Duyne—lived in the Ninth Ward outside of the Weeksville/Carrsville/Crow Hill cluster. The boundaries of Weeksville, then, can roughly be defined by this distribution of twenty-seven families. Census records do not indicate the density of this cluster, and it most likely contained several smaller groupings inside it. For purposes of this study, we will refer to this whole area as Weeksville.[46]

Sales of Lefferts's family land (especially in 1829, 1834, and 1839) and completion of the Long Island Railroad in 1834 help explain Weeksville's location. To understand why Weeksville was organized, however, we have to look at the intellectual and social context of African Americans in the 1830s.

Weeksville's Origins: Context

In the 1830s, there was reason to think that the future for African Americans would be better than the past. Slavery had ended at last in New York State. And people—both African American and European Americans—were organizing to ensure the abolition of slavery across the nation. In 1831, William Lloyd Garrison began to argue for immediate abolition in the United States in his new newspaper, the *Liberator*. Samuel Cornish and John B. Russwurm in New York City successfully published *Freedom's Journal* and *Rights of All*. Great Britain abolished slavery in 1834. In 1837, Samuel Cornish established the *Colored American*.

Beginning in 1831, African Americans organized national Negro conventions to advocate for African American rights. Junius C. Morel, who became the principal of Colored School No. 2 in Weeksville in 1847, was a major participant in these conventions. James W. C. Pennington, who escaped from slavery in Maryland to become a teacher and minister, represented Brooklyn at the first two conventions. In 1833, European Americans and African Americans organized the American Anti-Slavery Society in Philadelphia, and hundreds of statewide, county, and local antislavery societies followed. In October 1835, more than four hundred delegates met first in Utica and then in Peterboro, New York, to form the New York State Anti-Slavery Society.

In the late 1830s and early 1840s, abolitionists from across the country (both African American and European American) sent petitions to Congress protesting slavery in the District of Columbia and the territories, the admission of Texas as a slave state, and the slave trade. Within New York State, 140 African American men and 92 women in Brooklyn joined abolitionists from several upstate counties in 1837 to petition the state legislature for jury trials for people accused as fugitive slaves and for immediate freedom for enslaved people brought into New York State. In 1840, New York State passed legislation granting these requests.[47]

In this context, many African Americans were attracted to the idea of establishing an independent community where they could create a safe haven, work to ensure a better future for themselves and their children, and assert their full rights as free Americans.

Besides simple entrepreneurship, African Americans had at least five compelling reasons to create an African American land base. Weeksville's founders intended to

1. Define themselves as **free people,** after slavery ended in New York State in 1827
2. Assert their **political rights as American citizens,** especially their right to vote
3. Create **economic opportunities** for African Americans
4. Create a **safe haven** for themselves and for freedom seekers from slavery, who were subject to kidnappers and slave catchers
5. Challenge those who promoted European American–sponsored **emigration** to Canada or Africa (particularly Liberia)

"Too Long Have Others Spoken for Us": From Slavery to Freedom in New York State, 1626–1827

Weeksville was born in a time of transition from slavery to freedom.[48] Shortly after slavery ended in New York State in 1827, Weeksville began as a community of free African Americans. We do not know how many of its earliest residents had at one time been enslaved. We do know, however, that slavery was embedded into the economic and social system of colonial New York. Most African Americans on Long Island lived in close proximity to Dutch slave-owning families, and their skills and labor brought wealth to the colony of New York.

Although African Americans had always resisted enslavement, events leading up to the American Revolution brought antislavery debates among European Americans as well. In 1767, Quakers in Flushing formally enacted an antislavery resolution, condemning slavery as unchristian. In 1771, Quakers in the province of New York disowned members who refused to manumit their slaves. Some non-Quakers, too, began to advocate antislavery. How could Americans fight a war based on the ideal that "all men are created equal," they wondered, when they themselves maintained slavery? As Edgar McManus has pointed out, slaveholders were often responsive to this logic, and manumissions increased dramatically after 1774, as enslaved people themselves became "infatuated with a desire of obtaining freedom."[49]

British occupation of New York City during the Revolution led to freedom for many enslaved people, as the British offered freedom to anyone who became a Loyalist. More than three thousand African Americans from all over the country also received their freedom for serving with the Continental Army. So did many thousands more who served with state and local militias.[50]

Antislavery sentiment among European Americans was so strong in the Revolutionary period that a clear majority of delegates at the first Constitutional Convention in 1777 endorsed a resolution that "every human being who breathes the air of the state shall enjoy the privileges of a freeman." By 1785, the legislature was ready to act on this idea. Although almost unanimous in their agreement on emancipation, delegates disagreed on how to do it. Ironically, they failed to pass an emancipation law because the Council of Revision would not agree with the assembly's insistence on limiting the right of suffrage for freed people of color. African Americans, decreed the council, could not "be deprived of these essential rights without shocking the principle of equal liberty which every page in that Constitution labors to enforce."[51]

Perhaps impelled by these arguments, European American antislavery advocates, including John Jay, Alexander Hamilton, Philip Schuyler, and Chancellor Livingston, organized the New York Manumission Society in 1785. This group formed the most vocal and effective opposition to slavery in New York State. In spite of their efforts, however, the New York State legislature did not pass an emancipation law until 1799, and then it was a gradual one. It provided that all male children born to enslaved women after July 4, 1799, would become free at age twenty-eight and all female children would become free at age twenty-five. In 1817, another act freed everyone born into slavery before July 4, 1799, as of July 4, 1827. Some slave owners managed to avoid even these provisions, however, by smuggling those they had enslaved into other states and selling them.[52]

In spite of these antislavery sentiments, 33 percent of Kings County's population in 1790 were enslaved, the largest proportion of any county in New York State. In 1790, 63 percent of Kings County European American families counted at least one enslaved person in their households.

Of the 1,478 African Americans in Kings County in 1790, only 46 were free. As late as 1820, 879 people still lived in slavery in Kings County. This was the geographic and social context for what would become the village of Weeksville.[53]

Edgar McManus argued that slavery disappeared in New York State not only because it was morally reprehensible but also because it was increasingly unprofitable for European Americans. "In the final analysis," he wrote, "the slave obtained his freedom only because his labor was no longer needed." The implications of this for African Americans were potentially disastrous. Competing with cheap European American labor, excluded from skilled crafts dominated by European Americans, no longer bound to elite European American families in a patron-laborer relationship, and lacking a political voice, African Americans had to fend for themselves with few resources. In McManus's view, "what happened to the Negro in New York after emancipation forms one of the darkest chapters in the history of the state."

McManus's conclusions are not without substance but are too broad in scope. By emphasizing what happened to African Americans instead of what African Americans did for themselves, he painted a picture of passive helplessness instead of active and creative resistance. Events among African Americans in Weeksville, New York City, and New York State as a whole suggest a different aspect to the story.[54]

As soon as slavery ended in New York State in 1827, African Americans organized to promote their own rights. Presbyterian minister Samuel Cornish and Bowdoin College graduate John Russwurm began publication of *Freedom's Journal* in New York City, a paper that James Oliver Horton and Lois E. Horton called "the national voice of African America."[55] "We wish to plead our own cause," said the first editorial. "Too long have others spoken for us. Too long has the publik been deceived by misrepresentations, in things which concern us dearly."[56] Two years later, Boston tailor David Walker published his *Appeal to the Colored Citizens of the World*, urging complete equality for all African Americans, to be attained by violence if necessary. Walker died suddenly in 1831. One of his associates was Maria W. Stewart, the first American-born woman to speak to public audiences. Rejected by Boston African Americans, she moved to Brooklyn, where she taught in Colored School No. 3 in Williamsburgh.

Freedom's Journal, Appeal to the Colored Citizens of the World, and those African American newspapers, pamphlets, memoirs, novels, and historical writings that succeeded them became, as Patrick Rael has suggested, "the great mechanism for constructing a unified, even pan-African black identity, one that could protest the interests of the free and slave, African and African American. Those otherwise divided—by free or slave status, regional cultural style, or a host of other factors— were at least rhetorically united by this sense of blackness."[57]

Weeksville performed a similar function in physical form. It represented an opportunity for African Americans to define themselves as free people of color, united across lines of class and regional background, to speak with their own voices, in their own community, in their own ways.

"The Endeared Name, Americans": Political Equality for All

A second issue of vital concern to African Americans was the right to be recognized fully as citizens, especially to have the right to vote. Commitment to American citizenship ran deep among African Americans. When Samuel Cornish became editor of the *Colored American* in 1837, he noted the significance of the paper's name:

> Many would rob us of the endeared name, "Americans," a distinction more emphatically belonging to us than five-sixths of this nation, one that we will never yield. In complexion, in blood and nativity, we are decidedly more exclusively "American" than our white brethren; hence the propriety of the name of our people, Colored Americans, and of identifying the name with all our institutions, in spite of our enemies, who would rob us of our nationality and reproach us as exotics.[58]

More than offering African Americans an opportunity to create a distinct cultural community, Weeksville offered them an opportunity to own land, which in New York State was, for African Americans, the basis of political rights. In the late eighteenth and early nineteenth centuries, land was the basis of economic and political independence for everyone. Citizenship itself was tied to property ownership. In 1777, the first New York State Constitution incorporated this ideal, giving voting rights only to male citizens (both European American and African American) over the age of twenty-one who possessed property worth $250. In 1821, New York State revised its constitution. One of the main debates concerned voting rights. Should all men or only white men be allowed to vote? Partly, the debate centered on the idea of natural rights. Was suffrage a natural right, inherent in citizenship, or a right that could be granted or taken away, based on pragmatic decisions by those who held power?

Ultimately, delegates at the 1821 convention decided to grant universal white male suffrage but to keep the $250 property requirement for black male suffrage. They explained their decision in overtly racist terms. The chair of the committee on suffrage asserted that African Americans "are a peculiar people, incapable . . . of exercising that privilege [of voting] with any sort of discretion, prudence, or independence. They have no just conceptions of civil liberty," any more than "a monkey or a baboon." Samuel Young declared,

> This distinction of colour is well understood. It is unnecessary to disguise it, and we ought to shape our constitution so as to meet the public sentiment. If that sentiment should alter—if the time should ever arrive when the African shall be raised to the level of the white man . . . —when the colours shall intermarry—when negroes shall be invited to your tables—to sit in your pew, or ride in your coach, it may then be proper to institute a new Convention, and remodel the constitution so as to conform to that state of Society.

Underlying these racist sentiments was a partisan political issue: the Democratic-controlled Constitutional Convention feared that African American voters would flock to the Federalists. If African Americans voted, explained one delegate, the whole state would "be controlled by a few hundred of this species of population in the city of New-York."[59]

In protest, African Americans organized actively and loudly for equal suffrage. They held public meetings, gave speeches, and wrote articles. They sent petitions (which contained hundreds of names of both men and women) to the state legislature. In 1834, New Yorkers sent a petition to Albany with 200 to 300 names. In 1836, they sent another with 620 names. By then the movement had also attracted the support of

European American citizens. Petitions were sent from Brooklyn, Albany, Troy, Oswego County, Genesee County, and elsewhere, probably containing both European American and African American names.[60]

Weeksville represented an alternative to attacking the system from outside, and that was to undermine it from within. If African Americans themselves could own $250 worth of land, they could vote under existing law. Weeksville gave African Americans an opportunity to become independent landowners and therefore to become politically active citizens, instantly, peacefully, and unquestionably.

"Grounds Owned and Occupied by Our Own People": Economic Opportunities

After the American Revolution, African Americans in New York City found themselves increasingly excluded from skilled occupations.[61] By the early nineteenth century, as many as one-third of the African American population in New York City worked as domestics in the homes of European Americans. Domestic labor placed people in subservient positions, closer than many would have liked to their former status as enslaved workers. Others worked as laborers at the docks, as sailors, or as waiters, barbers, or chimney sweeps. Even well-educated, middle-class, professional African Americans—teachers and preachers—often worked also in low-paying jobs to maintain their families.

In 1831, Henry Thompson, Rev. James W. C. Pennington, and George Woods described the economic position of African Americans in a letter to the *Long Island Star*: "In our village and its vicinity, how many of us have been educated in colleges, and advanced into different branches of business; or taken into merchant houses, manufacturing establishments, etc. Are we not even prohibited from some of the common labor, and drudgery of the streets, such as cartmen, porters, etc.?"[62]

European Americans often conflated class with race. They argued that African Americans could not be trusted with citizenship as long as they behaved with working-class values. In response, some African Americans in New York City attempted to reshape class values, urging African Americans to minimize showy public parades, protest through legal means instead of through street violence, send their children to school, and attend church.[63]

Education became a major tool for economic betterment. The African Free School, established by the New York Manumission Society in Manhattan in 1788, encompassed seven buildings and fourteen hundred students before its absorption into the New York City public school system. In Brooklyn, a few African Americans attended school beginning in 1815, when Peter Croger established a private school in his home on James Street. Beginning in 1818, African Americans used a room in a tax-supported public school, but in 1827 they were no longer allowed into that building. Responsibility for black education fell to the African Woolman Benevolent Society of Brooklyn. President of the Woolman Society was none other than Henry C. Thompson, blacking manufacturer, who would become one of the founders of Weeksville.[64]

When the cornerstone for the new school was laid on September 25, 1827, the proceedings were marred by class conflicts. The Woolman Society wanted a sedate ceremony, but another group calling themselves the African Tompkins Society decided to march through the streets with music and "caused much disturbance in the streets." "We hope . . . that the respectable population of this village will not impute those irregularities to the Woolman Society," Thompson wrote in a letter to the *Long Island Star*, "for we aim at the general good of the people of color of this village, and have been associated for that purpose more than seventeen years; but we are opposed by these enemies."[65]

Land ownership epitomized not only voting rights for males but also economic independence, education, and nuclear family stability. Weeksville offered a chance for Africans Americans to define themselves as equals with European Americans and to challenge the dominant culture's attempt to keep them in subservient positions. Weeksville represented a refusal to live, as Leslie Harris suggested in the title of her study of African Americans in New York City, "in the shadow of slavery."[66]

An "Alarming Fact": Physical Safety for Free People

Always an issue for African Americans as individuals, physical safety was also a concern for African Americans as a group. On July 4, 1827, for example, official Emancipation Day, African Americans in New York City held celebrations indoors in churches rather than outdoors, because members of the New York State legislature feared that white citizens might resent African Americans celebrating on the "white" Fourth of July. About two thousand African Americans held their own parade instead on July 5, organized by members of lodges, joined by "a number of newly liberated slaves," from New York City and Brooklyn.[67]

As abolitionism became more visible, rioting increased throughout the northern states. In 1829, efforts to enforce stringent black codes forced one thousand free African Americans to flee Cincinnati. In 1834, racial violence erupted in New York City. For three days in July, mobs attacked African Americans and European American abolitionists, destroying, among other places, Arthur and Lewis Tappan's home on Rose Street and St. Philips's African Episcopal Church on Center Street. The Tappan brothers left their house unrepaired, as a "silent Anti-Slavery preacher." Mob action increased in the mid-1830s throughout the Northeast, in proportion to abolitionist organizing.[68]

At the same time, abolitionists began to publicize the problem of kidnapping. Slave catchers worked not only in the South but also in the North, brazenly kidnapping not only people fleeing from slavery but also free people of color. In 1834, Elizur Wright, a European American abolitionist, published a series of articles in the *Emancipator* about specific incidents of kidnapping in New York City, including stories of men, women, and children kept in horrendous conditions and sold irretrievably into slavery.[69]

African Americans, supported by European American allies, responded by establishing vigilance committees to assist both those who escaped from slavery and free people of color subject to kidnapping and enslavement. Friends of Human Rights organized the first vigilance committee in New York City in November 1835. "Impressed with the alarming *fact* that any colored person within this State is liable to be arrested as a *fugitive from slavery* and put upon his defence to prove his freedom, and that any *such person* thus arrested is denied the *right of trial by jury*, and, therefore subject to a hurried trial, often without the aid of a friend or a counsellor—We hold ourselves bound by the Golden Rule of our Saviour, to aid them, *to do to others as we would have them do to us*." Out of this meeting came the New York Committee of Vigilance, which published its first annual report in 1837.[70]

The Vigilance Committee, under the direction of secretary David Ruggles, defined kidnapping as carrying "an unoffending colored person, or any other person, into *slavery . . .* whether done *legally* or *illegally*."[71] The Vigilance Committee worked with three groups of people: those brought as slaves into New York State, free people of color escaping from the South, and people escaping from slavery in the South. Some of those enslaved illegally in New York State were brought as domestics; others were smuggled on slave ships directly from Africa. In late 1835, proving the widespread and blatant nature of the problem, Ruggles himself was captured and threatened with sale into slavery. Historian Carol Wilson noted that by 1837, "the kidnapping of free blacks had become so extensive that no free black person was safe. And that is the crucial issue." Every person of color lived "in perpetual fear."[72]

The Vigilance Committee assisted people through direct action— spreading the word about slave catchers in the city, providing safe houses for people needing refuge, taking offenders to court, publicizing cases in the newspaper, threatening mob action on behalf of fugitives, helping accused fugitives recover their property, and, if necessary, purchasing the freedom of accused fugitives. They were very successful in getting the attention of sympathizers throughout the state. In 1840, after free-born James Watkins Seward was captured and enslaved in Louisiana, the New York State legislature passed a bill authorizing the governor of New York to send an agent to rescue those kidnapped and taken to other states. Solomon Northrup would later be rescued under the provisions of this bill.[73]

Weeksville was established in this context of fear for the physical safety of African Americans, both individually and as a group. As a separate community, set apart from dense urban areas, Weeksville offered a retreat where African Americans, no matter their place of origin or legal status, could settle in relative safety and where slave catchers could not easily follow. Weeksville quickly became a refuge for people who sought freedom. More than 44 percent of adult Weeksville residents in 1850 were born in the South, over twice the proportion of southern-born African Americans in Brooklyn as a whole. Some may, of course, have been free people of color. Others were almost certainly people escaping from slavery who came north on the emerging Underground Railroad.

"Shall We Flee to an Unknown Land?" Emigration to Canada and Liberia

In the face of continued stress for African Americans in the United States, one other option presented itself: emigration to another country. In 1815, Paul Cuffe, African American, Quaker, merchant, and ship-owner, led a group of African Americans to Sierra Leone, the British colony on the west coast of Africa. Cuffe died in 1817, however, and the movement died with him.

European Americans revived the idea of emigration when they formed the American Colonization Society in 1817. They established the colony of Liberia and named its capital Monrovia after James Monroe, president of the Colonization Society and future president of the United States. African Americans, however, spoke out vociferously against this movement. They viewed it, with considerable justification, as a proslavery effort to rid the country of free people of color. Between 1820 and 1833, the American Colonization Society sent 2,886 people to Africa, and only 169 came from the North. Emigration did hold an allure for some, however. John Russworm, coeditor of *Freedom's Journal*, left for Liberia in 1829, where he spent the rest of his life. Even Samuel Cornish could sympathize with those who wanted to leave Cincinnati after the riots in 1829. Canada, he suggested, might make a congenial home for those who prized freedom.[74]

For most African Americans in the 1830s, however, emigration, especially African emigration, held little appeal. After all, almost no African Americans still alive had actually been born in Africa. African Americans did not reject their African heritage, but increasingly they identified it as part of their past rather than as part of their future. Their basic identity was as American people of color. They asserted their rights as American citizens, and they intended to see that America carried out its own revolutionary ideals. The American Colonization Society was designed to rid the United States of free African Americans, and most people of color opposed it with their whole soul.

In 1831, African Americans met in organized nationwide protests against the American Colonization Society. They gathered on June 3, 1831, at the African Hall on Nassau Street in Brooklyn. Henry C. Thompson chaired the meeting. George Hogarth, African Methodist Episcopal minister and later national African Methodist Episcopal book agent and Weeksville resident, was secretary. Rev. James W. C. Pennington, a self-emancipated man from Maryland, was one of the speakers.[75] "We know of no other country," the meeting resolved

> in which we can justly claim or demand our rights as citizens, whether civil or political, but in these United States of America, our native soil: And, that we shall be active in our endeavors to convince the members of the Colonization Society, and the public generally, that we are *men*, that we are *brethren*, that we are *countrymen* and *fellow-citizens*, and demand an equal share of protection from our federal government with any other class of citizens in the community. . . . We are not strangers; neither do we come under the alien law. Our constitution does not call upon us to become naturalized; we are already American citizens; our fathers were among the first that peopled this country; their sweat and their tears have been the means, in a measure, of raising our country to its present standing. Many of them fought, and bled, and died for the gaining of her liberties; and shall we forsake their tombs, and flee to an unknown land? No![76]

In a letter to the *Long Island Star*, Thompson, Rev. Pennington, and George Woods pondered the credibility of the American Colonization Society: "It is a strange theory to us, how these gentlemen can promise to honor, and respect us in Africa, when they are using every effort to exclude us from all rights and privileges at home." When an agent from the society spoke at the Presbyterian Church in Brooklyn later that summer, five hundred African Americans, sitting in a segregated gallery, walked out, one by one. At the agent's second talk, only two African Americans, one of them a journalist, appeared in the audience.[77]

In the mid-1830s, opponents of the American Colonization Society helped found Weeksville as a concrete alternative to colonization abroad. Four years after Henry C. Thompson chaired the Brooklyn meeting against the American Colonization Society, he invested in land that became the nucleus of Weeksville. George Hogarth, one of the leaders of this meeting, later moved to Weeksville.

In 1839, Francis P. Graham, who became Weeksville's largest resident landholder, also took a public stand against colonization. Graham was one of the secretaries of a large anticolonization meeting held in New York City on January 8, 1839. Dr. James McCune Smith offered the first resolution: "That the first principle of republic government is, 'that all men are by nature free and equal,' and the American Colonization Society, by denying that the colored men can rise, in this republic, to the full enjoyment of its institutions, denies the eternal principle of freedom and equality, and is anti-republican in its principles and tendency." Philip Bell, one of the speakers, might have had Weeksville in mind when he pointedly remarked, "'Tis principle that actuates our opposition to this scheme. It is not opposition for opposition's sake, but principle, moral, political, and religious principle. Here will we take our stand. And we will tell the white Americans, that their country is and shall be our country, we will be governed by the same laws, and abide by the same institutions, which we, like them, revere and honor and [we] will worship the same God at the same altar." "We may be driven to build on the barren sands," Bell intoned, perhaps a specific reference to the sandy hills and hollows of Weeksville, but we will make our offerings on the altar of our childhood."[78] It would be surprising if Francis P. Graham, as secretary of this meeting, had not been strongly influenced by these ideas. Later that year, he purchased his first large block of land in Weeksville, and he immediately began selling this to other African Americans.

In effect, Weeksville in the 1830s provided an alternative within the United States, controlled by African Americans themselves, to African colonization.[79] Weeksville allowed Henry Thompson, Francis P. Graham, and other opponents of African colonization to establish a community on U.S. soil, created by and for African Americans, where African Americans could be safe, free, and independent, living their lives both as people of color and as Americans.

For Thompson, Graham, and others, Weeksville had all the advantages of emigration—physical safety, economic stability, a chance to create a community controlled by and for African Americans—and none of the disadvantages. People would still be close to relatives and friends, within the borders of the United States. Most of all, they would still be able to exert their rights as American citizens. They could be, in the American tradition, a city upon a hill, offering a chance for the whole country to live up to its own ideals.

Weeksville: Family and Work in 1840

By 1840, Weeksville was clearly an established African American community. Twenty-four of the twenty-seven families (88.9 percent) in Weeksville were African American. Of the three European American families, two were headed by Moses Suydam and Lewis Suydam, Dutch farmers. Three African Americans—two men and one woman—lived in their households. Fredrick R. Hulbut, listed in the census as working in "learned professions and engineers," headed the third European American family with his wife and three children.[80]

In 1840, 112 people lived in those twenty-four African American families in the Weeksville cluster. Of the twenty-four heads of households, all but one, Elizabeth Brown, were male. All families except Brown's were almost certainly two-parent households (although since the 1840 listed only age and sex for household members, we cannot be sure). These households held a mean of 4.14 people. Family size ranged from two (in the homes of Joseph Tillman, Jorden Harris, Isaac Day, and Robert Tillman) to six (in the families of Robert Wood, Stephen N. Rogers, and William Gray), seven (in Jacob Thompson's family), and nine (in John Willis's home). Forty-seven of Weeksville's residents (42.9 percent of the population) were under twenty-four years old.

In 1840, most families earned their living from the land. Of the twenty-nine workers, eighteen (62 percent) worked in agriculture. Six (or 20.7 percent), including people from the households of Samuel P. Tucker, Stephen Rogers, John Field, William Mitchell, and John Powell, worked in manufacturing and trade. Three (10.3) worked in ocean navigation (including people from the homes of Stephen Rogers, James Weeks, and Rodrick Hazens). Two (6.9 percent) worked in commerce.

Many people who owned land in Weeksville actually lived not there but in downtown Brooklyn. Between 1833 and 1846, city directories listed Sylvanus Smith, for example, as a hog drover living at 189 Pearl Street. Smith very likely used his Weeksville lands to raise these hogs. Samuel Anderson lived near the Smith family at 93 or 193 Pearl Street from 1822 to 1835, before moving to Weeksville in 1839 and then back to downtown Brooklyn at Prince and Tillary in 1841–42. Through deed searches, Robert Swan located at least thirty-eight African Americans who owned property in the Weeksville/Carrsville area who were not listed in the 1840 census for the Ninth Ward.[81]

Hunterfly Road

At the eastern edge of Weeksville, Hunterfly Road ran south from the Long Island Railroad near the Suydam house on Atlantic Avenue and then rose on high ground to cross Crow Hill. Just south of the current site of the Hunterfly Road houses, travelers reached Keuter's Hook and Hunterfly Woods, where people came from miles around to hold "pic nics" and celebrations. Farther south, Citizens' Union Cemetery and the elegant Duncan house stood west of Hunterfly Road, looking east and south toward Jamaica Bay. Beyond Hunterfly Road, to the east, lay the wilder lands of New Lots, mostly pastures and unkempt farms.

In the early nineteenth century, on land that became part of Weeksville, the estate of Samuel Garrittsen owned a large farm whose eastern boundary was Hunterfly Road. At Garrittsen's estate auction on July 9, 1839, Samuel Bouton purchased parcels 11, 21, and 22 bordering Hunterfly Road. Parcels 11 and 22 contained about seventy-one lots of 2,500 square feet each. Parcel 21 contained about sixty lots of 2,500 square feet each. It would become block 1356 of Brooklyn, the present site of the houses now owned by the Weeksville Heritage Society.

At the same auction of Samuel Garrittsen's estate in 1839, Francis P. Graham purchased property on what would become block 1350 (listed on the Garrittsen map as block 20), along with the southwest corner of what is here noted as block 19, just north of Bouton's purchase. Graham's land was located south of where the Long Island Railroad intersected Hunterfly Road and east of the most concentrated settlement of Weeksville.[82]

By 1850, a dynamic cosmopolitan neighborhood had grown up on Graham's land. Among those who lived there was Lydia Ann Elizabeth Simmons Dixon LeGrant.

2

"Owned and Occupied by Our Own People"

Weeksville's Growth: Family, Work, and Community, 1840–1860

On a sunny June morning in 1850, Lydia Ann Elizabeth Simmons Dixon LeGrant stepped off the front porch of her house in the village of Weeksville in eastern Brooklyn.[1] Most likely, she was intent on her morning chores—feeding the chickens and geese, perhaps a goat or two, and maybe also a cow or horse—but she took a moment to savor her surroundings. She smelled the fresh green of early summer. Around her were sandy patches of scrubby grass interspersed with clumps of bushes and large trees. Just north of her neighborhood stood a large park filled with oak, spruce, and pine trees. Just south stood another large forest, Hunterfly Woods. People often came to both these parks for Sunday school picnics, dances, and large parties.[2]

She looked up at a steep hill just east of her house and down to a deep hollow just north. These banks were crisscrossed at odd angles by streets that were wide dirt paths, dusty in the summer heat, muddy in spring rains, and frozen in winter snows. Across the street, Suydam's Pond stretched a quarter of a mile west, providing fish for food, water for washing, ice for cooling, and ice skating in the wintertime. Just north of her house, near the corner of Rochester Avenue and Dean Street, several of her neighbors lived in a deep gorge between two hills, where stormy winds often blew.[3]

Like many of her neighbors (but not many women she knew), Lydia Simmons LeGrant owned her own land. In 1842, when she was only twenty-two years old, she had purchased two lots from Francis P. Graham, Weeksville's wealthiest resident, at the eastern edge of Weeksville, where Rochester Avenue crossed Bergen Street, just west of Hunterfly

Road. Graham's own house stood on Hunterfly Road, where it crossed the steep hill just east of Lydia's new lots. In the 1840s, when he was most likely more than fifty years old, Graham brought his new bride, teenager Sarah Ann, to live in this house.[4]

LeGrant's neighbors included people born in Virginia, Maryland, Pennsylvania, Washington, D.C., and Africa, as well as at least three people from South Carolina. They built homes and established a small neighborhood along Hunterfly Road. People worked as laborers, seamstresses, and shoemakers. Among them were Charles Lewis, boot maker, born in Virginia; James Moody, born in Africa, and his wife Jane Moody; Nathan C. B. Thomas, preacher from Maryland; and Rev. Thomas's wife Henrietta Thomas.[5]

Lydia Simmons had once been married to landowner Henry Dixon, with whom she had a daughter Ann. After Dixon's death, Lydia married James LeGrant, eight years her junior, who had come to Weeksville from South Carolina in the mid-1840s. James had his problems, having in 1849 been accused of stealing $4.50 from "his mother," perhaps young Sarah Graham, his stepmother. James spent sixty days in the penitentiary at Flatbush because he could not pay the $10.00 fine.[6]

As the only carpenter in Weeksville, however, James had skills the whole community found useful. He may have built Lydia's own house— a two-family dwelling at the northeast corner of Rochester Avenue and Bergen Street. Lydia, James, and Lydia's daughter, four-year-old Ann C. Dixon, lived in one part of this house. In the other part lived Edward Butler, shoemaker, born about 1820 in South Carolina. Butler was small and misshapen, perhaps as a result of a beating in his youth. A newspaper reporter in the 1870s called him "a dwarf, stumped in youth from a white swelling." Two more small girls, also named Ann, lived on Edward's side of the house—Ann E. Connor, three months old, and Ann E. Weeks, one year old. All three adults brought money into the household, James as a carpenter, Edward as a shoemaker, and Lydia most likely as a caregiver and seamstress.[7]

When Lydia and her family went to church, they may have attended Bethel African Methodist Episcopal Church, just two blocks west on Dean Street. They may, however, have walked up Crow Hill, just south of their house, to Berean Baptist Church, often called the "little church on the hill." Francis P. Graham was one of thirteen trustees of Berean

Baptist, organized just that year, in 1850. Most people who attended Berean Baptist were African American, but four of the trustees and the current minister, Rev. Daniel Underdue, were European American.

James Weeks lived two blocks west of the LeGrant home. In the 1840s, he expanded his property holdings, buying several more lots contiguous to his original purchase. By 1850, Weeks was fifty-six years old, working as a "superintendent." In 1850 he built a "handsome dwelling" worth fifteen hundred dollars at the corner of Schenectady and Atlantic Avenues. He also expanded his family to include many people who had emigrated from Virginia. He married Virginia-born Elizabeth Weeks, perhaps his second wife, since at age thirty-four she was twenty-two years younger than he was. They raised at least four children in Weeksville—Maria (age fourteen), Anna (or Sarah, age eleven), James (five), and Louisa (three). James and Elizabeth were surrounded by a large extended family, born in either New York State or Virginia. Cesar Weeks (perhaps a brother) was a laborer, aged forty-six, born in New York, who lived with his wife Isabella, born in New Jersey, aged forty-three, and their daughter, Isabella (eleven), in a house worth five hundred dollars. John Weeks was also a laborer, age thirty-two, born in Virginia, who lived with his wife Jane Weeks (twenty-three) and their four children—Mary (seven), John (five), Rosana (four), and Sarah (two), all born in New York.[8]

To outsiders, Weeksville was "terra incognita," full of "woods, wastelands, and wild gullies," known primarily for "peace, fresh air, and chickens," "hickory nuts and blackberries." To its residents, Weeksville was home. When Lydia Simmons LeGrant, James LeGrant, Edward Butler, James Weeks, and Francis P. Graham looked around them, almost everyone they saw was a person of color. Until the late 1850s, only three European American families lived in this African American enclave. Here, LeGrant and her neighbors had a chance to control their own lives. They could grow their own gardens, feed their own chickens, and keep dogs or goats, pigs, a cow or two, and a horse if they wished. People could walk everywhere. And if they wanted more than they could buy in local stores or more work than they could find in Weeksville, they traveled to downtown Brooklyn, just a ten-minute ride on the Long Island Railroad, where work was plentiful and ferries crossed the river to Manhattan.[9]

The two and a half decades from 1840 to 1865 were years of prosperity and growth for Weeksville, the high point of its identity as a separate African American community. By 1850, just fifteen years after it began, this community was an extraordinary thriving hamlet of almost four hundred people, a haven for people of color from all over the eastern United States, the West Indies, and the west coast of Africa. Its population more than tripled, from 165 African Americans in 1840 to 366 in 1850 to 521 in 1855. Weeksville's residents worked in a variety of urban and rural occupations, developed churches and a school, owned land, and worked for political equality, asserting their rights as free people of color in a land of slavery.

Weeksville Institutions and Events

From 1840 to 1865, Weeksville developed its identity as a predominantly African American community by creating institutions that reflected a vibrant community life. These included at least two churches (A.M.E. Bethel and Berean Baptist), a school (Colored School No. 2), the Citizens' Union Cemetery, and several recreational activities (including a baseball team, the Weeksville Unknowns).

Weeksville also became significant statewide and nationally as a center of activism against slavery and for the rights of free people of color. Weeksville was the home of a nationally known journalist (Junius C. Morel); a safe place for African Americans on the Underground Railroad; a key area of activism for the rights of free African Americans (including voting rights); a focal point for a nationally significant debate about emigration (especially to Liberia and Canada); the national headquarters of the African Civilization Society; a haven for African Americans escaping the draft riots in New York City during the Civil War; and a source of African American soldiers and sailors for the Civil War.

Churches and Religious Activities in Weeksville

By 1860, Brooklyn had so many churches—139 to be exact—that it was known as the "city of churches." Several of these were African American churches—including the African Wesleyan Methodist Church (formed in 1818, meeting on High Street and then, after 1854, on Bridge Street),

A.M.E. Church, Weeksville, built after 1848. Courtesy Weeksville Heritage Center.

African Society (organized in Williamsburgh in 1818, which became Varick A.M.E. Zion Church in 1827), Concord Baptist (formed in 1847), Siloam Presbyterian Church (formed in 1849), and two churches in Weeksville (Berean Baptist and Bethel A.M.E. Church).[10]

In Weeksville, as in the rest of Brooklyn, these churches became the basis of community life. In 1847, the same year that Concord Baptist organized in downtown Brooklyn, a small group of Weeksville citizens founded an A.M.E. church in Weeksville, under the care of High Street (later Bridge Street) African Wesleyan Methodist Church. In 1848, during the annual New York Conference, the Weeksville congregation laid the cornerstone for a small building at 90 Schenectady Avenue and Dean Street, on land purchased from Sarah Lefferts. On January 29, 1849, they incorporated as the Bethel African Methodist Episcopal Church "at Weeksville in the Ninth Ward of the City of Brooklyn." For the first few years, pastors from the High Street Church served the Weeksville congregation.[11]

When Bethel Church became part of a regular circuit, Edward C. Africanus became the first regular pastor. Africanus had been born about 1821 in New York State. In 1843, after an education in

Rev. Edward Africanus served African Methodist Episcopal congregations in Weeksville and Flushing, New York, before his untimely death. This lithograph was published about 1853 by the Tappan and Bradford Lithography Company, probably based on a daguerreotype. Courtesy National Portrait Gallery, Smithsonian Institution.

local schools, he became a member of the New York Conference of the A.M.E. Church. There he quickly learned both Latin and Greek. Many considered him, as Alexander Wayman noted in the *Cyclopedia of African Methodism*, "the most talented minister in the New York conference." Africanus left Weeksville to become pastor of Macedonia A.M.E. Church in Flushing, New York, where he died an untimely death about 1853.[12]

Even though women typically outnumbered men at least two to one as church members in this period, they did not have legal rights as citizens. So official representatives of the church were always male. Trustees of A.M.E. Bethel included Samuel Bowman, James Moody, Anderson Thompson, Michael Ward, and Henry Wright. Bowman, Thompson, and Ward were not listed in the 1850 manuscript census, but James Moody was listed as fifty-eight years old, born in Africa, married to Jane, age fifty-five, born in North Carolina. Henry Wright was thirty-one years old, a measurer of grain, born in Kentucky. Neither Moody nor Wright was literate, according to this census. Nathan C. B. Thomas ministered to this church. Born in slavery about 1791 in Prince George's County, Maryland, Thomas came to New York when he was young. There he was licensed to preach in the A.M.E. Church. He joined the New York Conference and traveled from one church to another for many years before he settled in Weeksville. He married Henrietta, born in Maryland about 1808. They purchased a lot on Hunterfly Road in 1841, where they still lived in 1850. By 1850, he owned property worth eighteen hundred dollars. In 1872, the city directory listed Thomas at 1519 Bergen Street.[13]

Bethel A.M.E. Church became an anchor for Weeksville's community development. Through the New York Conference, it was in regular contact with churches in Pennsylvania, New England, Maryland, western New York, Ohio, Indiana, and Upper Canada. The Upper Canada Conference was organized July 21, 1840, in Toronto, whose residents showed "such a magnanimous and generous spirit" toward people who sought refuge from slavery. Presumably, Weeksville A.M.E. members used this network to facilitate escape from slavery.[14]

By the 1850s, Bethel A.M.E. Church also supported two nationally significant people, one editor and one journalist. The editor was George Hogarth. Born in Annapolis, Maryland, Hogarth first appeared at an A.M.E. conference in Baltimore in 1828, when he was steward of a mission church in Haiti. After he moved to Weeksville, he used his Haitian connections to start merchant business, trading with Port-au-Prince. He also taught at Colored School No. 1 and in 1841 became one of the first trustees (with Sylvanus Smith and Henry Thompson) of Colored School No. 2.[15]

As teacher and merchant, Hogarth was a mainstay of the national African Methodist Episcopal Church from at least 1831, when he represented the New York Conference at the national A.M.E. meeting, until his death in 1850. Beginning in 1832, he served regularly as secretary for the New York Conference, and he also acted as book steward, first for the New York Conference and then, from 1835 to 1848, for the national body, headquartered in Philadelphia. In 1835, Hogarth's charge was to "publish such religious books, tracts and pamphlets as may be deemed best for the interests of the Connection," and he was given twenty-five dollars to revise and publish the hymnbook and discipline. To be closer to Hogarth, the national conference moved its headquarters for the book concern from Philadelphia to Brooklyn. Hogarth had a reputation for speaking and writing clearly and convincingly, without flowery rhetoric. Since he was a merchant by profession, he was used to business life. "He was no mere enthusiastic admirer of his own denomination. . . . He weighed things before he undertook to express their value by words, and then he employed just such words as really represented their value."[16]

Hogarth's business expertise made him especially useful, since he constantly had to raise money. In 1839, he outlined a plan for each member to give two cents per month to the book concern, with profits to be applied toward the care of aged and infirm ministers and the education of young ministers. In 1840, he wrote the prospectus for a new national A.M.E. magazine, the *Monthly Magazine*. Its major goals were espousing a "primitive Christianity," vindicating the rights of the church as "African Methodists," promoting union among Methodists, regardless of color, and expanding their outreach both to "brethren of color in this country" and to those who still lived in Africa, "the land of our fathers." Its first issue appeared in September 1841. By 1845, however, the magazine suspended operations for want of funds. Hogarth worked on a committee with Edward C. Africanus to compose a letter to the "World's Convention of the Christian Church," to be held in London. In it, he emphasized the history and organization of the A.M.E. Church, but he also appealed for financial help.

Throughout his tenure as editor, Hogarth espoused ideals of an educated ministry and congregants. In 1843, he celebrated with the rest of the church the "glorious outpouring of the Holy Spirit," which affected African American churches of several denominations. "Like priest, like people," he argued. "As the priests are, so will the people be. If the priests are ignorant, unacquainted with human nature, unacquainted with the human mind, their manners low and unimproved, so will the people be. That we need an enlightened, educated ministry no one ought to deny."[17]

Bishop Daniel A. Payne was an enthusiastic admirer of George Hogarth. In Payne's *History of the African Methodist Episcopal Church*, published in 1891, he eulogized Hogarth as "one of the most intelligent ministers in the A. M. E. Church," "among the most useful of the useful—one of the leading members of this Conference."

> In business tact and knowledge he had few equals and no superior. His publications in the form of Disciplines and hymn-books were remarkable for the beauty of their mechanical execution. His own productions were always simple, clear and pointed. And, although not distinguished for oratory, his sermons were always full of that warmth which belongs to the man whose heart is right with God. He was cut down in the midst of life and in the midst of his usefulness, respected and loved by all who knew him.[18]

Weeksville was also the home of a nationally known journalist, activist, and educator, Junius C. Morel. Raised in a southern slave cabin, he became one of America's most prolific journalists, writing for the *North Star* and other abolitionist presses, as well as for the A.M.E. national newspaper, the *Christian Recorder*.

Born at Pembroke Hall in South Carolina (or perhaps North Carolina) between 1801 and 1806, Morel was the son of a European American planter and an enslaved African American mother. Morel left his home with his father's blessing. An article signed "Junius of Cedar Hill" in the *North Star*, May 19, 1854, described his leave-taking. There were "weeks of busy preparation," "a dear mother's ever remembered embrace and admonition," and "the direction and benediction of to me, an affectionate father," before he left Pembroke Hall, the "slave plantation where I was born." He sailed north on the schooner *Olive Branch* of Shrewsbury, New Jersey, whose captain, Jonathan Rial, was a man of color and a "devoted Christian." His son George, "a very genteel mulatto young man," was cook and steward. The mate and crew were white. Captain Rial treated "Junius" as a son and seated him at the dinner table next to him every evening, along with the three white passengers. Captain Rial offered a prayer the first night, and it was, wrote "Junius," the first intelligible prayer that I had ever heard." He had been "sprinkled and crossed and blessed, and my father had read prayers out of a large book in Latin and French, and kissed and caused me to kiss the pictures in the book, but what of all that—what did I know about it? But when I heard Capt. Rial pray, I was amazed and lost in wondering."[19]

"This first intelligible prayer to me brought forcibly to my remembrance," Junius remembered,

> that I had often witnessed sufferings and stumbling and heard efforts made to pray as I have knelt down on the damp earth floor of the slave cabin, in the quarters where on the earth was spread a mat made of a species of flag, over which were a few rags and shreds. This we called a bed. Often at the side of such bed I have knelt down with a group of other little slave children, girls and boys, all in a State of nudity, while some kind old "auntie or uncle," groping in the thick mental darkness was aiming to instruct us in the Lord's prayer. Ho! the place, the group, the scene and the trembling embarrassment with the language of the instructor are so deeply engraven on the tablets of my heart's memory, that neither space nor time nor place nor the change of position nor any other change saved reason or death can even obliterate it.

Junius recalled scenes of cruelty from his childhood—a blacksmith unjustly accused of theft and beaten horribly; Sukey, who refused improper advances from a white man and whose master punished her by forcing her husband to lash her bare back; a free colored man named Overton who hunted runaways with his pack of dogs.

Finally, he recounted the story of seeing, in the streets of Philadelphia, a man in a broad-brimmed Quaker hat, Isaac T. Hopper, stopping George F. Alberti, a notorious kidnapper, from beating an enslaved man. This was, wrote Junius, "THE FIRST WHITE MAN THAT I EVER SAW, WHO PITIED THE COLORED MAN." When he arrived in Philadelphia, Morel stayed with a British family, Mr. and Mrs. G.— and their two sons. Mr. G. was a hardware importer and an Anglican. Mrs. G. was a Quaker. Both, wrote Junius, were "exemplary members of God's universal Church."[20]

In 1829, Morel initiated his lifelong career as a journalist and reformer by becoming a subscription agent for Samuel Cornish's paper the *Rights of All*. He helped organize the first national black convention in 1831, and, according to C. Peter Ripley, editor of the *Black Abolitionist Papers*, "played a prominent role in five of the first six black national conventions." Morel also organized the "Political Association" in Philadelphia, asserting the right of African Americans to vote. "Funds were collected, eminent counsel consulted, and matters . . . made ready to assert our claim," he wrote, but "a vain temerity on the part of some, and a suicidal apathy on the part of others prostrated my designs." In an article for *The Colored American*, Morel explained the source of his passion. "I speak knowingly on this subject, for am I not the son of a slaveholder, by his 'chattel personal?'—Have I not long resided among them, and am I not familiar and conversant with all its pagan—no! its tender, Christian and republican cruelties?—for Christian Republican Slavery is grown so licentious, as to know no law, and to be guided by no rule, save the will of the brutal slaveholder."[21]

Morel settled in Philadelphia and married Caroline Richards, a member of the local elite, but he condemned Philadelphia's leadership for their "criminal apathy and idiot coldness." Morel was, as the historian Julie Winch has noted, "fiery" and "vociferous." In 1836, Philadelphia leaders such as James Forten and William Whipper turned from the black convention movement to a new organization, the American Moral Reform Society, and organized a convention for "every American," black or white, who worked for "EDUCATION, TEMPERANCE, ECONOMY, and UNIVERSAL LIBERTY." Believing that they were Americans and not "colored" Americans, they broke with Samuel Cornish and the New York group over terminology. They also broke with radicals such as Junius C. Morel, who scorned them as "the modern elements" and urged that they call off "this unsound experiment" and give the money instead to the American Anti-Slavery Society.[22]

Looking for more congenial allies, Morel moved to Harrisburg, Pennsylvania, in 1837 and then to Newark, New Jersey, before he settled in Weeksville about 1847.[23] As principal of Colored School No. 2 (later P.S. 68) and as a resident of Weeksville, Morel became a major community leader and a nationally recognized African American activist and journalist, and (noted Elisha Weaver, book agent for the A.M.E. Church) a "much esteemed . . . gentleman and scholar." He taught both black and white students and laid the foundation for integrating Brooklyn's school system after the Civil War. He also became a member of the A.M.E. Church.[24]

By 1850, Morel was living near the school on "Morell's Lane" and was actively promoting land sales to African Americans on the school block itself, through advertisements in Frederick Douglass's *North Star*. He listed his own address as both the Brooklyn post office and his apartments in Weeksville. Morel must have been acting as an agent for someone else, since he did not purchase land in Weeksville himself until 1855. That year, he bought a 100-foot square lot on the north side of Pacific Street, 270 feet west of the corner of Troy Avenue on block 1334. In 1865, this property was listed in the census as worth two thousand dollars. He lived there until his death about 1874.[25]

Nationally, Morel began to write prolifically for African American newspapers. He became an agent for the *North Star* in 1851 and a national correspondent for the *Christian Recorder* under the pen name "Junius." In 1853, in an article in the *North Star*, "C. W." listed Junius C. Morel as one among several distinguished African American editors. "It is not a little remarkable," C. W. noted, "that [of] the editors above named, not less than one third were fugitives from the 'house of bondage.'"

Morel may or may not have been legally free. Although he claimed to have been born on a plantation, to a slave-owning father and an African American mother, he never claimed to be enslaved. In an 1837 speech against colonization, for example, he spoke as an "American Citizen," "Yes, Sir, a Southern born man, the son of one who lived and died a slave-holder."[26]

Morel's probable free status did not protect him from fear of capture, however, and he continued to take precautions. In 1850, the year the Fugitive Slave Act passed Congress, the U.S. census taker listed Morel as "Joseph Merrill," born in the West Indies. This may have been a mistake. More likely, however, it was an attempt by either Morel or the census taker to obscure Morel's paper trail, in case someone tried to capture him. In 1850, Morel's position in terms of the Fugitive Slave Law may have been doubly precarious, since he was one of the semisecret Committee of Thirteen, organized in the New York City area to assist people escaping from slavery. It is quite likely that this committee used Weeksville as at least a temporary place of refuge for freedom seekers. New York State census records in 1855 and 1865 listed Morel under his own name but noted in 1855 that he was born in South Carolina and in 1865 that he was from North Carolina.[27]

Morel helped rejuvenate the national black convention movement in the 1850s. In 1853, he received more votes (346) than any other of the forty-six candidates for the New York State Convention of Colored People. He acted as a Brooklyn delegate to the National Council of the Colored People in 1855 and promoted the national convention held in Syracuse in 1864.[28]

Morel's attitude toward emigration was complicated. He opposed the work of the European American–dominated African Colonization Society, but he endorsed Canadian emigration as early as 1830. He clearly opposed emigration to Liberia in the early 1850s, expressing his "utter abhorrence of the Colonizationists and their designs." "No one who hears him on that important subject," he wrote in the third person 1851, "can doubt whether he really hates them or not. Were they, the Colonizationists, to hear him, I really think they would afterwards hate themselves."[29] He defended the rights of African Americans to American citizenship after the Dred Scott decision in 1857. In 1863 he criticized President Lincoln's proposal to resettle African Americans in South America and the Caribbean. At the same time, he encouraged initiatives by African Americans themselves to settle in Honduras and to create new communities in the South and Southwest, and in the 1860s he became a supporter of the African Civilization Society.[30]

After the death of his first wife, Caroline, in 1838, Morel married a woman named Sarah, born in New York County in 1835. They had a daughter, Alice, born in 1860. He continued to live in Weeksville until his death about 1874.[31]

Members of the Weeksville church regularly supported the *Christian Recorder*, national newspaper of the A.M.E. Zion Church. Junius Morel wrote regularly for this paper under the pen name of "Junius." In 1861, Elisha Weaver, General Book Steward for the A.M.E. Church, gave a talk in Weeksville and collected three dollars for the cause, and Weeksville residents continued to contribute. In 1864, Weeksville women formed the first Daughters of Conference society of the A.M.E. Church, designed to raise money to support A.M.E. ministers.[32]

On August 15, 1850, a year after the official incorporation of Bethel A.M.E. Church, Berean Baptist Church was incorporated, also in the Ninth Ward. Unlike Bethel A.M.E. Church, Berean Baptist was originally a biracial church. The names of thirteen males plus two ministers

Berean Baptist Church, ca. 1851. Courtesy Weeksville Heritage Center.

of Berean Baptist Church were listed as founding members, either on the deed or on church incorporation papers. Of these, eight were African American (George Baker, Francis P. Graham, Charles Lewis, William Mitchell, Stephen Murray, Elijah Overton, Jeptha Reed, and John Weeks). Five of them (George Baker, Francis P. Graham, Charles Lewis, William Mitchell, and Jeptha Reed) had either lived in Weeksville or owned land there since 1840 or before. One, Francis P. Graham, shoemaker, minister, and land speculator, some of whose land holdings adjoined Hunterfly Road, had property worth eight thousand dollars. At least five of the original members (William Oliver, George Evans, T. J. Hutchinson, Peter Balem, John Treslow, Rev. Daniel Reese, and Rev. Daniel Underdue) were European American.[33]

Berean Church was originally built on Warren Street, now Prospect Place, on land purchased for $240. The original deed noted that it was in Carrsville, on block 1367. The site was high on a hill, earning the

church the name Little Church on the Hill. Sometime after its incorporation, several European American members left the church, claiming
that the hill was too difficult to climb. They built a second church on
the corner of Herkimer Street and Rochester Avenue, under the pastorate of Rev. Daniel Reese, leaving Rev. Daniel Underdue as pastor at
Berean Church. Peter Galem, one of the original European American
members, took a twenty-year mortgage of fifteen hundred dollars on
the original church, ensuring its survival.[34]

About 1863, Berean received its first African American pastor, Simon
Bundick. Rev. Bundick, born in Virginia, moved to Weeksville about
1847 with his wife Johanna and their five children (Isaiah [probably
Obadiah], age eleven; Margaret, ten; Simon, eight; Cornelius, five; and
Barsella, two). Johanna Bundick listed her birthplace as New Jersey, but
all of their children were New Yorkers by birth. Simon Bundick listed
his occupation as a laborer, but he had done very well for himself economically. In 1850, the family owned a frame house worth one thousand dollars. In May 1854, Simon Bundick bought a lot from Samuel
Howard at the corner of Troy and Bergen Street. In October 1869, he
bought another lot from Horetta Horton.[35]

Bundick may have worked as a tailor as well as a minister. In 1859,
the *Brooklyn Eagle* published an article about a tailor named Bundick
at 76 South Seventh Street, "an alchemical genius in the garment line,
who can renovate the most ancient, seedy coat into a bright an shining
vestment, rivaling a new one in appearance and durability, for a mere
trifle. If you have an old coat just try him," advised the *Eagle*. "You will
not need a new one for six months, and can save the money and buy
your wife a new hat." Johanna Bundick could not read, but she and her
husband valued education, and their two school-age children, Margaret
and Simon, attended school.[36]

From 1852 to 1856, Rev. Bundick served as pastor of the Concord
Baptist Church in downtown Brooklyn, known for its abolitionist sym-
pathies and its work on the Underground Railroad. Rev. Bundick succeeded Rev. Leonard Black, who had escaped from slavery and been
forced to leave Brooklyn after the Fugitive Slave Act threatened his
freedom. This may be the same Leonard Black, born in Ann Arun-
del County, Maryland, who escaped from slavery to become a minister, serving churches in Portland, Maine, and Boston in the 1840s. He

published his autobiography, *The Life and Sufferings of Leonard Black, a Fugitive from Slavery*, in 1847, recounting his life in slavery, where he was "owned like a cow or a horse."[37]

In 1856, Concord Baptist had twenty-seven members, while Berean Baptist, pastored by Rev. John R. Goings, had twenty-three members. From 1863 to 1874, Rev. Bundick served the Weeksville Baptist Church, located on the hill on Warren Street, where he earned a reputation as "a man who thinks for himself" and holds opinions "tenaciously."[38]

Like many churches, Berean Baptist had a strong tradition of both spiritual strength and social activism. A history of Berean Baptist, called *The Little Church on the Hill*, explained their theology:

> Berean Missionary Baptist Church was founded on the solid foundation that Jesus Christ is Lord and Savior of all. Understanding that the Christian faith addresses the holistic needs of humanity, beginning with the spiritual and encompassing all other needs, the members of Berean have always had one foot planted firmly on the spiritual path and the other rooted in helping to improve conditions for our community and our people. Guided by that faith, and with a strong belief in the words of Christ when He said, ". . . Inasmuch as ye have done it unto one of the least of my brethren, ye have done it unto me," our members have continually struggled to be doers of the Word and not hearers only.

The Little Church on the Hill noted that church members supported efforts to gain voting rights for African Americans, assisted freedom seekers from the South, and helped those fleeing from the 1863 draft riots in New York City.[39]

Berean Church was destroyed by fire on September 18, 1865. Members met in the home of George and Mary Elizabeth Joan Baker until they were able to build a new church, buy a pump organ, and start their own choir. In 1879–80, under the leadership of Rev. Samuel Christian, the church paid off its original mortgage. By 1890, they had thirty-five members.[40]

These churches anchored the Weeksville community and bound it into the larger network of religious institutions in Brooklyn. Often, churches throughout Brooklyn held joint celebrations for Sabbath school graduations, West Indian Emancipation Days, and other community affairs. African Americans in Brooklyn and Weeksville, as elsewhere, celebrated the anniversary of British Emancipation in the West Indies on August 1. The gathering of 1854 was typical. The Bridge Street African Methodist Episcopal Church held a citywide program, featuring talks by Weeksville's own Junius C. Morel, as well as by William Wilson, principal of Colored School No. 1; Rev. Dr. J. W. C. Pennington, who had escaped from slavery in Maryland to become a Brooklyn minister; and Rev. A. N. Freeman, Presbyterian minister and Underground Railroad activist. A decade later, in 1864, schools and churches held "one of the grandest affairs of the season" in Lefferet's (sic) Park, where local ministers (including Baptist minister J. Sella Martin and S. T. Jones of Zion Church) gave speeches. "The union of the churches in this matter warrants the hope that the young people, as well as the old, who wish to spend a pleasant day in the grove, will find there all that the heart can wish for; and the lovers of eloquence will listen to such appeals as will stir their patriotism," wrote Junius C. Morel to the *North Star*. These celebrations continued at least through the 1880s, attracting thousands of African Americans and a few European Americans.[41]

On January 1, 1863, Junius C. Morel from Weeksville helped carry out a typical a Sunday school celebration in the Bridge Street A.M.E. Church. He later reported it for the *Christian Recorder*:

Four beautiful trees, tastefully hung with books and presents for the lovely children, graced the altar. The little ones being seated, the pastor opened the services, then addressed the scholars, then they sang, led by one of their own number. Mr. J.C. Morel, an old and experienced teacher of public schools, addressed them, illustrating the scientific process of evaporation in his peculiar and happy manner; the boiling of the tea kettle, being the example of the mode of evaporation, the sticking of your finger in the molasses, that of adhesion, &c., then came the crowning of the queen of the school, a lovely, modest, and gentle little creature, who was presented and crowned with a beautiful white wreath, by Mr. Morell, and the scholars were rejoiced to greet their fair queen. After this came the distribution of presents. It was pleasant to see the children with smiling faces and sparkling eyes, receiving their books and presents as tokens of good conduct, they seemed happy in knowing that they have some one who cares for them. After this part of the exercises, they all retired to the basement, where the teachers had prepared amply for the comfort of the little ones.[42]

In 1978, A.M.E. Bethel moved to old P.S. 83 building at 1630 Dean Street, across the street from its original site. A cornerstone dated 1847 is attached to a small building on the corner of Dean and Schenectady, the site of the original building.[43]

Berean Baptist Church also expanded in the late nineteenth century. Destroyed once more by fire in 1891, the church began to meet in the Howard Colored Orphan Asylum. In 1894, under the leadership of Rev. Dr. Leonard Joseph Brown, they completed a new building on a lot measuring one hundred by ninety feet on Bergen Street, at a cost of $16,500. This was the first African American church in the New York City area to build its own building from the ground up, and it remained in use into the twenty-first century. Under Rev. Brown's leadership, the congregation continued to grow. By 1896, the church had 60 members, with 165 people in the Sunday school. By 1900, there were 100 members of the church, with 200 people in the Sunday school. Two wings were added to the church in 1915. In 1961, the church built a new sanctuary adjacent to the old one.[44] As the exhibit catalog for *Black Churches and Brooklyn* noted in 1984, Berean Church "stands as a living symbol of the centrality of the church to the concerns and aspirations of the black Brooklyn community almost from its beginning."[45]

Besides A.M.E. Bethel and Berean Baptist, two more churches entered Weeksville at the turn of the century. St. Philip's Protestant Episcopal Church began at 1887 Pacific Avenue. The following year, it moved to a former Baptist Church at 1610 Dean Street between Troy and Schenectady, then to 334 McDonough Street in 1904. This church established the first African American chapters of the Brotherhood of St. Andrew and the Boys' Brigade, a forerunner of the Boy Scouts.[46]

In 1910, African Americans founded the Newman Memorial United Methodist Church as a mission church in the Old Embury Church at Herkimer Street and Schenectady Avenue. It was named after bishop John P. Newman, who helped reestablish Methodism in the southern states after the Civil War.[47]

Berean Baptist Church, twentieth century. Photo by Alexander Moore. Courtesy Weeksville Heritage Center.

Schools

Brooklyn had a school for black children beginning in 1815, when Peter Croger set up a school in his own home on James Street. They moved to a public school in 1818 and then to a schoolhouse constructed by the Woolman Society, whose president, Henry C. Thompson, would within a few years become a founder of Weeksville. This school later became Brooklyn's Colored School No. 1. Its teachers included George Hogarth, who resigned in 1840 to become book agent for the A.M.E. Church and who would later move to Weeksville; Augustus A. Washington, who resigned about 1841 to become a well-known daguerreotypist before emigrating to Liberia; William J. Wilson, who served as principal until about 1863 when he became a teacher in a Freedman's school in the South and who also wrote for *Frederick Douglass's Paper* under the pen name "Ethiop," and Miss Wilson. In 1851, this school had a seating capacity of 450, with 300 pupils registered and an average attendance of 200.[48]

In February 1841, three "intelligent colored citizens," George Hogarth, Henry Brown, and Sylvanus Smith," became Trustees for Colored School No. 1. Carleton Mabee has suggested that this was an early instance of African American control over a public school. Robert Swan has disputed this, arguing that while African Americans did control black schools in Brooklyn, such schools were essentially independent black schools, not part of the public school system. When black schools did become part of the public system in 1845, African Americans lost control of them until after the Civil War.[49]

In the rural Ninth Ward, people in Carrsville formed an African Union Society, which built a small schoolhouse and opened a second school for African Americans in Brooklyn in September 1840, known as Colored School No. 2. In 1841, white trustees of the Bedford school district took over its operation because it was "as yet too feeble to sustain itself." African American Junius C. Morel became its principal in 1847. In 1851, it had sixty students registered and an average attendance of forty, twelve of whom were white.[50]

In 1853, the school moved to a new board and batten structure on Troy Avenue at the corner of Dean Street. When school inspectors visited Weeksville in 1855, they were very pleased with the new building, "a fine tasteful home," they reported, "that will comfortably seat 250 pupils," "in a beautiful grove of oaks, surround by the small, neat white houses of a hamlet, consisting of some thirty or forty colored families." The school had 115 students, both black and white, on the register. Junius C. Morel, principal, was "a very superior man and most devoted teacher," with Charlotte DeWitt as his assistant. "We have examined a large number of pen sketches, pencil drawings, and penmanship, the best we have met in any of the schools thus far," noted the committee, and "the school is in excellent condition."[51]

Colored School No. 2, 1853. Courtesy Weeksville Heritage Society.

In July 1841, Willis A. and William J. Hodges organized a third African American school in Williamsburgh. Maria W. Stewart, the first American-born woman to speak to racially mixed audiences, taught more than sixty students there by 1845. Hezekiah Green became principal in 1847, with Maria W. Stewart his assistant. E. Jinnings also taught there. In 1851, this school had 194 children registered, with an average attendance of 99. An evening school had 69 registered pupils and an average attendance of 16. Jane Williams kept a private school with 40 people registered and an average attendance of 27. Samuel Rankins was principal from 1852 to 1872, when Catherine T. Clow became the first African American female principal in Brooklyn. Sarah Smith Tompkins Garnet and Georgiana F. Putnam also taught in the Williamsburgh school. Putnam later became Assistant Principal at the Weeksville school.[52]

Weeksville adults had a relatively low literacy rate. Almost three-quarters of adults in Buffalo in 1850 were literate, for example, compared to only 57.4 percent of adults aged twenty-two to thirty-four, 47.7 percent of those aged forty-five to fifty-four, and 64 percent of those aged fifty-five to seventy-four in Weeksville. In spite of such a high rate of illiteracy, adults in Weeksville very strongly supported education for their children. Compared to New York City and Buffalo, Weeksville had a remarkably high school attendance. In New York City in 1851, a Committee on Education of the Convention of Citizens of Color reported that only about one-eighth of African American children in New York City attended public schools.[53] In Buffalo in 1850, only 41 percent of African Americans children attended school. Compare these figures to those for Weeksville in 1850, where 63.7 percent of children between the ages of six and sixteen were in school (fifty-eight of ninety-one children). Weeksville's school attendance continued to increase. By 1865, more than 85 percent of children aged six to fourteen attended school.[54]

School attendance paid off. In every adult age group, literacy rates increased between 1850 and 1865. By 1865, adults aged twenty-two to thirty-five had a literacy rate of 93 percent (compared to 56.4 percent in 1850). Even for the oldest adults, those between fifty-five and sixty-four, literacy increased from 64 percent to 86.8 percent.[55]

Citizens' Union Cemetery

America in the nineteenth century developed a passion for rural cemeteries. The third one in the country, established in 1838, was Greenwood Cemetery in Brooklyn. Not far away, African Americans also participated in the rural cemetery movement, using Weeksville as an anchor. On September 1, 1851, Alexander Duncan, Robert Williams, and Charles Lewis purchased 29.5 acres of land in the Ninth Ward, west of Hunterfly Road, between Butler Street (now Sterling Place) to the north and Sackett Street (now Eastern Parkway) to the south, and between Rochester Avenue to the west and Buffalo Avenue to the east, just south of the current site of the Hunterfly Road houses.

Alexander Duncan was an undertaker from New York, and, with his encouragement, these three investors sold the land on November 3, 1851, to the Citizens' Union Cemetery Corporation. Twelve acres of

Nineteenth-century house at 219 Buffalo Avenue, Weeksville, once part of Citizens' Union Cemetery. Photo taken in 1923. Collection of the New-York Historical Society.

this became the Citizens' Union Cemetery, and the rest was set aside for building lots. The founders advertised that the cemetery had no "rule which excludes any person from sepulture within its borders, on account of complexion," although they had organized especially to provide "a burial place for the colored." Those who were poor could be buried for free, with a charge only for opening and closing the graves.[56]

About this time, Duncan built a two-story frame house with wings and stained glass Gothic windows, perched high on the "bold and bare" hill just east of the cemetery. From there, he could see for miles to the south and east, all the way to Jamaica Bay and the Atlantic Ocean. The house still stood thirty years later, when a reporter for the *Brooklyn Eagle* described it. At least four other houses were built on the cemetery grounds by the time that Matthew Dripps published his map in 1869. Several more stood along the edges. A house at 219 Buffalo Avenue, photographed in 1923, was one of them, but it is not known whether it was built in that location or moved there after the cemetery closed.[57]

On May 4, 1853, the original trustees (Alexander Duncan, Robert Williams, Charles Lewis, William T. Nicholas, George H. Dixon, James Jeffers, Thomas Jackson, Cary N. Harris, Sylvanus Smith, George E. Baker, and William T. Dixon) sold their interests to Alexander Duncan, Robert Williams, and Charles Lewis, who worked with real estate developer Paul Pontou to reorganize the original cemetery into the Mount Pleasant Cemetery Association. Ten purchasers bought the land from the original owner, a man named Leake. In 1872, the *Brooklyn Daily Eagle* reported that "the new corporation was no better in any respect than the one preceding it—proving themselves totally incompetent to manage the concern, taking no pains to make the spot attractive as a place for burying the dead, and keeping their records of interments with a looseness that was positively culpable." Alexander Duncan seems to have buried many people, often at night, without keeping records of the location of their graves.[58]

Just before final incorporation of the Mount Pleasant Cemetery on April 12, 1865, Paul Pontau (Pontou), owner of one-tenth of the corporation, died. His widow, Nanette Pontau, took his place as owner and trustee, but failed to indicate that she was executrix and only life owner of the property. When the cemetery was sold once more in 1870, she had remarried and moved to South Carolina, leaving a complicated legal tangle.[59]

By 1870, Mount Pleasant owed the city of Brooklyn four thousand dollars in back taxes. Brooklyn intended to construct new streets leading from Prospect Park toward New Lots and Bedford-Stuyvesant, right through the cemetery lands. With permission from New York State, cemetery trustees sold the cemetery to Edward G. Kidder on June 6, 1872, for twenty-five thousand. The next day, Kidder sold it to Richard Bowne and George Rudd, from New York City. With some of the proceeds, cemetery trustees bought one acre of land at Cypress Hills Cemetery for two thousand dollars, where they supposedly removed all bodies from Mount Pleasant Cemetery. In his study of this cemetery, Richard Sens-Castet included a list of ninety-four bodies reburied in Cypress Hills Cemetery. The *Brooklyn Daily Eagle* reported, however, based on an interview with Mr. Williams (probably the son of Robert Williams, one of the original trustees), that many people had been buried in unmarked graves, and their bodies were "carried off to the dump before anything can be done."[60]

New York State inherited an interest in this property from Paul and Nanette Pontau when they died without issue. By 1910, questions arose about the legality of the cemetery sale in 1870. Not until 1911 did New York State pass a bill that finally cleared up these legal issues.[61]

Abyssinian Benevolent Daughters of Esther

African American men in the New York City area were active in benevolent societies. The New York African Society for Mutual Relief, formed in 1808 and rooted in black churches, provided a model for other male societies, including the Brooklyn African Woolman Benevolent Society, formed in 1810, headed by Weeksville land investor Henry Thompson.[62]

Women in Weeksville most likely supported at least one benevolent organization. During the big dig at Weeksville, before demolition of houses near the corner of Troy and Dean Streets, one of the young archaeologists found a copy of the Constitution for the Abyssinian Benevolent Daughters of Esther Association, originally printed in the office of the *Colored American* in 1839 and republished by African American publishers Zuille and Leonard in 1853. Craig Wilder characterized this group as "the era's premier black women's society." It was organized in New York City in April 1839, perhaps by members of New York City's Abyssinian Baptist Church, and its name reflected the courageous Queen Esther (also called Hadassah) and conveyed an image of strong, independent, and intelligent women. Its structure reflected that image, including only women as members and officers. Its purpose was to provide burial insurance, both for female members and for male spouses and children. Two male "guardians" were appointed to ensure that the society's property, including a cemetery, would be legally protected.[63]

Recreation

In the decades before the Civil War, Weeksville became the center of organized recreational activities for African Americans from the entire region, as well as for excursions for European Americans. In 1851, a Brooklyn correspondent for the *Frederick Douglass' Paper*, writing under the name "Observor," described a celebration of West Indian emancipation held at a picnic "between the villages of Weeksville and Corsville [*sic*], both colored settlements, about four miles from this place." (Probably "this place" was downtown Brooklyn.) "The object in having it there," he noted, "was not only to celebrate West Indian emancipation, nor yet to see a little pleasure, but it was mainly to congregate there from the surrounding country, on the grounds owned and occupied by our own people, and if we had anything to spend for nick-nacks, to spend it with them."[64]

The 1851 celebration attracted several thousand people from Brooklyn, New York City, Williamsburg, and Flushing, as well as "a number from other places more distant," who filled ten cars on the Long Island Railroad and several omnibuses. Speakers included William Johnson, blind abolitionist speaker from Ithaca, New York, and William Wilson and J. C. Morel, principals of two of the African American schools in Brooklyn. An unexpected highlight of the day was the appearance of the Hannibal Guards, a group of young men training as a military unit.[65]

Weeksville's rural character remained an alluring attraction for African Americans who wanted to have picnics and excursions. From 1862 through the early 1870s, George Pool organized annual picnics in an area called Atlantic Park, six acres on the south side of Atlantic Avenue, east of Rochester Avenue. In 1873, children from the Howard Orphan Asylum and several schools came to the picnic, along with African Americans from New York City, Brooklyn, and Weeksville itself. The *Brooklyn Eagle* reported that there were "swings, a cart load of clams and oysters, and a few kegs of lager. Overshadowed by the oak, spruce, pine and other trees growing in Atlantic Park, is a spacious dancing floor, and it was kept constantly occupied in consequence of the strenuous exertions of two violinists, a harpist and a flutist."[66]

By 1860, Weeksville had its own baseball team, the Weeksville Unknowns. On January 21, 1860, the *Anglo-African* reported on a game between the Weeksville Unknowns and the Henson Baseball Club of Jamaica. Weeksville lost.[67] This was only fourteen years after the first official baseball had been played at the Elysian Fields in Hoboken, New Jersey, in 1846 and only three years after the formation of the first amateur league, the National Association of Base Ball Players. Weeksville residents continued to enjoy local baseball games for many years, naming one of their teams the Garnet Club, presumably after Rev. Henry Highland Garnet, minister and activist. By the 1880s, Weeksville women had their own baseball team. Sometimes they took their practice too far, as in 1889, when team members Mary Thompson and Mary Jackson, from Crow Hill, picked up a man named Luke Kenney "for a ball and knocked him all over the field with baseball bats."[68]

Garnet Club. Baseball became a popular sport in Weeksville in the mid-nineteenth century, as it did throughout the United States. Courtesy Weeksville Heritage Center, Percy F. Moore Collection.

Other forms of organized recreation also attracted Weeksville residents. In 1860, the "Ladies of Brooklyn and Weeksville" worked together, for example, for a "Grand Concert and Oyster Supper."[69]

Political Activism

Weeksville citizens did not neglect an active commitment to African American rights in the larger world. In 1846, as part of a revision of the state's constitution, voters in New York State were asked to decide whether African American men should have rights to vote equal to those of European American men. On Mary 32, 1846, "Colored Voters" in the Ninth Ward met at the "School House, Bedford, in the Village of Carrsville" to express their opinions. Those attending this meeting formed a list of leaders of Weeksville. James Weeks was chair. Robert Tillman and Jeptha Reed, who were two of Weeksville's earliest landholders, were vice presidents, and Rev. James Gloucester (who would later start Siloam

Presbyterian church and with his wife Elizabeth would befriend John Brown) was secretary. Rev. George Hogarth offered a prayer. Five men, including Francis P. Graham, William J. Wilson, Isaac Reed, William Brown, and Constant Hesdra, were appointed to a committee to draft resolutions. Based on the idea that "the whole is incomplete without its parts," they concluded "that the disfranchisement of a portion of the citizens of the State, leaves a void in our democratic system of government, and forms an impenetrable barrier to the true progress of Republicanism," and "that in their efforts for their enfranchisement, the people of Color contribute no more to their own interest as citizens, than to the best welfare of the state; and the perfectibility and perpetuity of Republican institutions," and finally "that we will not vote for any man as delegate to the Convention who will not pledge himself to vote for the Elective Franchise, free from any property or complexional qualifications."[70]

In 1855, the Brooklyn City and Kings County Record described a group called the Colored Political Association of the City of Brooklyn and Kings County. It was "an association of colored property holders in Kings County, formed for the purpose of consolidating their political power as voters, and bringing that power to bear on each political contest in such a way as shall best serve their interest in tending to bring them just and equal rights as native born Americans, and conduce to the cause of true democratic freedom, without partiality and without hypocrisy." At each election, they recommended which candidates should received their votes, and in 1855 they petitioned the state legislature once more to pass an equal suffrage amendment, giving the right to vote to "all citizens, without regard to complexion."[71] Rev. Amos Freeman, of Siloam Presbyterian Church, and Dr. Peter W. Ray, physician and pharmacist, were among the officers of this group. Given the high proportion of Weeksville residents who owned enough property to qualify as voters, it is almost certain that Weeksville, too, was heavily represented in this organization.

Underground Railroad: A Safe Haven for Freedom Seekers

Weeksville's origin was rooted in a search for safety, self-reliance, and citizenship. These goals rested on the solid premise that people in Weeksville were free. But freedom was not easy to define. Legally, the line between slavery and freedom was clear. Emotionally, socially, and culturally, however, the boundary was often blurred. Free people of color often shared values with those they had grown up with in slavery in Virginia or South Carolina. Family members might be both free and enslaved. Free people as well as those legally enslaved feared capture and enslavement.

The situation in New York State seemed to improve in the 1840s. In 1841, supported by Governor William H. Seward, New York State passed a personal liberty law, giving freedom immediately to any enslaved person brought into the state. Previously, the state had allowed slaveholders to bring enslaved people into New York for up to nine months. The U.S. Supreme Court's decision in *Prigg v. Pennsylvania* in 1842 overturned this law, declaring that no state could pass a law contradicting the 1793 U.S. law relating to fugitive slaves. While some abolitionists were distressed, others argued that *Prigg v. Pennsylvania* actually meant that no slaveholder could expect any assistance at all in retrieving freedom seekers from within New York State.

The Fugitive Slave Law, passed on September 18, 1850, changed all that. Nowhere in the country could states protect the rights of people accused of escaping from slavery since federal officials could legally recapture anyone, anywhere. To make matters worse, accused people had no right to testify on their own behalf.

African Americans throughout the North were in crisis. The greater New York City area was a special focus of concern. Large numbers of people escaped from slavery to and through New York. In 1851, for example, the superintendent of Common Schools for the City and County of New York noted the "increasing numbers of fugitives and ignorant black people, who are constantly coming into the city." Large numbers of slaveholders also had business and personal connections in New York City and Brooklyn, especially because it was the major point for the cotton trade with Europe.[72]

In a dramatic test case, James Hamlet was taken back to slavery from Williamsburgh in Brooklyn. Reaction from the African American population in the greater New York City area was intense and immediate. On October 1, 1850, fifteen hundred people (almost all of them African American, two-thirds of them women, "with a slight and visible sprinkling of white Abolitionists") crowded into Zion Church on Church

Street in New York City. Some of those who attended were from Weeksville. The audience recognized that slavery threatened every free person
of color. "Your Liberty, your Fire-side is in danger of being invaded!"
read the call for the meeting. "Shall we resist Oppression? Shall we
defend our Liberties? Shall we be FREEMEN OR SLAVES?"

President William P. Powell opened the meeting with a stirring
appeal to the African Americans and the American revolutionary
tradition:

> A more important subject than this, never in the history of this country,
> came before the American people, and it is nothing nor less than this—
> Shall the iniquitous Fugitive Slave bill, which subjects every free colored
> man, woman and child, to be seized upon, handcuffed, and plunged into
> perpetual Slavery? Shall the blood-thirsty slaveholder be permitted by
> this unrighteous law to come into our domicils, or workshops, or the
> places where we labor, and carry off our wives and children, our fathers
> and mothers, and ourselves, without a struggle—(loud cries of "No,
> no,")—without resisting, even if need be, unto death . . . upon your deci-
> sion this night hangs suspended the fate of millions.

"This 'covenant with death, and agreement with hell,'" noted Powell, "must be trampled under foot, resisted, disobeyed, and violated at
all hazards. (Cheers) . . . Throughout the revolutionary and late war,
colored men stood side by side with white men, and achieved a most
glorious victory in the name of liberty. We have met this night to
decide . . . whether we will suffer ourselves and families to be made
slaves."[73]

Those at the meeting addressed a letter to C. S. Woodhull, mayor of
New York City, asking what protection they could expect, as free people of color, from local officials. They heard lengthy discussions of the
constitutionality of the Fugitive Slave Law from local leaders such as
George Downing, James McCune Smith, and Junius C. Morel himself.[74]

Several speakers advocated violent resistance. John S. Jacobs, freedom seeker and son of the better known Harriet Jacobs, advised "my
colored brethren, if you have not swords, I say to you, sell your gar-
ments and buy one. . . . If there be any man here tonight who wants to
know my name, tell him it is John S. Jacobs, of South Carolina, and that

I am an American citizen. . . . They say that they cannot take us back to the South; but I say, under the present law they can; and now I say unto you, let them only take your dead bodies. (Tremendous cheers.)"

Junius C. Morel advised people to keep the peace, not to be aggressors, but to be prepared. "I would not tell you what to do, but I will tell you what I will do," he said. "I am a freeman, and I care not for the constitution or the laws made by man. There is a law above them; and I tell you that before they drag me into Slavery they will have to take my life." Reporting the proceedings for the *North Star*, Morel added, "It would be exceedingly difficult to take a fugitive publicly from this city, but unfortunately the work is done secretly and in the dark."[75]

The meeting took up a collection to defray the expenses "of a number of fugitive slaves who are now in this city on their way to Canada." They raised eight hundred dollars, enough to buy James Hamlet out of slavery, and Hamlet eventually returned to his wife and children in Williamsburgh.[76]

A Committee of Thirteen was organized to oppose colonizationists and to aid freedom seekers. It had three members from Brooklyn: William J. Wilson, Junius C. Morel (from Weeksville), and Dr. T. Joiner White. Maritcha Lyons remembered that no one outside the members themselves knew exactly who was on the committee. "Without officers, headquarters, passwords or treasury, this band was liberally supported," she remembered. "Aid was given to escaping slaves, financially or otherwise, by those who required no other details save that such help was needed. Any adventurer who had the courage to set out on a life or death journey from bondage to freedom, knew by the 'grape vine telegraph,' New York City would never prove indifferent to his needs in the exigency." Lyons's own parents, who lived both in New York City and Brooklyn, assisted about one thousand people on the Underground Railroad. "Thanks to mother's devotion and discretion," Lyons remembered, "refugees were kept long enough to be fed and to have disguises changed and be met by those prepared to speed them on in the journey toward the North Star. Father used to say humorously this part of his business was 'keeping a cake and apple stand.'"[77]

The Fugitive Slave Act touched off the most active decade of the Underground Railroad. Several documented references to the Underground Railroad relate to Brooklyn. Rev. J. W. C. Pennington, the "fugitive blacksmith," escaped from slavery in Maryland, settled in Long Island and then in New York, became a well-known antislavery activist, and wrote his autobiography, *The Fugitive Blacksmith*. Rev. Amos Freeman of Siloam Presbyterian Church helped one young woman, Maria Weems, sent to him from William Still in Philadelphia, reach Canada. Rev. Henry Ward Beecher, European American minister at Plymouth Congregational Church, auctioned a young slave girl from his pulpit to raise money for her purchase from slavery. Willis Hodges, born free in Virginia, moved to Williamsburgh, and became an outspoken activist against slavery and for the rights of free African Americans. When he received a land grant from Gerrit Smith, he moved to the Adirondacks, where he wrote his autobiography, *A Free Man of Color*. Maritcha Lyons, who later became assistant principal in P.S. 83 in Weeksville, remembered, "Every thinking man and woman was a volunteer in the famous 'underground railroad.'"[78]

Considerable evidence suggests that Weeksville was an important haven for African Americans from the South. Local tradition highlights Berean Baptist Church, whose members reputedly assisted freedom seekers, for example. Of the eight original African American members, all but one (Stephen Murray) were born in the South. Four were born in Virginia, one in Maryland, one in North Carolina, and one (Francis P. Graham) in South Carolina.[79]

Census reports suggest that many of Weeksville's residents had been born in the South. We do not know whether southern-born people were born free, were manumitted, bought their freedom, or simply left. In any case, they certainly had experience with a slave system. In 1850, 29.5 percent (or 105 of Weeksville's 366 African Americans) were southern-born. Most of these were from Virginia (60 people) or Maryland (27 people). Thirteen were from either North or South Carolina. Fewer than 3 percent of Weeksville's total population was foreign-born (seven from the West India, two from Africa, and one from England). Those from the West Indies and Africa may also have been freedom seekers.

Weeksville's proportion of southern-born African Americans was one of the highest of any city in the United States. In 1850, Cincinnati (on the border of a slave state) and Buffalo (on the border with Canada) had a larger proportion of southern-born African Americans than did Weeksville. Almost 60 percent of Cincinnati's black population was southern-born in 1850, compared to 42 percent in Buffalo and 29.5 percent in Weeksville. In contrast, in 1850, only 16.6 percent of Boston's black population had been born in the South. By 1860, the percentage of southern-born African Americans in Boston had risen to 24.1 percent.[80]

If we look only at those African Americans over the age of sixteen in 1850, Weeksville more closely resembles key Underground Railroad centers than it does other northern cities. In 1850, 44.7 percent (96 out of 215 people) of those in Weeksville were born in the South, double the percentage for Brooklyn as a whole. Of the ten northern cities for which Leonard Curry compiled nativity data for 1850, only Cincinnati, Buffalo, Pittsburgh, and Philadelphia had African American populations with larger proportions of southern-born people over the age of sixteen (Cincinnati had 71.9 percent, Buffalo 58 percent, Pittsburgh 50.7 percent, and Philadelphia 49.4 percent). With the exception of Pittsburgh, these were all on the borders of slave states or Canada. As a major port on the Ohio River, Pittsburgh would have been an attractive destination for freedom seekers. (In contrast, figures were 22.4 percent for Brooklyn as a whole, 21.4 percent for Boston, 19.5 percent for New York City, and 20.6 percent for Providence, Rhode Island.)[81] As ports, all of these cities (including Boston, New York City, and Providence) would have been attractive destinations for freedom seekers. They also acted as funnels and primary channels for freedom seekers who went farther north. Cincinnati, Pittsburgh, and Philadelphia were the first free cities that freedom seekers encountered on their journey north. For some, these cities would also have been their final destination. For others, they would have been jumping off places for points farther north. Buffalo was a major point of embarkation for Canada (as were Detroit and Oswego). With 44.7 percent of its adult population born in the South, Weeksville more closely resembled these major funnel points than it did other urban centers.

Weeksville: Family and Work in 1850

Most urban neighborhoods where African Americans lived in the nineteenth century were mixed-race communities, including both European Americans (often from many parts of Europe) and African Americans (often from many parts of West Africa and the southern United States).

None of them resembled twentieth-century ghettoes. As Leonard Curry concluded, "Nowhere did racial residential segregation remotely resemble that common in American cities in the second half of the twentieth century." In *Black Bostonians*, James Oliver Horton and Lois E. Horton reached a similar conclusion. Even Boston, the most racially segregated city in the country, "was a racially separated but not totally segregated city." The West End of Boston, on the north side of Beacon Hill, was the most segregated neighborhood of the most segregated city in antebellum America. Yet even here, African Americans lived intermixed with European Americans. And such cities as Detroit and Cleveland showed "no evidence of the existence of well-defined ghettoes before 1890."[82]

Weeksville, however, was different. If you walked along the hilly dirt roads of Weeksville in 1850, almost every person you met was African American. Compared to any other known urban population in the United States in 1850, Weeksville displayed an extremely high concentration of African American residents. By 1850, 82.2 percent of Weeksville's 443 people were African American. Only 17.8 percent were European American. Looked at another way, of Weeksville's 133 families, 115 (86.5 percent) were African American.

Weeksville's 82.2 percent African American population in 1850 is a startling contrast to the 2.5 percent African American population in Brooklyn as a whole or to the proportion of African Americans in ten northern cities in 1850, which ranged from a low of 1.46 percent of the total population in Boston to a high of 8.85 percent in Philadelphia. Even in southern cities, the proportion of African American residents never reached Weeksville's concentration. Among five southern cities, the African American population ranged from a low of 16.14 percent in Louisville, Kentucky, to a high of 53.44 percent in Charleston, South Carolina.[83]

Weeksville was not, however, a ghetto. Instead, this residential separation was a conscious attempt by Weeksville's land investors to create an independent land base for African Americans within the boundaries of the United States.

In terms of family size, Weeksville's African American families averaged four people each. Family size varied considerably, however. Some were single-person households (such as that of fifty-seven-year-old Aurora Weldon, born in New York and owner of one hundred dollars worth of property). Some were households with young married couples without children (such as that of newlyweds Elija and Matilda Van Mater, aged thirty and twenty-eight, born in New Jersey and Virginia). Many families had five or more children. Many families also included people whose last names were different from those of the head of household. These people may have been relatives, boarders, or foster children. There were a few single-parent households, suggesting the death of a spouse. Cornelius Anderson, for example, aged forty-five, was raising his three sons, Joseph (aged twenty-one), Solomon (aged twenty), and Moses (aged seventeen) by himself. Stephen Murray, aged sixty, a laborer and owner of three hundred dollars worth of land, shared his home with Hana S. Abrams, aged thirty-six and probably a widow, who mostly likely acted as housekeeper for Murray and her own children, Rachel (aged fourteen), Lois (aged eleven), Thomas (aged eight), James (aged six), Eliza (aged four), Stephen (aged two), and William (aged one). Amanda M. Johnson, born in Virginia and twenty-one years old, also lived with them.

In 1850, this population worked in both urban and rural occupations. The census listed 103 African American men who worked in twenty-three different occupations. (The 1850 census did not list occupations for women.) None worked in named occupations related to agriculture, although the largest number (70, or 58.5 percent of the total) listed their occupation as laborer, and these might have included agricultural workers.

Some of the laborers may have worked on farms—including hog farms, dairies, and horse farms—owned by European Americans who lived outside the village. Others certainly worked for local African Americans on small-scale farms of an acre or two, growing corn, vegetables, and melons. Some people kept large numbers of pigs. Sylvanus Smith, for example, lived with his family in downtown Brooklyn, but he purchased land in the Weeksville area, where he kept pigs. An 1897 article in the *Brooklyn Eagle* emphasized the importance of these piggeries both in the local economy and local politics. "Pigs exercised a much more powerful influence on Flatbush politics than party principles. To take sides against them was to invite political ruin," asserted the journalist. Hogs were so common that one observer called recipes to combat cholera "as plenty as hogs at Crow Hill."[84]

Judging by the number of cows advertised in the *Brooklyn Eagle* as lost on Crow Hill, many people were also involved in raising either dairy cows or beef cattle. Some local farmers had whole herds of cattle. Roger Laney, European American, listed his address as Crow Hill when he advertised for someone to purchase three to four hundred quarts of milk a day. Most people who owned cows, however, kept only a cow or two for their own use. In 1863, for example, William Hanford advertised, "COW LOST—$5 REWARD—STRAYED FROM the premises of the subscriber, Butler street, corner of Albany Avenue (Crow Hill) on the night of July 1st, a dark red cow, small size, black legs and face, small handsome horns sawed off at the end. Also had a rope tied around her neck when she left the premises."[85] Horses were also common. Frequently advertised as lost, they also formed the core of at least one horse dealing business, owned by an African American. After the death of Major James Davis in 1853, "a well-known horse dealer," his estate included "one superior Bay Stallion, sired by St. Lawrence; also several horses of different colors, style, speed, and age." The 1850 census listed James Davis, black, age forty-two, born in the West Indies, with real property worth $5,800. His son, James Davis, Jr., was black, age eighteen, and born in New York. Both were listed as horse dealers.[86]

Entrepreneurs capitalized on the large numbers of animals kept locally to establish fat-rendering establishments and fertilizer factories, producing fertilizer from bone, for sale to Britain, New Jersey, Philadelphia, and southern states. These seem to have been operated primarily by German Americans or Irish Americans. Swanmitel, Pieper & Co. was the first to render fat and grind bone on Crow Hill. They sold their fat and fertilizer primarily to British markets. Joseph Oechsler started a similar factory in 1852, selling some of his product on Long Island but most of it to Philadelphia and southern states. In 1855, Frederick Langman joined this production, selling most of his fertilizer in New Jersey. Mr. Kelly had a bone mill on Crow Hill in 1850, judged by the health inspector to be not a nuisance.[87]

Several people also built ropewalks on Crow Hill. These were long covered platforms in which strands of hemp could be laid out and braided by steam-powered (or human-powered) machines into ropes. These were sold mostly for sailing ships. John Morrison's ropewalk, erected on Crow Hill at the southeast corner of Troy and Warren

Streets, offered employment to a handful of people, including Morrison's son Otto. Morrison was well known, and people relied on him for a variety of neighborhood needs, from locating stolen horses to providing bail. In July 1850, one Jonathan Beecroft, accused of assault with intent to murder, appeared at the door of Morrison's ropewalk, asking for fifteen hundred dollars for his bail.

"Can't do it," replied Morrison, "for if I should have to pay that amount, it would ruin me!"

"Well, if you can't go my bail, I must bid you good-bye," retorted Beecroft, who proceeded to walk out the back door of the ropewalk, leaving the deputy sheriff who had accompanied him waiting patiently with his horse and carriage out front.

Morrison did well for himself, judging by his advertisement in 1862 for the loss of "a large gold, open face, English lever watch and gold chain," to be returned to Mrs. Morrison. The Morrison family was European American, but African American Charles Bloom owned a second ropewalk in Weeksville by 1855.[88]

Shoemaking was perhaps the largest manufacturing business in Weeksville, employing four local African Americans and three European Americans nearby. Where these shoemakers obtained tanned hides and where they sold their work remains an open question. These seven shoemakers surely produced more shoes than people in Weeksville alone would have needed. And what were their final products? Did they make work shoes? Fashionable shoes? Shoes for men, women, or children? Charles Lewis listed his occupation in one source as "boot maker" rather than shoemaker. Did he produce boots or shoes, and if so for whom? Was he allied with Henry P. Thompson and his downtown bootblacking business? Francis Graham, largest resident landholder in Weeksville, listed his occupation in the census as shoemaker, and he may have used his capital to create this shoemaking business for markets outside Weeksville.

In the context of this mixed economy—with employment possibilities in agriculture, service occupations, and manufacturing—fifty workers in Weeksville specified a specific occupation. Many people, for example, worked in transportation. Thirteen of these were related to the sea and shipping, including eight seaman, one sailmaker, and four stewards, probably ships' stewards. One of these was Jacob Thompson. Many of these may have worked in all-black crews. They may also have found themselves working side by side with European American seamen. Increasingly, they may have found their options limited to occupations such as cooks or stewards. Some of these may have been involved with coastal trips, including voyages to southern ports. Others may have signed on for deep-sea voyages to Europe, the West Indies, or Africa.[89]

Other Weeksville residents worked with local land transportation. One person was an engineer. One more was a coachman, and two were horse dealers (including James Davis), making seventeen people associated in some way with sea or land transportation.

Sixteen were service workers in one capacity or another. Six of these were porters. Two were measurers of grain. Five were waiters; one was a packer (although of what, we do not know); and two were cooks.

Twelve (9.2 percent of the total) were small manufacturers. Of these, four were shoemakers (including Francis P. Graham and Edward Butler); two were coopers; two were cigar makers (or segar makers); and one each was a basket maker, upholstor (sic), stamp (?) maker, sailmaker, and carpenter.

Five were businesspeople. Two of these were grocers. (Two European American grocers also lived in this area.) One other person listed his occupation as speculator. Perhaps this person was a land speculator. Finally, three were professionals—one preacher, one teacher (Joseph Merrill, aka Junius C. Morel), and one (James Weeks himself) who listed his occupation as superintendent, although we do not know what he supervised. One man was blind and listed his occupation as "none."

Probably the businesspeople (especially the two grocers) and professionals (the teacher and preacher) dealt primarily with residents in Weeksville itself. Service workers, especially those related to transportation and the port, probably earned their living primarily by commuting to downtown Brooklyn.

While the 1850 census did not list occupations for women, we can infer that many kept boarders in their homes. Many families survived by sharing child care, either caring for others' children or leaving their own children with friends or relatives so they themselves could go to work for pay. Many women worked as laundresses or seamstresses, jobs they could combine with child care in their own homes.

Whatever their work, families supplemented their income and food supplies by growing small plots of corn, vegetables, potatoes, and melons. Reports in the *Eagle* of small-time thefts reveal the value of these items. In August 1848, for example, Mary Elizabeth Decato was sentenced to fifteen days in the Flatbush Penitentiary for stealing "green corn and watermelons from Stephen Murray at Crow Hill." John Bunce was taken into custody when police discovered him "strolling homeward with a bag of potatoes on his back, and armed with a hoe with which he had been driving in somebody's field during a foraging expedition." People also picked nuts from local trees and foraged for wild berries.[90]

Certainly, measured by the rate of property ownership in 1850, Weeksville's experiment was a resounding success. The rate of property ownership in Weeksville was more than twice the rate of property ownership for African Americans in Brooklyn and almost twice the rate of property ownership for the whole population of Brooklyn, both white and black. Of the total number of residents in Weeksville, forty-two of them (9.5 percent) owned property. In the rest of Brooklyn in 1850, only ninety-eight African Americans (4.04 percent of the total African American population) owned property, and only 5.3 percent of the population as a whole owned property. Weeksville's property ownership was also far higher than that of Manhattan, where only seventy-one African American residents owned property in 1850. Only in the African American settlement of Seneca Village, in what is now Central Park, was the rate of property ownership higher than that in Weeksville. In Seneca Village, more than half the households owned property, compared to more than one-third of the households in Weeksville.[91]

Looking at Weeksville's property ownership in another way, of the ninety-eight African Americans in Brooklyn who owned property in 1850, forty-two of them (42.9 percent) lived in Weeksville. Of the eight African American women who were listed in the 1850 census as owning property in Brooklyn, five of them lived in Weeksville: Aurora Weldon ($100), Rachel Davis ($150), Sarah Corpsew ($250), Charlotte Johnson ($300), and Jane Stringham ($900). Lydia LeGrant was yet another woman landowner. Although the census listed her house in her husband's name, deeds show that she actually owned the property.[92]

Looking at these statistics still another way, of the total number of male residents aged twenty-one years and older, almost 30 percent owned property. Property values ranged from Jacob Thompson's $73 worth to that of Francis Graham, worth $8,000. Thirty-one of these men owned property worth at least $250, making them eligible to vote in New York State.[93]

In 1850, almost 70 percent of Weeksville's population had been born in a northern state and almost 60 percent of these had been born in New York State. About 30 percent, however (106 of Weeksville's 366 people) were southern-born. South Carolina–born residents are of particular interest. One of the houses now owned by the Weeksville Heritage Center (1702–03 Bergen Street) closely resembles houses built by and for enslaved people in South Carolina. South Carolina–born residents included Francis P. Graham. He listed his occupation in the 1850 census as shoemaker, but he was also the largest African American property owner in the Ninth Ward.[94]

James LeGrant, the only African American carpenter in the Ninth Ward, was also born in South Carolina. LeGrant was probably either Francis Graham's nephew or the son of Phebe LeGrant, who was most likely Graham's sister. He arrived in Weeksville about 1848 and married Lydia A. E. Sisson, who purchased land at the corner of Rochester Avenue and Bergen Street from Francis Graham in 1843.[95] Other South Carolina–born residents included four members of the Rogers family (Isaac, Rachel, and their two children, Caroline and Isaac) plus Edward Butler, shoemaker, who shared a two-family house with James and Lydia LeGrant. Junius C. Morel may also have been born in South Carolina. Although he was listed in the 1850 census as Joseph Merrill, born in the West Indies, he appeared in later censuses as born either in South Carolina or North Carolina. Rev. R.H. Cain became a major South Carolina politician after the Civil War. Finally, people outside of Weeksville may have had South Carolina roots. Was Paul Pontou (Ponto/Ponteau), African American real estate agent for Weeksville, part of a South Carolina family?[96]

Hunterfly Road

Hunterfly Road marked the eastern boundary of Weeksville. On the northeast corner of Bergen Street and Rochester Avenue, Francis P.

Graham sold lots in the 1840s along Hunterfly Road, on what would later become block 1350, to African Americans from all over the eastern United States and Africa. They built houses in this neighborhood, most of which still stood in the 1880s. This neighborhood, stable in population for more than thirty years, formed a key part of Weeksville's identity. On the block across the street, south of Bergen Street, Samuel Bouton purchased empty lots in 1839, where the houses now owned by the Weeksville Heritage Society stand.

After Graham purchased twenty-four lots in this area from the Garrittsen estate in 1839, he sold two lots at the corner of Rochester and Bergen in 1842 and 1843 to Lydia Ann Elizabeth Sisson. After he moved to Weeksville from New York City about 1844, he repurchased part of the lot on the corner of Rochester and Bergen. He married shortly thereafter and built a house on this block for his new wife, Sarah.

Francis P. Graham and Sarah Graham most likely lived in the house at the top of the hill on Hunterfly Road, where the road bent slightly southward. An 1851 article in the *Brooklyn Eagle* noted that Sarah Graham, Francis P. Graham's wife, lived on Hunterfly Road "between Carrsville and Weeksville." In 1869, Matthew Dripps noted a house in the middle of the block, facing Hunterfly Road, just where it bent slightly south. A building still stood in this location in 1888. As noted in the Sanborn map of that year, it was a one-and-a-half-story frame house with one-story wings on either side. Sometime between 1888 and 1904, this house may have been moved a block east, to 1759 Bergen Street, on the north side of the street just east of the new St. Joseph's School for the Deaf. It stood there until 1939, to be recorded by the New York City Housing Authority before it was demolished as part of the Kingsborough housing project.[97]

In 1850, Francis Graham listed his age as thirty-seven and his birthplace as South Carolina. Since he left a wife and two children in Charleston in 1822, he was more likely forty-seven or even fifty-seven years old. His new wife, Sarah, born in New York, was only eighteen. Also in their household lived Ann Sparks, age thirty-five, born in New York; and Stephen Locke, age forty, born in New York.[98]

Census records correspond roughly to the houses listed on Matthew Dripps's map of 1869. All but two families on this block are listed as African American. Graham began selling lots to African Americans

The house at 1759 Bergen Street. The small house with the overhanging porch, just left of the row of three-story Italianate houses, fits the plan of Francis P. Graham's house, once located a block west on Hunterfly Road, just north of Bergen Street. This house was still on Hunterfly Road on the Sanborn map of 1888, but it was no longer there on the 1904 Sanborn map. It was demolished after 1939 to make room for the Kingsborough houses. Photo by New York City Housing Authority, November 9, 1939. LaGuardia-Wagner Archives, LaGuardia Community College.

almost immediately after he bought the land, and from 1841 to his death in 1852, he created a viable African American neighborhood here. All its residents except the Morrison and Mott families were black, but they were diverse in terms of age, sex, occupation, and place of origin.

The European American family of William Morrison, grocer, age thirty-four, and his wife Mary, age thirty-two, was listed next to the Graham family in the census, with real estate valued at one thousand dollars. With William and Mary Morrison lived their daughter Ann E., age five, and Elijah Rayner, age fourteen, all born in New York State.

Garrett Wright, laborer, age twenty-seven, born in New Jersey, lived nearby with his wife Ellen, age twenty-five, born in the West Indies, and their son John H., age one, born in New Jersey, all African Americans.

William Potter, laborer, and Cynthia Potter, ages twenty-six and twenty-nine, both African Americans born in New York, were listed next to the Wright family in the 1850 census.

James and Jane Moody were between the Potter and Thomas families in the census. James Moody, fifty-eight, had been born in Africa, and Jane Moody, fifty-five, was from North Carolina. Although the census listed no occupation for either of the Moodys and no property value for their house, deeds suggest that James Moody purchased land (40 by 103 feet) facing Dean Street for $110 from Stokely Orker, who had purchased it from Francis Graham on Dean Street, on July 1, 1842.

Henrietta and Nathan C. B. Thomas lived near the Corprew and Mott families. Nathan Thomas was a preacher, ordained by the A.M.E. Church at its annual conference in New York City in 1844. In 1850 he was fifty-nine years old, with property valued at eighteen hundred dollars. Henreitta was forty-one. Both were born in Maryland. The Thomases had purchased their property in 1841.[99]

Listed between the Corprew and Thomas family in the 1850 census was the family of William and Sarah Mott, both European Americans born in New York. William was a laborer, and four children—William, David, Lucinda, and Betsey Raynor—lived with them.

Sarah Corprew, age forty-nine, born in Virginia, lived next to the LeGrant-Butler family with her children Catharine, age twenty-three, born in Virginia; Sarah A., eighteen, born in New York; Ceaser A., sixteen, a laborer born in New York; and David W., thirteen, born in New York. Their deed was in the name of Doxie Corprew, Sarah's deceased husband, and their land lay on Rochester Avenue just north of Lydia LeGrant's two lots.

In 1868, Sarah Corprew sold her house and land at the southeast corner of Rochester Avenue and Dean Street to an Irish immigrant grocer named John McMurn. McMurn ran a grocery store here. In 1875, a reporter from the *Eagle* interviewed him at his "place of business" about McMurn's role as a juror in the famous Beecher-Tilton trial. Henry Ward Beecher was perhaps the most famous Protestant preacher in the United States. As pastor of Plymouth Church in Brooklyn, he supported the abolition of slavery. In the late 1860s, however, he was tried for adultery. McMurn served as a juror for his trial. When the *Eagle* reporter interviewed him, McMurn sat in his shirtsleeves, reading the paper, on the porch of his house. His house was "a two story frame dwelling house and store on the corner of Dean street and Rochester avenue," noted the reporter. "It is a small, old fashioned building, with the remains of a broad piazza on two sides." Was this the house, similar in design to Graham's own house, originally owned by Sarah Corprew and her family?[100]

In 1850, Lydia and James LeGrant shared a two-family house. Although the census listed James LeGrant as owner of this house, worth six hundred dollars, most likely it stood on Lydia LeGrant's land near the corner of Rochester Avenue and Bergen Street. Edward Butler, shoemaker, also from South Carolina, was listed as owning real estate worth eighty dollars, and three small girls lived with them. LeGrant was most likely Graham's nephew, son of his sister Phebe LeGrant. Butler may have been related to the Butler family banished from Charleston along with Graham at the time of the Vesey Rebellion. In his will, written in 1852, Francis P. Graham left both men "the income and profits arising from my real estate for the use and benefit during their natural lives share and share alike," as well as all the income from the sale of his personal property "such as horses waggons furniture &c" invested at 7 percent interest.[101]

By 1855, the LeGrant-Butler household had expanded to include Lydia's mother, Ann Simmons, and Ann Dixon, Lydia's daughter. The census taker reported that Lydia and her mother now owned the property, and that James and Edward lived in half the house while Ann, Lydia, and Ann Dixon shared the other half.

Isaac Day, age fifty, cook, born in New York, married to Rosanna Gibbons, age forty-nine, born in Ireland, lived nearby, along with Rosanna's Irish-born daughter Rosanna, age eighteen.

Rebecca and Charles Lewis, both born in Virginia, ages forty-eight and fifty, lived at the very edge of this neighborhood, on the northeast corner of Rochester Avenue and Dean Street. Charles was a shoemaker. An 1844 deed listed his occupation as a boot maker. Although the 1850 census did not list them as owning any property, deeds suggest that Charles Lewis purchased two pieces of property in 1841.

Between 1846 and 1848, Francis P. Graham also sold land on block 1850 to Charles A. Horton, John Flamer, and Cecelia Powell. John Flamer was a major Weeksville landowner and politician, but none of these people appeared in the 1850 census in this area.

Just north of this small African American neighborhood lived the Suydam family, Dutch Americans, whose farmhouse stood on the east side of Hunterfly Road, near Atlantic Avenue, at least until 1887. In the late eighteenth century, Lambert Suydam had married Mary Lefferts. In 1850, their descendents included Phebe Suydam, who lived here along with Ann Suydam, Joel Concklin, and George Lindley. Just west of Hunterfly Road, across from the Suydam farmhouse, a large spring-fed pond, twenty-five feet deep, measured about six hundred feet wide and three-eighths of a mile long. James Weeks and his family lived on the other side of Suydam Pond, along with Junius P. Morel, principal of Colored School No. 2.[102]

Other landowners in Weeksville before 1860 included both European Americans and African Americans: Amos Powell (perhaps Cecelia's spouse), Jacob Durling, Robert and Ellen Lane, Alfred Decker, Rem and Maria R. Lefferts, Paul Ponto, Albert G. Thorp, J. Carson Brevoort and Elizabeth Brevoort (a Dutch American banker and land developer), and Patrick Heney, whose estate provided funds to sustain Roman Catholic orphanages nearby. It is not known whether any of these people ever lived in Weeksville.

Francis P. Graham had served for more than a decade as minister of the A.M.E. Church, with a congregation on Third Street in New York City. When he came to Weeksville, he also worked as a pastor in the A.M.E. Church. He had been ordained as elder in the church's annual meeting in Brooklyn in 1834. In 1850, Graham listed his occupation not as minister, however, but as shoemaker, and he most likely hired both Charles Lewis and Edward Butler in his shoemaking business. Graham owned land valued at eight thousand dollars (including his land on block 1850 as well as several lots elsewhere in the area), more land than any other resident of Weeksville. As minister, landowner, and shoemaker, Graham took an active part in Weeksville's political life. In 1846, he attended the meeting in the Ninth Ward for the right of suffrage for African Americans, along with "a large and respectable" group of African American voters in the Ninth Ward. He served on a committee of five to draft resolutions.[103]

Life in the Graham household was full of drama. In 1844, shortly after Graham moved to Weeksville, he was arrested for assault and battery. A boy named John T. Sudor, who lived next door to Graham, complained that on January 18, 1844, Graham had tied him with a rope wound tightly around his neck and body. He "struggled and writhed upon the floor, causing the rope to chafe his neck and wrists in no gentle manner, and producing a partial congestion of the brain." His eyes were "one mass of blood." Testimony suggested, however, that Sudor had been "conducting himself in a manner quite terrific to behold, so much so as to cause alarm to the members of his family," who requested Graham's help to subdue the young man. The judge instructed the jury that Graham was right to help the boy's family but not "to use more force than was necessary to restrain him." "If the boy, by his own rage during his struggles, inflicted the injuries upon his person, Graham was not accountable." The jury's verdict? Not guilty.[104]

Graham's marriage to eighteen-year-old Sarah, a woman dramatically younger than he, elicited all kinds of stories, some of them probably even true. The *Brooklyn Eagle* insinuated that Graham had a way with the ladies, "who had been in the habit of pillowing his head in their laps until soothed to sleep by their lullabies." Perhaps Sarah was one of those smitten. She did not, however, take easily to her new situation. The *Eagle* suggested that she entertained other men and that Graham knew it. And she had continuing troubles with her neighbors. In 1851, Lydia LeGrant paid Sarah a visit and ended up verbally and then physically assaulting her. The judge decided that both of them were at fault and fined each of them for disorderly conduct, Sarah Graham for five and Lydia LeGrant for seven dollars.[105]

Perhaps this was the occasion when Graham caught "an old man" in bed with Sarah, which, reported the *Brooklyn Eagle*, "to a man of Graham's high moral character was unendurable." He beat the man, tied him down on an old wood wagon, and "amid the shouts of hundreds of black and white youngsters he drove him down to City Hall." There he sued for divorce. The case was called, the jury sworn, and Graham's testimony given when the court called a break for lunch. When they returned, they were surprised to find that Graham and his wife had made up and left for home.[106]

Francis Graham did not have to suffer these familial disputes for long. He made out his will on February 3, 1852, and died a year later. He left only ten dollars to his wife, Sarah Ann, "over and above what the law allows her." He gave his house to his sister, Phoebe LeGrant, and life income from his real and personal property to James LeGrant and Edward Butler (probably his nephews). This property included five acres near where the Boulevard would be built in the 1860s, twenty-four lots on Hunterfly road, and twenty-six lots on Albany, Troy, and Rochester Avenues, as well as a building at 371 Broadway in New York City and a church in New York on Third Street. Except for the token ten dollars to his wife Sarah and the house he gave to his sister, Graham left everything he owned, including "all my several houses and lots of ground and all real estate that I may die seized of and entitled unto either at law or in equity situate and being in Ninth Ward of the City of Brooklyn and also all personal estate of whatever nature or description including money in the house at the time of my decease and debts due unto me" to N. Bergasse La Bau of the city of New York.[107]

As might be expected, Graham's will resulted in several years of litigation. Family members were not happy to be put in second place, and they had good reason to question the document's validity. The will was particularly suspicious because it was in the handwriting of N. Bergasse La Bau, who was both Graham's lawyer and his officially designated heir. La Bau had been born in 1822 in Trenton, New Jersey, to Jonathan and Margaret Bergasse La Bau, descended from French Huguenots on his father's side and Greek grandparents on his mother's side. He became a lawyer in New York City by 1850, and in October 1852 he married Mary Vanderbilt, daughter of railroad tycoon Commodore Vanderbilt. He supported Millard Fillmore and the Know-Nothings in 1856, served in the New York State legislature, and died in 1873.[108]

When Judge Jesse C. Smith received the will for probate, he rejected it. La Bau appealed the decision in front of a jury and lost his case. But he did not give up. When he brought suit once more, several lawyers volunteered their time on behalf of the LeGrant-Butler family. Finally, after a full day of hearings and another jury trial in March 1857, the court directed the jury, on a technicality, to rule that this was indeed Francis P. Graham's last will and testament and that La Bau had not exercised undue influence over Graham in order to get his land. Without money to appeal, Graham's family—including presumably James LeGrant, Phebe LeGrant, and Edward Butler—were forced to let this ruling stand.[109]

Settlement of Francis Prince Graham's will cleared the way for the sale of Graham's land in 1862, just in time for the expansion of Weeksville's population in the 1860s. Meanwhile, however, Weeksville attracted the attention of the outside world. It became a place of refuge after the Fugitive Slave Act of 1850 and the draft riots of 1863, the anchor of the African Civilization Society, and a source of support for the Civil War.

3

"Shall We Fly or Shall We Resist?"

From Emigration to the Civil War, 1850–1865

By 1860, the Weeks, Bundick, Morel, and LeGrant families and their neighbors had lived in Weeksville for many years.[1] They continued to work, attend school and church, and contribute to their community. At the same time, they were caught up in local, state, and national affairs that would change their lives forever. James Weeks and his immediate family had died or moved away from Weeksville by 1860, but two individuals named Weeks remained. One, Sarah Jane Weeks, was a seamstress, aged thirty. The other, Ann Weeks, was four years old and living in the same household with Sarah Jane Weeks and three other young women, aged twelve, thirteen, and seventeen, all born in New York.

Simon Bundick, too, had experienced change and loss. Johanna Bundick died in the late 1850s, leaving Simon a widower. In 1860, Margaret was nineteen years old, Simon seventeen, Cornelius fifteen, Barsella twelve, and Eliza nine. Obadiah, the baby, was not listed as part of the household. Simon Sr. owned real estate valued at two hundred dollars and personal property valued at three hundred. His occupation was indecipherable in the census, but Simon, the son, was working as a whitewasher. Both Eliza and Barsella attended school, probably Colored School No. 2, taught by Junius C. Morel. Interestingly, all of the family except Eliza, whose place of birth was indecipherable, listed their birthplace as Virginia, in contrast to earlier censuses, in which only Simon Sr. had listed his birthplace as Virginia. Had this entire family escaped from slavery? Or did the census taker make a mistake in listing places of birth?

In 1860, Junius C. Morel, now forty-eight years old, was at the height of his career as an energetic teacher, journalist, and activist. "Mr. Morel has few equals and still fewer superiors," noted one admirer. He was a member of the Committee of Thirteen, made up of key African American leaders in the New York City area, and he had become nationally significant through his writings in the *Christian Recorder* and the *North Star*. He had a "flourishing school" of "the most pleasant and agreeable nature." He had done well economically, too. He owned real estate worth two thousand dollars and personal property worth two hundred. Morel listed his birthplace as North Carolina in 1860 (compared to earlier census reports of South Carolina and the West Indies).[2]

Junius and his twenty-four-year-old wife Sarah shared a double house with the Buchanan family (Thomas, Samuel, and another male Buchanan, ages twenty-six, twenty-six, and twenty-one, who may have been brothers); Susan Butler and Amantha Butler, ages fifty-six and twenty-three, who may have been mother and daughter; and Julia Thompson, age thirty, all born in New York State.[3]

Throughout his literary career, Morel used the pseudonym "Junius," and many people continued to wonder who this literary intellectual really was. In 1863, James Jones from Indiana wrote to the *Christian Recorder*, "Now sir, who this Junius may prove to be, I know not. I am likewise uncertain as to what his profession, religion, or politics may consist of. I am wholly at a loss to know from what stand-point he has viewed the rapid strides of the 'grand march of events,' which he so eloquently notices in his communication."[4]

Morel responded with a description, half romantic fantasy, of his own situation in Weeksville:

> If it be any satisfaction to him to know who Junius is, I would lead him to a lonely cottage, surrounded with shrubbery of native growth, where birds flit through the boughs, and warble their sweet notes. The books he studies are first the Bible, and second Nature. In these he finds all the enchantment of soul that mortals can enjoy. From these sublime readings he ascends to the Giver of them all, and in profound adoration he bows before his throne. His religion is that of revelation; his politics are even-handed justice to all mankind; and his name is Junius.[5]

But in the 1860s, Weeksville was at a crossroads. The rural enclave that Morel described was about to be lost forever. Locally, European Americans began to move into Weeksville, bringing new buildings, new streets, and new problems. Nationally, people confronted momentous changes in the debate over slavery and freedom.

The decade of the 1850s had opened with the Compromise of 1850. The new Fugitive Slave Act allowed slave catchers to demand the return of any person accused of being enslaved anywhere in the United States, without giving the accused person a right to testify on his or her own behalf. Efforts to enforce the Fugitive Slave Act met strong resistance throughout the North, but the stark reality was that no one could guarantee the safety and freedom of any person of color, free or enslaved, South or North. In 1854, the Kansas-Nebraska Act opened western territories to a popular vote on slavery and abrogated the Missouri Compromise, which since 1820 had kept slavery out of territories north of the Missouri line.

In 1857 came perhaps the worst blow of all. Dred Scott, a man enslaved in Missouri, argued for his freedom based on his residence in what is now Minnesota (then part of Wisconsin territory). Not only did the Supreme Court deny Scott's appeal; they also asserted that the federal government had no right to keep slavery out of any territory. Chief Justice Roger B. Taney of Maryland added that Scott had no right to sue in federal court since he was not a citizen. In fact, no person of African descent—free or enslaved—could be a citizen of the United States. The nation's founders, argued Taney, believed that African Americans were "altogether unfit to associate with the white race, either in social or political relations, and so far inferior that they had no rights which the white man was bound to respect."

The Dred Scott decision severely deepened national tensions. It led directly to the expansion of the Republican Party and, some argued, made possible the election of Abraham Lincoln as president of the United States. Among African Americans, the Fugitive Slave Act and the Dred Scott decision rekindled the debate about emigration. Weeksville had been born as an alternative to Liberian emigration. Now, so dismal did prospects for African Americans within the United States seem that national African American leaders such as Martin Delany and Henry Highland Garnet began to argue once more for emigration.

In 1858, they organized the African Civilization Society to promote colonization to Liberia, with the goal of Christianizing Africans and developing a free-labor cotton economy. In 1864, they chose Weeksville as its headquarters.

Civil War in the 1860s convulsed the nation—black and white alike. To African Americans, it promised a strange juxtaposition of liberty, opportunity, and death. The Emancipation Proclamation took effect January 1, 1863, and seemed to portend a change in national policy toward slavery. But when draft riots in New York City made African Americans of all ages vulnerable to attack, Weeksville became a safe haven. By late summer in 1863, African American men from Weeksville and across the nation joined Union troops. Their experience as part of this national military experience convinced them of their essential rights as free people and citizens of this United States.

Emigration: Liberia and Canada

Events in the 1850s, particularly passage of the Fugitive Slave Act in 1850 and the Dred Scott decision in 1857, rejuvenated interest in emigration. Attention focused primarily on Liberia. Established by the American Colonization Society in 1821, the African nation of Liberia named its capital Monrovia, after U.S. (and American Colonization Society) president James Monroe. Supported by many slave-owning European Americans in the South, as well as by antislavery leaders in the North, the American Colonization Society promoted emigration to Liberia as an alternative to enslavement in the United States. Most people of color—and increasing thousands of white abolitionists—opposed emigration, however. Only about four thousand free people and seven thousand people in slavery actually went to Liberia. Weeksville itself had been organized as an alternative to Liberian emigration.[6]

By the early 1850s, some African American leaders believed that the situation had changed. Liberia had become an independent country in 1847, with its own constitution, president, and legislators, all people of color. And after the United States passed the Fugitive Slave Act in 1850, escape from the country assumed new urgency for many formerly enslaved people.

Weeksville residents were at the focal point of this debate, as key national leaders publicly took adversarial positions. Some opposed emigration, as the founders of Weeksville had once opposed the American Colonization Society. Some, however, organized the African Civilization Society, whose specific goal was to promote emigration to Liberia, under the control of African Americans.[7]

William J. Wilson, principal of Colored School No. 1 in Brooklyn, adamantly opposed emigration plans. Writing to *Frederick Douglass' Paper* under the pen name "Ethiop," Wilson reported on his attendance at a meeting in 1851 to discuss emigration to Jamaica. "A distemper long prevalent among the whites, has broken out here among the blacks," he wrote.

It must be speedily cured: aye, if need be, burned out with caustic, ere it spread, and drink out the very life-blood of the people. I allude to what is commonly called African Colonization or negro Colonization. . . . I always thought, up to this time, that what we most wanted, and continually sought after, was full admission into, and not secession from these institutions of our country; that even that meeting was to express our determination to stay here, and be fully incorporated into all the institutions of the country, and to let go no hold already gained, either in church, school, or state. Was I mistaken?[8]

Junius Morel, long an outspoken opponent of African emigration, seemed to be wavering when it came to emigration to the West Indies. In 1851, he "made an out-and-out Colonization speech." He cut "himself loose from all institutions, whether Church or State, at all favoring proslavery doctrines, and denouncing those holding any connection therewith, as two-faced, and unworthy of confidence, actuated only by a few paltry dollars and cents. . . . Dr. Pennington and Rev. S.E. Cornish came in for a full share of the dose, for their connection with the Presbyterian Church."[9]

In the fall of 1851, a group calling itself the New York and Liberia Emigration and Agricultural Association petitioned the New York State Legislature for funds to transport African Americans in New York State to Liberia, claiming to have 277 people ready to go. The Committee of Thirteen, including both Junius Morel and William J. Wilson, publicly protested this action. They knew of no more than twelve people who would actually leave, they said, and these could easily be accommodated by the New York State Colonization Society. From 1849 to 1851, the Colonization Society collected $50,547.58, but they spent only $1,784.34 for transporting emigrants. Clearly, African Americans were not interested in leaving the United States for Africa in large numbers.[10]

One of those who did choose Liberia in the early 1850s was Augustus Washington. In 1841, Washington briefly taught in Weeksville, before attending Dartmouth College in 1844 and moving to Hartford, Connecticut, in 1846. There he established himself as a daguerreotypist. One of his earliest portraits was a famous image of John Brown, taken about 1846–47 when Brown lived briefly in Springfield, Massachusetts. In 1853, Washington closed his successful business in Hartford and emigrated to Liberia, where his clientele was exclusively African American. His portraits of Liberian merchants and political leaders—all emigrants from the United States—document Liberia's earliest existence as a free and independent nation.[11]

To many African Americans, Canada seemed a more attractive destination than did Liberia. Mary Ann Shadd, born to free middle-class parents in Delaware, moved to Canada and became editor of the *Provincial Freeman*, published in Chatham, Canada West. In 1852, she published *A Plea for Emigration, or Notes of Canada West*, a sanguine assessment of Canada, declaring, "land is cheap, business increasing, with a steady increase of population, no lack of employment at fair prices, and no complexional or other qualification in existence."[12]

Weeksville formed a key anchor for this debate. In essays for the *Provincial Freeman*, John N. Still, who owned a secondhand clothing store in Brooklyn, advocated strongly for emigration. In May 1854, he reported a story about "a large tract of land sold a few days ago in the neighborhood of the colored settlement, called Wiessville [Weeksville], adjacent also to their cemetery." The sellers, however, "most abruptly refused to sell to colored persons. . . . Heretofore we have had no resort but to grin and bear it, but now that we have begun to move, it will cause a change of feeling with them. I mean the whites." A local white gentleman, never before interested in "colored people," had recently asked Still for letters of introduction to "respected colored fugitives" in Canada, specifically so that he could investigate their living conditions.

"I know of nothing that is doing more good than the general stir about emigration," Still concluded. "It is indicative of enterprize, say the whites, and they seem doubly willing to do something for us. They are satisfied that we now mean something more than talk, and that we are really dissatisfied and mean to better our condition."[13]

On May 30, 1854, Brooklyn African Americans held an informational meeting about Canadian emigration, chaired by Francis Champion, with John N. Still as secretary.[14] "We have been and are still being ousted from many of the domestic occupations which custom had consigned us to," Still argued in January 1855. "Men say we must stay here and bear it, stay here and help to fight for the slave. Bless your dear soul, my considerate friend, do you not know that a half a dozen black 'merchant princes,' plying between the city of New York and Canada, clothed with all the rights of the British subject, would be more help to the slave than a whole State full of such defenceless and unprotected menials as we are here."[15]

In March 1854, Mary Jane Robinson, a former Weeksville resident, wrote a letter to her friend Sarah Ann Harris, still living in Weeksville, describing her new home in Buxton, Ontario, Canada West. After describing their trip from Weeksville to Buxton, via steamboat to Troy, railroad to Buffalo, steamboat across Lake Erie to Detroit and Chatham, and then by road for six miles to Buxton, where they purchased a farm, Mary Jane Robinson waxed eloquent about Buxton itself:

> O, my dear friend, how I do want to see you again; I do wish you would try and come to Buxton, Canada West. Come to a land of liberty and freedom, where the coloured man is not despised nor a deaf ear turned to them. This is the place to live in peace and to enjoy the comforts of life. In September, we got a fine cow, with a heifer calf ten months old. So I have been quite a country-woman. I both churned my own butter and milked my own cow. We have got three nice sows, and, by and by, I shall have some geese, and chickens, and ducks, and all those things. Here is nine thousand acres of land now taken up by coloured people in Buxton, where we live; and Mr. King, the government agent, who sells the land, has purchased eight thousand more to sell at the same rate; and the people are coming in from all parts, and the place is filling up fast. I hear that OLD FILLMORE is a screwing you all up tighter still, but don't

stay there, come to Queen Victoria's land, where they are not making laws to oppress and to starve you. I raised a fine sight of tobacco. We had turnips as big as the crown of your husband's hat, and cabbage as large as a water-pail. O, don't laugh, for it's a fact—for the ground is so rich it raises everything up in no time. We were late, so we had only Fall things. There is a saw-mill and a grist-mill building in Buxton, and a school now here, with seventy or eighty scholars. O, we are just beginning to live well enough without the white man's foot on our necks. Away with your King Fillmore, I am for QUEEN VICTORIA. GOD SAVE THE QUEEN. We have all kinds of game, deer, raccoon, ground-hogs, black-squirrels, hens, pheasants, quails, wild turkey, wild duck, woodcock and red-headed woodpeckers, and sapsuckers, wild red raspberries and plumbs, crabapples and wild gooseberries, and all kinds of nuts. Not as cold as I thought. We have Methodist, Baptist and Presbyterian meetings, too. We are to have a log-rolling soon, and then we will have ten acres cleared. They (the people) all will help you to raise and log, and you help them again. Whatever you raise in the ground, you can sell it in Chatham, six miles from here. My husband walks up and down once or twice a week, and thinks nothing of it; but I hope soon we'll have a team of our own. There is a number come from Toronto to this place, as land can be got cheaper—20s, an acre and ten years to pay it in, and land that will bring anything you plant just as I did in Weeksville (only it wanted more manuring); only put in the seed and pray to the Giver of rain, and they will come up. O, dear, how I want to see you again. Do come to Buxton, Canada West.[16]

The *Provincial Freeman* editorialized that "our coloured friends," "we think, will agree with us, that here is a pleasanter picture than that recently presented to them in Augustus Washington's letters from Liberia."[17]

It is very likely that Mary Jane Robinson was living in Weeksville in 1850, listed in the census for that year as Mary J. Robertson, thirty years old, born in New York, married to forty-five-year-old Ohio-born John Robertson, porter, and living with their five sons (John, thirteen; Henry, eleven; Albert, eight; Thaddeus, five; and Homer, three) in a house worth twelve hundred dollars. All four of the older children attended school. Mary Jane Robinson sent her letter care of William Dolly, Zion's

Church, New York, so she may have been affiliated with the African Methodist Episcopal Zion Church in Manhattan rather than with the African Methodist Episcopal Church in Weeksville. The Robertsons lived only four houses away from Sarah Harris, recipient of Mary Jane Robertson's letter from Buxton, and her husband James Harris. In 1850, Sarah Harris was thirty-five years old, born in North Carolina. James was forty-seven and a laborer, born in Virginia. They lived in a house worth four hundred fifty dollars.[18]

Junius C. Morel, an outspoken opponent of the American Colonization Society in the 1830s, changed his mind in the 1850s, exploring issues of emigration controlled by African Americans themselves. Why should we wait "three centuries for the deep-seated prejudice in this country to subside," he asked, "before we should assume responsibilities of government as other nations do"?

> "What is to be my status in the coming events?" The father must ask. "For what position am I rearing my children? . . . Are my children, after I have spent my hard-earned means to educate them for any position in commercial, scientific, or philosophical business, doomed to be bootblacks, or waiters in hotels, or drivers of some gentlemen's fine carriages, or porters in some store?" The mother should be concerned abut the position her daughter is to occupy in the future; whether she is to take pains to qualify her to wait on some white man's daughter, or to be the mistress of her own house—the director of her own business matters.

We need four things, wrote Morel: "1st. We must possess the soil. 2. We must have all political rights. 3. We must possess all educational facilities without restriction. 4. We must then be where the accursed prejudices of a dominant race are not preponderately [sic] over law and justice." Honduras, he thought, offered a chance to start over, much as the pilgrims had started over in colonial New England, much as Germans were starting over in nineteenth-century New York. "Why will not colored men follow the example of the pilgrim fathers," he asked, "and hew out for themselves a nationality—a reputation? Why not run some risks in order to arrive at some practical results?"[19]

Morel's exploration of Honduras perhaps prepared him to look once more at Africa. When he did so, he emerged as a strong supporter of

Liberian emigration. Inspired by a group of Brooklyn ministers, Morell enthusiastically endorsed the African Civilization Society.

Henry Highland Garnet (minister of Shiloh Presbyterian Church in Brooklyn), Martin Delany (often called "the father of black nationalism"), and others founded the African Civilization Society in 1858, a year after the Dred Scott decision. Their goal was to promote the emigration of African Americans to Africa as a way first to Christianize Africans and second to develop a viable free-labor cotton economy. Whereas European Americans controlled the American Colonization Society, African Americans led the African Civilization Society.[20]

Henry Highland Garnet was one of this country's most brilliant, committed, and creative leaders. Born in slavery in Maryland in 1815, he and his family escaped from slavery and came to New York City when Garnet was only ten years old. While his father worked as a shoemaker, Garnet attended the African Free School and then the Noyes Academy in Canaan, New Hampshire. In 1839, he graduated from the Oneida Institute in Whitesboro, New York. He became pastor of the Liberty Street Presbyterian Church in Troy, New York, in 1842. From there, he gave two of his most famous speeches. In 1843, at the National Colored Convention in Buffalo, New York, he electrified his audience and the world with his famous "Call to Rebellion." "Rather die freemen than live to be slaves," he urged. "Let your motto be resistance! *Resistance!* RESISTANCE!" In 1848, Garnet reviewed the remarkable history of African Americans. Notably, he opposed colonization, declaring, "America is my home, my country, and I have no other. I love whatever of good there may be in her institutions. I hate her sins. I loathe her slavery, and I pray Heaven that ere long she may wash away her guilt in tears of repentance."[21]

The following year, however, he began to explore emigration. The new country of Liberia had officially formed in 1847, and Garnet was impressed with its possibilities. "I would rather see a man free in Liberia than a slave in the United States," he declared. In 1850, he went to Britain to lecture on free produce, working to create free-labor sources for goods such as cotton and molasses. In 1853, he served as a missionary in Jamaica. Ill health forced him back to the United States in 1855, when he became pastor of the Shiloh Presbyterian Church. There he united with other local clergymen to form the new African Civilization Society.[22]

Martin Delany was born of a free mother, Pati Delany, and an enslaved father, Samuel Delany, in Charles Town, Virginia, in 1812. His grandparents on both sides had been born in Africa, and Delany considered Africa his spiritual home. In 1822, his mother took her children to Chambersburg, Pennsylvania, to ensure their freedom. In 1831, Delany attended the first black convention, held in Philadelphia, and became interested in setting up a "black Israel" in Africa. That same year he moved to Pittsburgh, where he worked as a barber, attended college, studied medicine, and, in 1843, started a newspaper called the *Mystery*. In 1847 Delany joined Frederick Douglass to start the *North Star*, which Douglass edited and published in Rochester, New York.[23]

In 1850, Delany was one of the first three black students admitted to Harvard University Medical School. When a group of students complained, Harvard dismissed all three students. Delany returned to Pittsburgh, increasingly convinced that the United States held no place for free people of color. In 1852, he published *The Condition, Elevation, Emigration, and Destiny of the Colored People of the United States, Politically Considered*, a succinct review of the history and current condition of African Americans. He affirmed his commitment to American ideals: "Our common country is the United States . . . , and from here will we not be driven by any policy that may be schemed against us. We are Americans, having a birthright citizenship—natural claims upon the country—claims common to all others of our fellow citizens—natural rights, which may, by virtue of unjust laws, be obstructed, but never can be annulled. Upon these do we place ourselves, as immovably fixed as the decrees of the living God." At the same time, Delany argued that the Fugitive Slave Act made all African Americans "slaves in the midst of freedom." "What can we do? What shall we do?" he asked. "Shall we fly, or shall we resist?" Delany's conclusion was to fly, preferably to Central America, South America, or the West Indies.[24]

In 1854, Delany called for a convention to discuss emigration. Meeting in Cleveland, Ohio, this group elected Delany president pro tem. In 1856, Delany moved to Chatham, Canada, where he practiced medicine. After helping to organize the African Civilization Society in 1858, he spent a year exploring the Niger Valley in central Africa.[25]

Frederick Douglass remarked once, "I thank God for making me a man simply; but Delaney [sic] always thanks him for making him a 'black man.'" That pride infused all of Delany's political and personal life. He and his wife Kate Richards named their children after black heroes. (Their first son was Toussaint L'Ouverture.) Delany's support of the African Civilization Society and his continued interest in Africa reflected that pride. The Civil War, however, diluted Delany's emphasis on emigration. In 1865, he received a commission as major of an all-black unit of troops. He worked for several years with the Freedman's Bureau before becoming inspector of the customs house and later judge in Charleston, South Carolina. The Reverend William Simmons, who published *Men of Mark: Eminent, Progressive, and Rising* in 1887, paid tribute to Delany's widespread interests and many gifts by calling him a "Scientist-Ethnologist-Lecturer-Discoverer-Member of the International Statistical Conference."[26]

In April 1861, supporters of the African Civilization Society from Brooklyn and New York City held a meeting that featured reports from Rev. A. A. Constantine, missionary from the Yoruba country of Africa, and professor Robert Campbell, who had recently returned from exploring the same area. The purpose was to raise ten thousand dollars to send Henry Highland Garnet himself to lead a group of twenty African Americans to settle the Yoruba country, "as a means of diffusing a Christian civilization." Their second goal, to grow cotton in Africa, would, they hoped, create an alternative to cotton grown by enslaved laborers in the United States. At the same time, it would allow Africans to become "producers as well as consumers."[27]

In November 1861, supporters met again, this time in conference with Martin R. Delany. Delany drew up a supplement to the constitution, explaining the society's aims more clearly. The movement was to be controlled by the "colored people of America," Delany assured doubters, but "their white friends" were welcome as "aiders and assistants." First, they explained, "the Society is not designed to encourage general emigration, but will only aid such persons as may be practically qualified and suited to promote the development of Christianity, morality, education, mechanical arts, agriculture, commerce, and general improvement: who must always be carefully selected and well recommended, that the progress of civilization may not be obstructed." Second, "the basis of the Society, and ulterior objects in encouraging emigration shall be: Self-Reliance and Self-Government on the Principle of an African Nationality—the African race being the ruling element of the nation, controlling and directing their own affairs."[28] Chair of this meeting was Rev. R. H. Cain, minister of the Bridge Street Church in Brooklyn, who lived at 20 Lawrence Avenue, near Weeksville.

By 1863, Junius Morel was impressed with how successful the African Civilization Society had become. Reporting on the annual meeting in May, he confessed "that although formerly an advocate of the 'stay-here' policy, I felt that if black men would come together and reason on the subjects which interest them as a nation, they would elaborate plans and execute them, which would do more for building up their race than anything that they have ever yet done in this country." "I felt to my own shame," wrote Morel, when the secretary reminded his audience "that black men were the greatest opponents of the Society, which they had met with since its existence."[29]

Rev. R. H. Cain, pastor of the Bridge Street A.M.E. Church and always a mainstay of the African Civilization Society, gave the main speech. He knew, he said,

> that in presenting the claims of Africa, he would be advocating what was, generally, distasteful to colored people; that every and any other subject would find admirers among his race, but the one, which should, of all others, interest them. He could not understand why the descendants of African ancestors should despise their father-land, when the Irishman from Cork, the Scotchman, Englishman, and German, all look back to their country with pride. He said that we owe more to Africa than any other class of men, by reason that we could sympathize more truly than others for our race.

Frederick Douglass, a strong opponent of colonization, was in the audience. He reluctantly agreed to speak. "This was the place black men were to develop and become great," he argued. The constitution of the African Civilization Society was "the fruits of the same vine as colonizationists" and "'the same old Robfit Colonization' with a new skin," charged Douglass.[30]

In October 1863, Morel described the transition of the African Civilization Society in detail. "In its beginning," he explained, "it was engineered, manned and worked almost exclusively by the white men, who lived comfortably on the profits. . . . Black men there were belonging to it, but they were mere ciphers. All money, and all offices of remuneration and trust were monopolized by the 'anglo' with the African left out." Morel was referring here to the original American Colonization Society.[31]

Now, asserted Morel, African Americans themselves had taken over the colonization movement, believing "that black men, of all others, were the best qualified to carry forward the work of establishing an association which looks to the recognition of the interests of 'colored people, wherever found on the face of the globe.'" They incorporated in New York State and redefined their mission to work with freed people in the South, as well as with people of color in Africa, Central and South America, and the British West Indies. "They work steadily and surely for the good of their race," Morel concluded. "The Society is composed of ministers and gentlemen of known and tried integrity, who believe that colored men are capable of thinking and acting intelligently for their own elevation. They believe that the great work of civilizing Africa is committed to the African race. They feel that black men have real sympathy—that which prompts to deeds of mercy more than the cold, stoical expressions of the Saxon. Hence their efforts to do something for themselves."[32] On January 2, 1864, the African Civilization Society adopted a new constitution:

> The object of this Society shall be the civilization and Christianization of Africa, and of the descendants of African ancestors in any portion of the earth, wherever dispersed. Also the destruction of the African slave trade by the introduction of lawful commerce and trade into Africa; the promotion of the growth of cotton and other products there, whereby the natives may become industrious producers, as well as consumers of articles of commerce; and generally the elevation of the condition of the colored population of our own country and of other lands.[33]

Finally, to emphasize how important their task was, they concluded that "aided by the Divine blessing we shall strive to make this Society to the interest of the colored people, what the American Bible Society is to the world."[34]

Supporters of the society came primarily from New York City, Brooklyn, and Philadelphia, but individuals and auxiliaries were located from Ohio to Washington, D.C., Connecticut, and Canada West. Brooklyn supporters included ministers such as President George W. LeVere, Presbyterian minister Theodore Cuyler (European American), James Myres, James Morris Williams, Episcopal minister Peter Williams, Rev. Amos N. Freeman, Baptist ministers Rufus L. Perry and John Sella Martin, and A.M.E. minister Richard H. Cain. Henry H. Wilson of New York City was corresponding secretary. Henry Highland Garnet remained a prominent supporter. So, finally, did Weeksville educator and journalist Junius C. Morel.

In 1864, the African Civilization Society established its national headquarters in Weeksville, at the corner of Dean Street and Troy Avenue, on the same block as Colored School No. 2. The building, heated by wood and lit by kerosene lanterns, tended by a woman janitor, quickly became a community center. Morel's support for the African Civilization Society was undoubtedly a key factor in promoting this move. They constructed "a splendid missionary building, the chapel being used for school and church purposes, and the remaining portion occupied as a residence, press-room, and . . . publication office." One supporter praised its "earnest and noble" leaders, with "goodness of heart and high, refined, mental caliber."[35]

At the same time that Morel advocated African colonization, he began to praise separate African American communities within the United States. "Just now, as a people," he wrote, "we want homes more than any thing else. We want to be owners of lands, houses and stocks. I am inclined to think we want these things more than political rights!" All other rights, he argued, depended on the ownership of property. "We must be equal to others in possessions and intelligence," he wrote,

> so that there will be a mutual dependence and independence on both sides. Then each will respect the other. We cannot expect this in the large cities of the North, because our poverty and ignorance of commercial relations disqualify us to enter into the contest with any hope of success.
>
> But we can go to the rural districts, with a small capital, and purchase lands of the Government, and become industrious farmers, mechanics

and small tradesmen, and there gradually rise to importance and position in the community, and becoming endowed with wealth and education, thus gradually rise into respect and esteem as good citizens.

African Americans can "look to making money, getting rich, being
educated, settling colonies in the South and South-west, removing the
masses from the cities, where they are now living in garrets and cellars,
to fine arable farms, where home will be what it should be, and their
children reared in industry and cleanliness, where they may feel that
they are entitled to the same degree of respect and consideration as others surrounding them."[36] In effect, Morel was advocating that African
Americans in the 1860s repeat the pattern they had developed a generation earlier in Weeksville: create their own communities based on land
ownership, where they could work as farmers, mechanics, and tradesmen, support education for themselves and their children, and become
politically powerful and respected citizens.

Morel's essay sparked a national debate, and not everyone agreed
with him. James F. Jones, from Richmond, Indiana, vehemently
opposed Morel's sympathy for colonization:

Many schemes of colonization have been introduced by prejudice and
have nearly all been a complete failure. The Hayti colonization, for
instance—why it was and has been a curse, rather than a blessing, to our
people. The colored people of the west are, and ever have been, opposed
to colonization in any form whatever. No sir, we are colored Americans;
our destiny is an American destiny; our interests are linked with the
interests of this country and people. . . . Away at once and forever, with
all ideas of colonization![37]

One of the strongest supporters of the African Civilization Society was
Rev. R. H. Cain. Richard Harvey Cain was born in Greenbrier County,
Virginia, of free parents, on April 12, 1825. He moved to Ohio as a young
man, where he worked on a steamboat in Cincinnati and then moved to
Hannibal, Missouri, where he was licensed as a Methodist preacher in
1844. Shortly thereafter, he returned to Cincinnati and joined the A.M.E.
Church. He received his first pastorate in Muscatine, Iowa, and became a
deacon in 1859. He studied at Wilberforce University.

In 1861, he moved to Brooklyn, where he became pastor of Bridge Street Wesleyan Church. He remained in Brooklyn for four years, becoming one of the primary supporters of the African Civilization Society. He lived at 20 Lawrence Avenue, near Weeksville, according to the Brooklyn City Directory. In 1864, he attended the national convention in Syracuse, New York, advocating universal manhood suffrage. Before he left for his new pastorate in South Carolina, women in Weeksville organized a benefit party for him.

In 1865, Rev. Cain went to South Carolina, to serve Emanuel A.M.E. Church in Charleston. The South Carolina government had closed this church in 1822 (which had nurtured Francis P. Graham, among others) because of the Denmark Vesey rebellion. Cain brought this church back to life and converted thousands of people. Noted his biographer, "Church after church sprang into existence as if by magic under his charge." He also founded and edited a newspaper, the *Missionary Record*.

Through his church and newspaper, Rev. Cain gained considerable political influence. In 1868, he served in the South Carolina Constitutional Convention, and he then became state senator from Charleston and U.S. congressman (forty-third and forty-fifth Congresses), where he supported the Civil Rights Act of 1875. "All that we ask is equal laws, equal legislation, and equal rights," he asserted. He also promoted emigration to Liberia.

In 1880, he was appointed a bishop in the A.M.E. Church, and he became founder and first president of Paul Quinn College in Waco, Texas (1876–80), the oldest historically black college west of the Mississippi, organized to serve people who had survived slavery. After he died on January 18, 1887, Bethel A.M.E. Church in Weeksville held a memorial service. He was eulogized as "one of the brightest lights" and "richest gems" of the A.M.E. Church, "a brilliant star."[38]

Civil War

The tsunami of the Civil War overwhelmed debates about colonization. Confronted with the genuine possibility of ending slavery in the United States, many emigrationists—including Henry Highland Garnet and Martin Delany—moved their primary focus to military support for the Union. They argued that a Union victory, especially after the Emancipation Proclamation took effect on January 1, 1863, became the best hope for dignity, respect, and economic and political power for African Americans. Building on their connections with prominent Republican politicians, these African American leaders changed the focus of the African Civilization Society from emigration to providing African American teachers for schools established in the South by the Freedman's Bureau.

The decade did not begin auspiciously for African Americans. In 1860, New York State voters confronted a state constitutional amendment proposing equal voting rights for African Americans. Voters had turned down such a provision in 1846. In 1860, they turned it down again, in spite of support from the Republican Party and extensive lobbying by African Americans. On January 16, 1860, Charles M. Briggs, representing the Fourteenth and Eighteenth Wards in Brooklyn, presented a petition supporting the equal voting rights signed by W. Hodges (probably Willis Hodges) and 130 other African Americans in Brooklyn. On January 30, 1860, George H. Fisher, representing the Seventh, Fifteenth, Sixteenth, and Nineteenth Wards in Brooklyn, presented a second petition signed by Willis J. Hodges and other African Americans, also supporting the amendment.[39]

All Brooklyn newspapers, including the Democratic *Eagle*, however, opposed the amendment, and they appealed to racial prejudices to attract Democratic support. Statewide, voters elected Abraham Lincoln but rejected the equal suffrage amendment by 63 percent. Brooklyn voters overwhelmingly rejected equal suffrage, 23,399 to 5,534.[40]

At the beginning of the Civil War, Lincoln's avowed purpose had been to save the Union. But on January 1, 1863, he brought new moral urgency to the war by issuing the Emancipation Proclamation, freeing those African Americans enslaved in Confederate states. African Americans and European American abolitionists in Brooklyn celebrated at the Bridge Street Church, with speeches by Rev. John Gloucester, Theodore Tilton, William Wells Brown, and others. Many Brooklyn residents also attended the huge rally at Cooper Institute in New York City, where five thousand people celebrated emancipation with Henry Highland Garnet, Lewis Tappan, and other stalwart abolitionist speakers in a "glorious meeting."[41]

The Emancipation Proclamation also included a provision for enlisting African Americans into the Union armies. African American soldiers had not always been welcomed. As early as July 1861, New York's Governor Morgan had offered "three colored regiments, armed and equipped, ready for immediate service, and to be sustained through the war at private expense." Lincoln rejected Governor Morgan's offer, but in November 1862 Thomas Wentworth Higginson, a European American abolitionist from Massachusetts, took command of the First South Carolina Volunteer Infantry in Beaufort, South Carolina, made up primarily of formerly enslaved men. In February 1863, a month after the Emancipation Proclamation, Massachusetts formed the first northern African American regiment, the Fifty-Fourth Massachusetts Colored Infantry. Men from New York City and Brooklyn joined both of these regiments.[42]

In the spring of 1863, however, African Americans in Brooklyn and New York City were reluctant to enlist in the army, and for good reason. While whites were often given bounties to fight, African Americans usually received nothing more than their monthly pay, which was less than that given to European Americans, $7.00 a month plus $3.00 for clothing for African Americans compared to $13.00 a month plus $3.50 for clothing for European Americans.[43] "While there is no lack of patriotism in the black man," noted Junius Morel, "men in the North will not leave their homes and families, their avocations, at wages of $25 and $30 per month, to be sent to South Carolina, or Georgia, to fight rebel white men, with the prospect of dog's death by the minions of Jeff. Davis, should they be captured, all for $10 per month, without bounty at that; no—no, we do not see any beauty or enough glory for such fool-hardy madness." "War is a reality, and the glory of dying for the privilege of riding in the 'Jim Crow car' in 6th Avenue, or standing with the driver on the 4th Avenue is not considered by some gentlemen a sufficient compensation."[44]

As the war droned on, new recruits became harder to find, and the U.S. government initiated a draft. Only European Americans were eligible, and the burden fell heaviest on the poor. Wealthy people could pay a bounty and buy their way out of service. But poorer Irish Americans in New York City took their rage out on African Americans. Over four days in July, Irish rioters attacked and burned the Colored Orphan

Asylum in New York City, killed about one hundred African Americans, and drove thousands of others from their homes. The *New York Sun* reported that

> attacks upon the colored people continue. They are not safe anywhere. They are driven from their homes, and it is not an unusual sight to see women and helpless children in search of some place of refuge, followed by crowds of idle men and boys. There were reports yesterday that attacks were expected upon the colored citizens of Weeksville, a village near the boundaries of the Ninth Ward. The residents of that neighborhood at once took precautionary measures, by procuring arms and organizing.[45]

Junius C. Morel reported in detail on the "fearful volcano of fire, blood, death, lamentation and wo":

> Many men were killed and thrown into the river, a great number hung to trees and lamp-posts, numbers shot down; no black person could show their heads but what they were hunted like wolves. These scenes continued for four days. Hundreds of our people are in station houses, in the woods, and on Blackwell's island. Over three thousand are to-day homeless and destitute, without the means of support for their families. It is truly a day of distress to our race in this section. In Brooklyn we have not had any great trouble, but many of our people have been compelled to leave their houses and flee for refuge. The Irish have become so brutish, that it is unsafe for families to live near them, and while I write, there are many now in the stations and country hiding from violence.[46]
>
> In Weeksville and Flatbush, [Morel continued], the colored men who had manhood in them armed themselves, and threw out their pickets every day and night, determined to die defending their homes. Hundreds fled there from New York, and rations were served up there daily by the benevolence of J.C. Morel, H. M. Williams and other noblehearted men whose names I have not learned. The mob spirit seemed to have run in every direction, and every little village catches the rebellious spirit. One instance is worthy of note. In the village of Flushing, the colored people went to the Catholic priest and told him that they were peaceable men doing no harm to any one, and that the Irish had threatened to mob them, but if they did, they would burn two Irish

houses for every one of theirs, and would kill two Irish men for every colored men killed by them. They were not mobbed, and so in every place where they were prepared they escaped being mobbed. Most of the colored men in Brooklyn who remained in the city were armed daily for self-defence.[47]

Merchants in New York City and Brooklyn organized the Committee of Merchants for the Relief of Colored People, Suffering from the Late Riots. They worked with African American ministers (including R. H. Cain, George LeVere, and Henry Highland Garnet) to raise money, collect food and clothing, and find shelter for families affected by the riots. Relief was desperately needed. Junius C. Morel was amazed at how "one eruption has thrown this whole class into indiscriminate confusion, left thousands penniless, and pauperized a whole community, in four days. One stands aghast, at the thought that in so short a time, by the hands of an infuriated, brutalized mob, the whole political, social and religious standing of a people can be so completely changed. The wonder is not that the mob was so furious, for that is the character of mobs, but that the foundation on which these relations rest should be so frail."[48] "I have been utterly astonished," he wrote, "to find such universal want among them. I had not prepared my mind for such a scene of wretchedness. . . . What crimes have we, an unoffending people, committed, that we should suffer these cruelties?"[49]

The Committee of Merchants described the situation in Weeksville itself. "On the Monday succeeding the riot," they wrote,

We visited Weeksville, a settlement of colored people, situated some three miles from the ferries, where we found a large number of refugees from the city of New York, and many that had been driven out from their homes in Brooklyn, the inhabitants having furnished them such shelter as they were able, with their limited means and small facilities for accommodating several hundred strangers thrown upon them. We found not only Weeksville, but Carsville, New Brooklyn, and the whole vicinity extending to Flatbush and Flatlands, had more or less refugees scattered in the woods and in such places as they could find safety and shelter. All being thrown out of employment and the means of support, your committee immediately made arrangements for furnishing them daily supplies of food. With the assistance of Mr. Edgar McMullen, who had for a few days previous been assisting them, we had food (as we think prudently and judiciously) distributed daily from July 20th, to August 14th. The amount so given out in Bread, Hams, Flour, Rice, Sugar, and Tea, and in some few cases of great need small sums of money, amounted to eight hundred and fifty 27-100 Dollars [$850.27].[50]

Local tradition suggests that some of these refugees took shelter in the Vanderveer windmill in Flatbush. Built in 1804, it formed a defensible position in case of further attack. Weeksville citizens also created a defensible earthworks around several homes, which they called Fort Sumter, after the federal fort outside Charleston, South Carolina, captured by Confederate troops at the very beginning of the Civil War.[51]

In Brooklyn itself, the relief committee found "so many cases of distress in the city, arising from injuries received during the riot, from losses, and from want of employment" that they opened a place where people could apply for assistance. "Four colored ministers of Brooklyn" visited the families. They helped 752 families, with 2,250 people.[52]

By September 1863, the situation seemed somewhat better. "I am happy to note a great change in the affairs of our people in the last few weeks," noted Junius Morel. "They are returning to their various occupations. In the tobacco factories they are at work at better wages than before. I have been informed that there is a call made for seventy-five colored men to take charge of a factory in this city. There is a great scarcity of colored servants; hundreds of neat respectable women could find situations here if they could be procured."[53]

One result of both the Emancipation Proclamation and the draft riots was a new interest in enlisting in the Union Army. Frederick Douglass worked diligently to recruit African Americans to serve in the war. "Once let the black man get upon his person the brass letters, U.S., let him get an eagle on his button, and a musket on his shoulder and bullets in his pockets, and there is no power on earth which can deny that he has earned the right to citizenship in the United States," he wrote. Other African American leaders agreed. William Wells Brown, African American novelist, historian, and orator, recruited in Brooklyn. People such as Garnet and Delany, once committed to leaving the United States, shifted their focus in 1863 from emigration to fighting for the

Vanderveer mill, Flatbush, built 1804. Brooklyn Historical Society, Adrian Vanderveer Martense Collection.

Union. Henry Highland Garnet joined the effort as chaplain. Delany received a commission as major of an all-black unit of troops.[54]

Governor Horatio Seymour opposed the organization of African American regiments in New York State, so African Americans at first joined regiments organized outside the state. Peter Vogelsang, from Brooklyn, joined the Massachusetts Fifty-Fourth, perhaps when William Wells Brown was recruiting after the draft riots. He became second lieutenant in April 1865 and later was promoted to first lieutenant. After the war, he moved to Weeksville. John Carraway, also from Brooklyn, served as a private with the Fifty-Fourth in Company A. Alfred Cornish, who later lived in one of the Hunterfly Road houses, served in the Massachusetts Fifty-Fourth. This regiment became famous in its attack on Fort Wagner, South Carolina, the subject of the film *Glory*.[55]

Lieutenant Peter Vogelsang, Massachusetts Fifty-Fourth Regiment. Courtesy Massachusetts Historical Society.

Lieutenant James R. W. Leonard came to New York City from Rhode Island (perhaps from the Fourteenth Rhode Island Heavy Artillery) to offer bounties of two hundred dollars plus ten dollars per month to new recruits. Connecticut regiments also recruited African Americans. "They are enlisting very fast," noted Morel. "Hundreds will go into this regiment, to get clear of the accursed prejudice in this state. There never was a time when colored men are so fully determined to leave as now." The *New York Tribune* confirmed this report. "A large number of colored families have left the city," it reported on August 3, "with the intention of never returning to it again."[56]

Instead of state sponsorship, the Union League Club of New York City organized three companies from New York State, beginning in December 1863. Between December 1863 and January 1864, at least sixty African Americans from Long Island joined a total of one thousand men in the first regiment, the Twentieth U.S. Colored Troop. Among them were Thomas Rix, from Weeksville, and John Anderson, from Brooklyn. Brooklyn minister Rev. George LeVere became chaplain for the Twentieth.[57]

The enlistment of African American soldiers dramatically changed European American attitudes. "One thousand colored soldiers [were] encamped in the city of New York," noted Junius C. Morel in December 1863, "and were served by white men with as much respect as all other soldiers belonging to the U.S. service, and marched through the principal streets of this city, where a few months past colored men were chased and murdered by an infuriated mob. How changed the scene! Thousands of people crowded the park to gaze on those sable warriors; even copperheads acknowledged that there was the appearance of fight in these men."[58] When the Twentieth U.S. Colored Troop received their flag on March 5, 1864, *Harper's Weekly* commemorated the event with illustrations in its magazine. "No scene of the war has been more striking or significant," they reported.[59]

Presentation of colors to the Twentieth United States Colored Troop. *Frank Leslie's Weekly*, February 26, 1864. Courtesy of the House Divided Project at Dickinson College.

One hundred thousand people crowded Union Square to watch the "Mothers, Wives and Sisters" of the Union League Club members present the soldiers with their colors. The message was clear: in the aftermath of the draft riots, African American soldiers could count on the support of some white men and, most especially, some white women. Twenty years later, LeGrand B. Cannon gave these women special attention at a commemorative banquet. "The potent influence of the women of position and power in our New York world stamped out prejudice, turned hisses into applause, exalted the humble and despised to places of honor, and in giving the black man not only the right but the invitation to fight for his liberty, created the force which emancipated the slaves and saved the Union."[60] While Cannon certainly overstated the impact of these women on the future of Africans and the Union, he did point out the dynamics of race and class that their actions illustrated.

A second unit, the Twenty-Sixth USCT, was sent to South Carolina on the *Warrior* at the end of March. John Jay and Henry Highland Garnet gave speeches in their honor. This regiment included James H. Abraham, Thomas Abrams, and Jacob Cato, all from Brooklyn, as well as many people from New England, Canada West, and the West Indies. Together the Twentieth and the Twenty-Sixth Regiments had more than twenty-two hundred men. The Union League sponsored three more companies of the Thirty-First USCT, which fought at Petersburg and elsewhere in Virginia.[61]

Altogether, at least seven men from Weeksville fought in the Union armies. Frank Anderson, age twenty-eight, a waiter born in Queens, enlisted as a private in the Eleventh Colored Volunteers in October 1863. George Burch, age seventeen, born in Virginia, enlisted as a private in October 1863. Oscar Clair, born in Kings County, age seventeen, enlisted as a private in the Fourteenth Rhode Island Volunteers, July 1863. Alfred Cornish (Massachusetts Fifty-Fourth), age twenty-eight in 1870, born in New York, became a cabinetmaker in Weeksville by 1870. Thomas Ewell, born in Virginia, enlisted as a private in September 1863, age nineteen in 1865. Thomas Rex (or Rix), age twenty-seven, born in Kings County, enlisted in 1864 in the Twentieth Infantry. So did Thomas Williams, age twenty-five, born in Kings County.[62]

In addition, at least five more men from Weeksville served in the Navy. Three of Simon Bundick's four sons (all but the youngest,

"Navy-Yard at Brooklyn, New York, June 1861," *Harper's Weekly*, July 20, 1861. Barcella Bundick and John Francis both served on the *North Carolina*, second sailing ship from the left in this image. Courtesy, Department of Art, Syracuse University.

Obadiah) enlisted as seamen. Barcella Bundick shipped as a cook on the *North Carolina* when he was eighteen years old, in March 1864, and then transferred to the *Connecticut*. The National Park Service's Civil War Soldiers and Sailors System listed Brazillai Bundicks, as a laborer/hostler, colored, age eighteen, in the Navy from New York. Simon Bundick, Jr. signed on to the *Vermont* as a captain's waiter in January 1865, when he was twenty-two years old, then transferred to the *Glaucus*. Bundick appeared in the National Park Service's list of Civil War sailors as a clerk/cook/cooper, age twenty-three, mulatto, from New York. He likely was on the *Glaucus* when it ran aground at Molasses Reef in the Bahamas and had to be towed for repairs. Cornelius Bundick, listed as living in Jamaica, also served. John Francis shipped as a seaman on the *North Carolina* in March 1865 at age twenty and then transferred to the *Susquehanna*. The National Park Service listed him as colored, age eighteen, a waiter from Long Island.[63]

James Matthews, baker, was a ward steward on the *Congaree* for three years, beginning in February 1862. James A. Matthews, mulatto, age twenty, barber, was listed in the National Park Service list, from New York. James Weeks, born in New Brunswick, served on the U.S.S. *Brooklyn* from July 25, 1864, until he was mustered out and the ship was decommissioned on September 11, 1867. The National Park Service listed no James Weeks from New York as serving in the Navy, but it did list Benjamin M. Weeks, mulatto, age twenty-seven, a steward from Long Island; Benjamin R. Weeks, Negro, age twenty-one, a shoemaker/ waiter from New York; Edward Weeks, colored, age twenty-three, a barber; and Major Weeks, mulatto, age twenty-eight, a cook from New York. Without more information about the ships on which these men served, we cannot know whether any of them may have been related to the Weeks family in Weeksville.⁶⁴

Weeksville soldiers and sailors were part of the largest military effort the United States had ever engaged in. By the spring of 1865, almost 180,000 African Americans had served in 163 different units in the Union Army. About 18,000 African American men and several dozen women served in the Union Navy on almost every one of the Union's seven hundred ships. African Americans formed about 10 percent of the total of the whole Union forces, both land and sea. About one-third of those who signed up were killed or wounded.⁶⁵

We can guess that Weeksville soldiers and seaman joined the military for both personal and political reasons. They fought for their own economic well-being, to feed their families. They fought to keep the Union together. And they fought for their own rights as free people.

Their participation in the war changed their lives forever. No longer was their vision limited, if it ever had been, to Weeksville alone, or even to Brooklyn, New York City, or the state of New York. Military and naval service took African Americans from Weeksville all over the United States, and they fought both as black men and as citizens of the United States. Weeksville residents, along with African Americans everywhere, were determined to assert their full rights as free people, citizens, and voters, and military service was a powerful weapon in that struggle.

"The participation of the black soldier was perhaps the most revolutionary feature of the Civil War," noted historian David Blight. "By 1863 the war to save the Union had irrevocably become as well the war to free the slaves, and black soldiers came to symbolize their people's struggle for freedom, a recognition of their humanity, the rights of citizenship, and a sense of belonging in a new nation."[66]

African Civilization Society and the Freedman's Bureau

The Civil War opened new opportunities for African Americans to serve in both the Union Army and the Navy. It also shifted the focus of the African Civilization Society away from emigration and toward meeting the basic needs of freed people at home. The number of freed people of color grew exponentially in the South in 1863, and the African Civilization Society devoted itself to recruiting African American teachers for them. "The African Civilization Society is fully in the field," reported Junius C. Morel. They are "holding meetings, collecting clothes, books, papers," and "they have employed a competent colored lady to go to Washington to open a free school for the freedmen, under the auspices of the society." "They are making arrangements to send colored teachers just as fast as they can find means and persons qualified to go."[67]

This first teacher sent by the African Civilization Society to teach at a Freedman's school in Washington, D.C., was most likely Maria W. Stewart, who had once taught in Colored School No. 3 in Brooklyn. A report in April 1864 from the Auxiliary African Civilization Society of Washington noted that "an estimable lady, Mrs. Stewart, of New York" taught eighty-five scholars in a free school that met at the Second Baptist Church.[68]

Stewart had a long record of activism for African American rights. While working as a teacher in Boston in the 1820s, she became the first U.S.-born woman of any race to speak to mixed-gender public audiences. Committed to justice for both African Americans and women, she befriended David Walker, whose *Appeal* became a clarion call for action. In the early 1830s, she wrote two pamphlets and gave four speeches, all published in the *Liberator*. In 1833, she moved first to Manhattan and then to Brooklyn, where she taught in Colored School No. 3. After 1852, she moved to Baltimore. During the Civil War, she moved to Washington, D.C., and became a teacher in a Freedman's school and then matron of the Freedman's Hospital in Washington.[69]

Morel was thoroughly impressed with this work of finding and supervising teachers. "It is truly refreshing," he wrote, "to see a combination

of colored gentlemen looking after the affairs of their people, and especially sending colored ladies and gentlemen to teach those persons
who are ushered into this new condition of life. There has not been
such a step taken by any society formed among the colored people in
this country before. . . . It is time that we should do our own thinking
and acting, for our own best interest," he concluded. "We should enter
heartily into this good work and form auxiliary societies all over the
country; collect means and send teachers into every part of the South
where we can get access, carry our newspapers and books, and impress
the love of liberty and the appreciation of freedmen upon the minds of
our brethren in the South. God speed these truths. Amen!"[70] By the end
of 1868, the African Civilization Society supported schools in Washington, D.C., Virginia, Maryland, the Carolinas, Georgia, Mississippi, and
Louisiana. At its height, the society employed 129 teachers educating
eight thousand students, at a cost of $53,700.[71]

Altogether, at least eighteen African Americans from Brooklyn
taught in Freedman's schools in the South after the Civil War, including Maria W. Stewart; William J. Wilson (formerly principal of Colored
School No. 1 and journalist writing as "Ethiop" for *Frederick Douglass'
Paper*), along with his wife and daughter; Peter Vogelsang, formerly first
lieutenant of the Fifty-Fourth Massachusetts, who moved to Weeksville
in the 1870s; Hardy and Susan Mobley, minister and tailoress (both children of enslaved people) and their three daughters; Celinda and Matilda
Anderson, teacher and principal; Laura Cardozo, teacher; James D. S.
Hall, minister; Martha Hoy; and Hezekiah Hunter, teacher and minister, and his wife, Lizzie Hunter. None of these except Peter Vogelsang
seem to have been associated with Weeksville, since none are listed in
the 1860 or 1865 census records for the Ninth Ward of Brooklyn.[72]

In 1866, the African Civilization Society began publication of *Freedman's Torchlight*, "devoted to the temporal and spiritual interests of the
Freedmen; and adapted to their present need of instruction in regard to
simple truths and principles relating to their life, liberty and pursuit of
happiness." Contributors read like a blue ribbon list of Brooklyn's African American intellectual elite. They included Rev. Rufus Perry, editor;
Rev. A. N. Freeman, minister of Siloam Presbyterian Church in Brooklyn; Henry M. Wilson; Junius C. Morel; and Martin R. Delany. Only
the first copy of this newspaper has survived, published at the society's

headquarters on Dean Street, near Troy Avenue, in the heart of Weeks-ville. It noted that the African Civilization Society was "officered and managed entirely by colored men" and that it employed sixty-nine col-ored people, served 614 scholars in Sabbath schools, had distributed 450 Bibles and more than 400 other books, and carried on a "large print-ing business in its own building, giving employment to a number of colored printers." In addition to *Freedman's Torchlight*, the society pub-lished a weekly paper called the *People's Journal*, edited by Rev. Rufus Perry. Apparently no copies of this survive.[73]

The African Civilization Society, operating from the same build-ing as the Howard Orphan Asylum and controlled essentially by the same people, did very well in the 1860s. As the *Brooklyn Eagle*, not a supporter, noted in 1870, "Between the receipts from miscellaneous charitable white people in Brooklyn, New York and all over the coun-try, toward civilizing our American citizens of African descent, and the contributions of the Freedmen's Bureau toward the Orphan Asylum Brothers Wilson and Perry made a good thing of it in money as well as reputation."

After its impressive work in operating a national institution com-pletely under the control of African Americans, printing a newspaper, and raising money to support teachers in Freedman's schools during the Civil War, the African Civilization Society dissolved in 1869–70. In 1869, three of its officers (Rev. Amos Freeman, president; Rufus L. Perry, general agent, superintendent of schools, editor of the newspaper, and chairman of the building committee; and John Flamer, director) brought a lawsuit against Rev. Henry M. Wilson, corresponding secre-tary, accusing Rev. Wilson of stealing the society's silver communion service when he left the society's employ. Rev. Wilson defended him-self, replying that he had returned the service to Junius C. Morel, act-ing treasurer. The following year, he won a judgment against the society for two thousand dollars for defamation of character. John Flamer took possession of the African Civilization Society's property on July 1, 1871, perhaps to pay this debt.[74]

Although the African Civilization Society dissolved, its legacy lived on. Institutionally, it gave birth to the Howard Orphan Asylum. Per-sonally, people associated with the African Civilization Society contin-ued their commitment to independence and self-determination. Henry

Highland Garnet narrowly escaped attack during the draft riots when his daughter misled rioters by ripping the nameplate off the Garnet family's front door. From 1864 to 1866, Rev. Garnet served as pastor of the Fifteenth Street Presbyterian Church (Liberty Church) in Washington, D.C. In that capacity, he became the first African American to speak to Congress, on February 12, 1865. After a brief period as president of Avery College in Pittsburgh, Pennsylvania, he returned to Shiloh Presbyterian Church in Brooklyn in 1870. There he met Sarah Smith Tompkins, first African American woman principal in the New York City schools and daughter of Weeksville founders Sylvanus and Ann Smith. They married in 1879 and went to Liberia in 1881, where Garnet served as U.S. minister. Garnet died just two months later and was buried in Palm Grove Cemetery in Monrovia. One observer noted, "They buried him like a prince, this princely man, with the blood of a long line of chieftains in his veins, in the soil of his fathers."[75]

Sarah Smith Garnet returned to Brooklyn, where she became a major leader of movements for women's rights and African American rights. She helped to form the Niagara movement, a precursor to the NAACP, and she worked for women's suffrage through the Equal Suffrage Club, a group she helped found in Brooklyn, and the National Association of Colored Women's Clubs. Although Garnet did not live in Weeksville, her parents had been early land investors, and she represented a coalition of dynamic organized African American women that emerged in Weeksville, Brooklyn, and the nation during and after the Civil War.

Rev. Rufus Perry continued to live in Weeksville during his long and illustrious career as a pastor, author, and editor. Rev. Perry, D.D., Ph.D. had been born about 1831 in Smith County, Tennessee, to parents Lewis and Maria Perry, both enslaved by Archibald W. Overton. Lewis Perry was a mechanic, carpenter, and cabinetmaker of some renown. He hired out his own time, so he was able to move his family to Nashville, where Rufus attended school as a free child. When Rufus was only seven years old, his father escaped to Canada. The rest of the family was forced to move back to Overton's plantation, where Rufus, partly because of his schooling, earned a reputation as dangerous. He was consigned in 1852 for sale to Mississippi, but before he could be sent away he joined his father in Canada.[76]

Rev. Rufus L. Perry in William J. Simmons, *Men of Mark: Eminent, Progressive, and Rising* (Cleveland, Ohio: George M. Rewell, 1887), 620. General Research & Reference Division, Schomburg Center for Research in Black Culture, New York Public Library, Astor, Lenox, and Tilden Foundations.

Receiving a call to the ministry in 1854, he attended Kalamazoo Seminary in Michigan, graduating in 1861. He served as pastor of Baptist churches in Ann Arbor, Michigan, St. Catherine's, Ontario, and Buffalo, New York, before he went to Washington, D.C., as superintendent of the Freedman's school kept there by the African Civilization Society. He came to Weeksville about 1868, where he published the *People's Journal* for the African Civilization Society. As a Baptist minister, he also worked as general agent of the African Civilization Society, superintendent of its schools, and chairman of the building committee. In 1870, he became editor and publisher of the *National Monitor*, published in Weeksville. The *Monitor* dealt with "racial subjects and matters touching the political rights of colored men." It was "a spicy paper," noted biographer William Simmons. For a time, Perry also served as coeditor of the *American Baptist*, which served primarily white Baptist congregations. Perry also served as secretary of the Consolidated American Baptist Missionary convention, which counted a membership of more than a million African American Baptists; the American Educational Association; and the American Baptist Free Mission Society. Perry founded and became pastor of Messiah Baptist Church, located in East New York, Brooklyn. In 1891, he was elected president of the New England Baptist Missionary Convention.[77]

In 1880, Reverend Perry was forty-five years old. He lived in a mixed-race neighborhood near Weeksville with his wife, Charlott Perry, age thirty-seven, at 999 St. Marks Avenue. They had eight children ranging from fifteen years to five months old: Edith, Rufus L., Jr., Arthur, Latha, Eudha, Minnie, David, and Hattie B. Their house was a simple frame dwelling with a porch and garden. Perry himself turned over the first shovel of sod on this lot.[78]

Reverend Perry was a scholar as well as an editor and educator, and he published several pamphlets, all of them related to African American history and religious texts. The first, published with T. McCants Stewart in 1887, was *The Cushite; or, The Children of Ham (the Negro Race) as Seen by the Ancient Historians and Poets*. In it, he argued that there were "three great and distinctly marked streams of people," "a white Europe, a black Africa, and a yellow Asia." "No race," he suggested, "can boast of a higher celebrity in ancient times than the Negro, then called Cushites by the Hebrews and Ethiopians by the Greeks." He first read this before the Brooklyn Literary Union, which published it and sold large numbers of copies. In 1893, he published what was likely a revision of this essay, *The Cushite; or, The Descendants of Ham: As found in the Sacred Scriptures and in the Writings of Ancient Historians and Poets from Noah to the Christian Era*. One of his sermons, titled "The Scriptures," appeared in a collection of writings by black Baptist ministers in 1890. In it, he used reason to explore Scripture as the word of God.[79]

Biographer William Simmons hailed Perry's "powerful intellect." "He has had a sword sometimes apparently dipped in wrath, and with giant force driven in the vitals of those who dared assail him and his cause; but he did it not for self but for the cause," Simmons noted. "He is revered for his zeal on behalf of his religion and his race," wrote the

Eagle. After Reverend Perry died in 1895, the *New York Age* eulogized him as "a man of large powers and great influence," "one of the scholars of his denomination as well as one of its ablest men."[80]

Perry's son, Rufus L. Perry, Jr., became both a Jew and a socialist and authored a book called *Man: Viewed from Science and the Talmud.*[81]

Weeksville: Family and Work in 1865

At the end of the war, Weeksville, like the rest of the nation, emerged from a period of intense stress and change. Attention from national leaders, through the African Civilization Society, faded by 1870, leaving Weeksville's citizens to cope with a growing population of immigrants from Germany, Ireland, Canada, and England. Key members of Weeksville's first generation of families remained, maintaining a stable infrastructure.

By 1865, several families named Weeks once again lived in Weeksville. We do not know whether they were directly related to the original settler James Weeks, but it seems likely that at least some of them were. One James Weeks, perhaps the son of the original, had served in the Union Navy on the U.S.S. *Brooklyn*, but he had not returned to Weeksville by 1865. Instead, Weeks families now included three nuclear family units plus one single woman, Agnes Weeks, age twenty-two, born in New York County. John Weeks, age thirty-nine, a chimney sweep born in Virginia, headed one household. His wife had evidently died, and he lived with his two children (John, age seven, and Sarah, age five) in a frame house worth twelve hundred dollars. William Weeks, age twenty-eight, headed the largest Weeks's household. His occupation was listed as "none." He lived with wife Maria, age twenty-eight, and their four children, Maria, age eight; twins Elizabeth and Edwin, age three; and baby Sally, age one and a half, all born in Kings County. Eliza Weeks headed the third Weeks household. At age thirty-six, Eliza was a single parent living with son Jacob, age four, both born in Kings County.

The Bundick family had undergone many transformations in the five years since the beginning of the Civil War. In 1863, Simon Bundick, age fifty, had become the first African American minister of Berean Church in Weeksville. The oldest three of Bundick's four sons—Barcella, Simon, Jr., and Cornelius—all served in the U.S. Navy. When the census was taken in June 1865, Simon, age twenty-two, had returned home and was working as a waiter. His sister Margaret, twenty-four, also lived in the household, along with Eliza, fourteen, and Obadiah, twelve. Another child, Alexander, nine, was now living with the Bundicks, although he had not appeared in their household in earlier censuses. Finally, Charlotte Bundick, eighteen, was listed as a wife, perhaps married to Simon. All of the family except father Simon were listed as being born locally, in either Kings County or New York County. Simon Bundick, Sr. was listed as owning a frame house worth one thousand dollars. Reverend Bundick also supported the African Civilization Society. He had become a yearly member, one of those who "contributed liberally to sustain the Society, and to cheer on those who are at work for the elevation of the descendants of the African ancestors, wherever they may be found."[82]

Junius and Sarah Morel, aged fifty-nine and thirty, now had a five-year-old daughter Alice. They owned a frame house worth two thousand dollars, and for the first time they were living in a single-family house, on the north side of Pacific Avenue. Their neighborhood reflected the economic prosperity of many of Weeksville's residents, as well as the varied places of birth of Weeksville's older generation. The Morels lived next door to William Tillman, porter, aged fifty-three, and Harriet Tillman, aged fifty, born in Maryland and North Carolina, who shared a house with one of William and Harriet's four children, twenty-nine-year-old Thomas, a seaman, and with Thomas's wife, Caroline, born in New Jersey, and their two children, four-year-old William and eighteen-month-old Ella.

Just beyond the Tillmans lived Ham and Maria Matthews, sixty and fifty years old, born in Maryland and the West Indies, respectively. Only one of their eleven children still lived at home, twenty-two-year-old James, a baker, who had recently served in the U.S. Navy. Ham Matthews worked as a packer. Although he could not read or write, Ham, his wife, and his son all owned land. They valued their frame house at two thousand dollars, and they had an Irish-born servant, a widow who had left her only child to earn her living in the Matthews household.

On the other side of the Morels, Juliana Dudley, fifty years old, headed a household with three of her four children. Juliana, born in the

West Indies, made a living as a laundress, with help from her children, Sarah, aged twenty-four, a cook; Edward, aged twenty-two, a waiter; and Mary, aged nineteen, a cook. No one in this family owned land, and neither Juliana nor Sarah could read or write. Just beyond their house, on the other side from the Morels, lived forty-year-old cook Merchat Dawsey, born in Maryland, and his twenty-five-year-old wife, Margaret, born in Virginia, with their five-year-old son Martin, living in a frame house worth eight hundred dollars. Neither Merchat nor Margaret could read or write. It is not clear whether or not the Dawseys owned their own home.[83]

The Weeks, Bundick, and Morel families were among the 472 African American residents in Weeksville in 1865, down by 9.8 percent from the 523 people in 1855. In the previous ten years, many European Americans had also moved into Weeksville. No longer was Weeksville an enclave dominated almost completely by African Americans. Now many German, Irish, and English immigrants, as well as European Americans born elsewhere in the United States, lived side by side with African Americans.

The largest number of African Americans in Weeksville in 1865 (287, or 60.8 percent) had been born in New York State. Only 9 came from New England, 16 from Pennsylvania, and 20 from New Jersey. Six came from the West Indies. A sizable number (112, or 23.7 percent) had been born in the South, in Virginia (63), Maryland (28), North Carolina (18), and South Carolina (1).

Weeksville residents worked in a wide variety of occupations, and a far higher percentage of them reported employment than they had in 1855. Of the 298 men and women aged seventeen and older, 38.6 percent (115 people) listed specific employment. Nineteen more (6.4 percent) listed "none" as an occupation. Of those who did not list employment, almost all were wives, mothers, or teenage or young adult children. A very few were servants, nephews, or boarders.

Compared to the pre–Civil War decades, we see an increased diversity in occupational opportunities. Not counting "none," there are thirty-four different occupations listed in the 1865 census. These included baker, bar man, barber (two), basket maker, blacksmith, boot maker, car man, clergyman, clothes cleaner (two), coachman (four), cook (six), doctor, dressmaker (eleven), embroidery, farmer, grocer, hostler, janitor, junkman, laborer (eight), laundress (four), mason (two), packer, porter (twenty-seven), salesman, school teacher (two), seaman (eight), steward (three), sugar maker (most likely "segar" maker Tubucio Agular, from Cuba), sweep, tailor, tobacconist, waiter (nine), and whitewasher (three).

Of the 115 workers who listed occupations outside the home, 18.3 percent (21 people) were women. Five of these were cooks (including sisters Sarah and Mary Dudley), eleven were dressmakers (including Sarah Usher and Julia Usher, both born in the West Indies), four were laundresses, and one listed "embroidery."

Opportunities in ship-related occupations were declining for African Americans in general, but people in Weeksville continued to work on the sea. W. Jeffrey Bolster noted in *Black Jacks* that 14 percent of sailors out of New York City had been African American in 1835, but only 4.5 percent were African American in 1866. A little more than 10 percent of Weeksville's workers (twelve people), however, worked in 1865 in jobs relating to the sea, as seamen, stewards, or cook. Some of the waiters may also have worked on board ships. Like other African Americans, however, Weeksville's seamen found few opportunities for advancement. As Jeffrey Bolster noted, "Occupational mobility on merchant ships was virtually all lateral, between cook and steward and seaman. Of 3,500 merchant ship crews outbound on foreign voyages from Providence, Philadelphia, and New York between 1803 and 1856, only three had an officer of color. George Henry, an ex-slave who escaped to Providence after years of commanding a coasting schooner in his native Virginia, curtly recalled, 'I found prejudice so great in the North that I was forced to come down from my high position as captain and take my whitewash brush and wheelbarrow and get my living in that way.'"[84]

By the end of the Civil War, Weeksville, like the rest of the country, had reached a turning point in its history. Established as a place where African Americans could assert their own rights to economic self-reliance, physical security, and political power, it largely fulfilled that dream. It became a community that was almost completely African American. Both its own residents and those outside the village identified the community as unique, "that colored settlement called Weeksville," as Brooklyn merchant John N. Still called it in 1851, or "the grounds owned and occupied by our own people," as Frederick Douglass referred to Weeksville and Carrsville that same year.

Weeksville offered a haven for freedom seekers, for people fleeing the New York City draft riots in 1863, and for those who wanted a safe place to raise their children. Weeksville residents could find employment both within the community itself and in the larger Brooklyn area. Many of them worked on the docks or on ships. Weeksville residents emphasized education for their children, and they supported at least two churches.

But Weeksville did not offer an isolated idyllic retreat from life. The presence of Junius C. Morel, principal of Colored School No. 2 and nationally known correspondent for the *Christian Recorder*, meant that no thinking person in Weeksville could escape debates about larger state, national, and international issues. Weeksville residents, like African Americans across the country, confronted voting rights, the Fugitive Slave Law, and emigration. When Junius C. Morel threw his support behind the African Civilization Society in 1863, the society moved its national headquarters to Weeksville, on the same block as Colored School No. 2. As the African Civilization Society shifted its focus to raise money for Freedman's schools in the South, one of the first people to go was Maria W. Stewart, the first American woman to lecture in public, who had been the teacher at Colored School No. 3 in the Williamsburgh section of Brooklyn.

When Lincoln signed the Emancipation Proclamation and the draft riots threatened the lives of every African American in New York City, African Americans began to enlist in the army and navy in large numbers. At least seven men from Weeksville enlisted in the army, and five men from Weeksville enlisted in the navy.

When they came home, they would return to a community that had changed. Up to the mid-1850s, Weeksville had been almost exclusively a semirural African American enclave, with frame houses separated by yards, built around small hills, woods, and ponds. After the Civil War, European Americans came to Weeksville in large numbers. Developers were buying up rural lots, cutting down hills, filling in low spots, and establishing a grid pattern that cut through yards and left people's houses standing at odd angles to the new streets. Many of the new buildings were row houses, some of them frame but many of them brick, designed to bring high-density housing to what had been relatively low-density landscapes. Locally, the city had come to Weeksville, and life would never be the same.

Weeksville's residents recognized that they were residents not simply of their own local neighborhoods but of New York City and the whole United States. Their challenge would be to make real the ideals of equality and full citizenship that the Civil War years had promised.

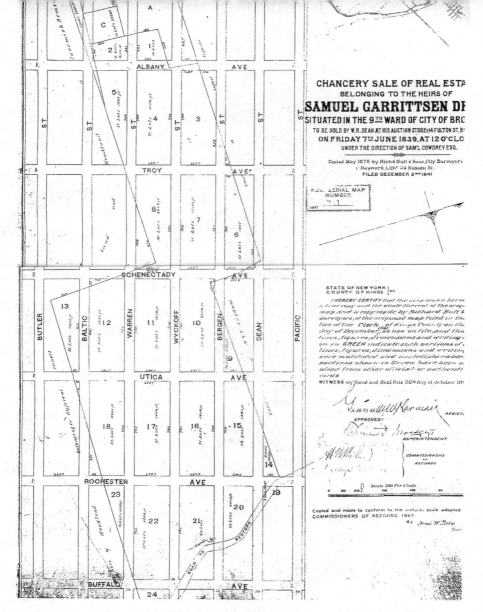

This map shows the boundaries of the estate of Samuel Garrittsen in 1839 (section contained within rectangles); Hunterfly Road forms the east boundary. Francis P. Graham purchased land on block 20 and elsewhere. He built his own house at the top of the glacial moraine, where Hunterfly Road takes a turn to the south, going over the top of the hill. The current Hunterfly Road houses, owned by the Weeksville Heritage Society, are located on the west side of Hunterfly Road, just past where the road turns toward the east (block 21 on this map, later block 1356; by 1869 this was block 592, by 1881 block 185). *Chancery Sale of Real Estate Belonging to the Heirs of Samuel Garrittsen, Dec'd* (Topographical Bureau, Office of the President, Borough of Brooklyn, 1839). Copy courtesy of Weeksville Heritage Center.

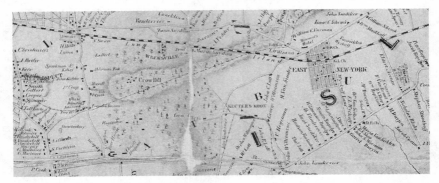

The very first map to show Weeksville was Sidney's 1849 map of the area around New York City (opposite, detail above). This section shows a cluster of houses labeled Weeksville, just south of the Long Island Railroad, between Bedford on the west and East New York on the east. Crow Hill runs east and west just south of Weeksville. The cluster of houses on the west end of Crow Hill may have been the area sometimes called Carrsville. Hunterfly Road runs south, east of Weeksville, between Maria Suydam's house on the east, just south of the Long Island Railroad, and the pond (often called Suydam's Pond) just west of Hunterfly Road. Francis P. Graham purchased land on the west side of Hunterfly Road, where it turns to cross Crow Hill in 1839. By 1849 he had sold much of this land to other African Americans. Although Sidney's map shows no houses in this area, the 1850 census shows people living here. On the south side of Crow Hill, where Hunterfly Road turns sharply south, Sidney shows three houses west of the road in approximately the same location as the houses now owned by the Weeksville Heritage Center. No other source shows houses on this location before the early 1870s. *Sidney's Map of 12 Miles around New York* (Philadelphia: J.C. Sidney, 1849). Courtesy New York Public Library.

In 1850, J. H. Colton published the second map reference to Weeksville, located here just south of the Brooklyn & Jamaica Railroad, between Bedford to the west and East New York to the east (opposite, detail above). Note Hunterfly Road stretched from northwest to southeast on the eastern edge of Weeksville. J. H. Colton, *Map of the Country Thirty-Three Miles around the City of New York* (New York: J. H. Colton, 1853). Courtesy Wiki Media Commons.

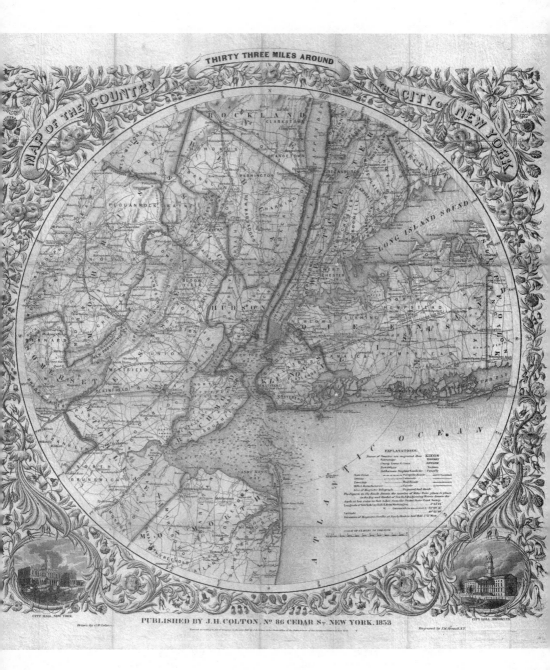

THIRTY THREE MILES AROUND

MAP OF THE COUNTRY

THE CITY OF NEW YORK

PUBLISHED BY J.H. COLTON, N° 86 CEDAR S⸱ᵀ⸱ NEW YORK. 1853

Matthew Dripps's 1869 map is the single most important source available for buildings and lots in the Weeksville area (opposite, detail above). As far as we can check this
information with other sources, Dripps has proven to be accurate. The Roman Catholic
Orphan Asylum (built between 1865 and 1868) forms a major landmark on the left (west)
of this map, between Wyckoff and Warren Streets. The cluster of buildings north of the
asylum includes Colored School No. 2 at the corner of Dean Street and Troy Avenue as
well as several houses (many of them still located in the middle of the blocks, off the grid
of streets) south of Atlantic Avenue. This area formed Weeksville's most built-up section.
Hunterfly Road ran across lots, generally northwest to southeast, along the east side of
this map. A cluster of buildings sold by Francis P. Graham to African Americans in the
1840s appears along the west side of Hunterfly Road on the northeast corner of Rochester
Avenue and Bergen Street. Lydia Simmons LeGrant's house stands directly on the northeast corner of Rochester Avenue and Bergen Street, while Francis P. Graham's house is at
the top of the hill, where Hunterfly Road turns more directly south. The block just south
of this is the site of the current Hunterfly Road houses owned by the Weeksville Heritage
Center. Ferdinand Volckening purchased lots here from the estate of Samuel Bouton in
1863, when it was still undeveloped. Shortly after this map was published, Volckening
moved to his property four houses, the same houses that remained on this site in the early
twenty-first century. Note the African Baptist Church ("Afric. B. Ch.") on the south side of
Warren Street between Utica and Rochester Avenues. Citizens' Union Cemetery occupies
a large swath of land running north and south along a ridge just west of Hunterfly Road.
Samuel Anderson, Paul Pontou, and other African American land investors purchased
strips of land running north and south just west of the cemetery. *Map of the City of Brooklyn, Being the Former Cities of Brooklyn and Williamsburgh and the Town of Bushwick* (New
York: Matthew Dripps, 1869), plate 3. Courtesy the Lionel Pincus and Princess Firyal Map
Division, New York Public Library, Astor, Lenox, and Tilden Foundations.

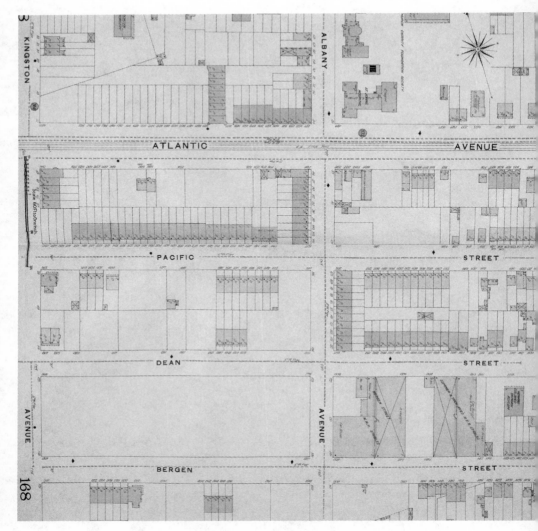

By 1888, the block bounded by Dean Street on the north, Bergen Street on the south, Albany Avenue on the east, and Troy Avenue on the west still held the core of Weeksville's historic institutions: the school, home for the aged, and Howard Orphan Asylum. The west of the block now held stables, a repair shop, and storage for horse-drawn railroad cars, hay, and feed for the Sumner and Troy Avenue and Bergen Street horse-drawn railroads. When Howard Orphan Asylum left Weeksville in 1911, it sold the rest of the block to Nassau Railroad Company. All of these smaller companies later became part of the Metropolitan Transit Authority, which still owned the entire block into the twenty-first century. Sanborn Map Company, *Borough of Brooklyn* (New York: Sanborn Map Company, 1888), 170. Courtesy New York Public Library.

4

"Fair Schools, a Fine Building, Finished Writers,
Strong Minded Women"

*Politics, Women's Activism, and the Roots of
Progressive Reform, 1865–1910*

In 1865, the military war was over, but the struggle for full citizenship continued, for Weeksville residents as for African Americans throughout the nation.[1] As historian Hugh Davis suggested, the movement for equal rights in the 1860s and 1870s "stands as the most important African American crusade for full citizenship rights prior to the modern civil rights cause of the 1950s and 1960s." This struggle focused on two main issues: black male suffrage and equal access to public education. Both involved government, the first in defining voter characteristics and the second in paying for public schools. Both dominated public discussion in Weeksville, as well as among African Americans nationally. In addition, however, residents of Weeksville (and many other African American communities) struggled to define respect and equality through nongovernmental community organizations: churches, benevolent institutions, and voluntary community groups.[2]

While African Americans were united on the goal of complete respect and equal rights for every person in every arena, they debated different methods of accomplishing that goal. Did racial integration lead to full respect and equality? Or did separation based on race actually provide more equal access to resources? In terms of voting rights, a strong consensus emerged that standards should be absolutely equal for males of whatever race or ethnicity. (Females remained excluded from this definition.) In terms of public schools, African Americans were divided over whether school integration or separation would result in a better education for their children. In terms of churches, benevolent institutions, and community organizations, African Americans most often developed separate institutions under African American leadership. Demands for equality thus roughly formed a scale from equal rights based on full integration (voting rights) to equal rights based on racial separation (nongovernmental institutions), with debates over schools falling in between.

By 1870, Weeksville was, noted the *Brooklyn Eagle*, "in a very flourishing condition," with "fair schools; a fine building, finished writers, strong minded women."[3] While the African Civilization Society lost its focus after the Civil War and closed its doors by 1871, three more community institutions—Colored School No. 2 (later called P.S. 68 and P.S. 83), Howard Colored Orphan Asylum, and Zion Home for the Aged—joined Weeksville's churches to maintain the community's collective identity. As a measure of their continuing vitality, Weeksville's school, churches, orphanage, and home for the aged all had new buildings constructed between 1880 and 1900. These helped form the local basis for Progressivism, a movement that would characterize national politics and reform by the turn of the century.

After the Civil War, Weeksville's development experienced a change in generations. Many of Weeksville's founding members died in the 1870s. James Weeks was one of the first to go. He died of consumption, age seventy-four, on May 28, 1864, on Pacific Street, most likely at his home. Junius C. Morel died in 1874. In 1871, the *Eagle* noted, "Nathan Thomas has resided in the ward for 26 years, and is 89 years of age." He died the following year, at age ninety. Lydia LeGrant died or moved away from Weeksville in the mid-1870s. Berean Baptist Church's longtime pastor Simon Bundick died in May 1879.[4]

The Bundick family offers a detailed example of these changing generations. At the end of his life, Simon Bundick endured a lengthy illness. In 1874, Bundick's illness and debates over finances split Berean Baptist into two camps. A reporter from the *Eagle* interviewed Bundick as he sat in an open window of his house, a three-story frame structure with a basement. It sat on the south side of Warren Street, just east of Albany. The builder obviously intended to build a "pretentious" house, noted the reporter, but "in its present unfinished condition," it was "a strange looking place," with no front stoop and only some rough boards for a front door. "I am Simon Bundick," Reverend Bundick announced and quickly added, "I'm very sick now. I am spitting up blood, but I expect to be well in a short time." Shortly after this interview, Bundick spent time in the Flatbush Asylum but moved back to his house before he died. He left property, including his house and four lots, worth between four and five thousand dollars, half to his daughter Margaret and the rest to be divided among his sons. His oldest son Obadiah contested the will. Although Obadiah won the case in 1879, the judge reversed this decision and upheld Bundick's will in 1881.[5]

Most of Simon Bundick's children continued to live in Weeksville. Simon Bundick, Jr. and Barsella Bundick apparently moved away from Weeksville after the war. But in 1880, Obadiah Bundick was a tailor, twenty-five years old, residing with his wife, Ella Bundick, age twenty, and their two children, two-year-old Obadiah and two-month-old Alexander, at 63 St. Marks Avenue. Alexander Bundick, twenty-three years old, perhaps a cousin of Obadiah, was also a tailor. He and his wife Sarah shared the house with Obadiah and Ella.[6]

Margaret Bundick married a man named Duers and lived at 1834 Dean Street. She died on December 29, 1902, at age sixty-two, and was buried from Berean Baptist Church.[7]

Cornelius Bundick never quite settled down to work at a regular job or own property. In 1875, he lived near the corner of Douglass Street and Rochester Avenue, where he fed his three hogs on swill and was arrested for beating a horse with a shovel. In 1880, the Bundicks lost their eleven-year-old son, who drowned in a pond near Rochester Avenue and St. Marks Place. In 1893, Cornelius Bundick lived at 12 Pleasant Place. The *Eagle* reported that his son Buel was arrested as a "disobedient child" for staying out late "and other sundry wicked things." Bundick described himself, noted the *Eagle*, as an "Immanuel laborer": "I earn my bread by the sweat of my brow." He later lived at 9 Willoughby Street, working as a janitor.[8]

Elijah Bundick, son of Lewis Bundick and most likely a nephew of Simon Bundick, became active in Republican politics. In 1874, he presided over a memorial service held by Brooklyn African Americans for Senator Charles Sumner. He lived near the corner of Dean Street and Rochester Avenue, in a "one and a half story frame shanty, filled in with brick." In 1876, a windstorm destroyed the house, killing his wife and one of his two children. Bundick also owned other property in the area, including two frame houses on South Fourth Street, which he rented as a candy store and apartments. In 1893, he bought property worth thirty-five hundred dollars at the corner of Buffalo Avenue and Butler Street, perhaps a commercial investment, where he later built a one-story frame stable.[9]

As the founding generation died, Weeksville incorporated a new generation of African Americans. Some of the most prominent of these were women. Although denied the vote, women in Weeksville and Brooklyn formed an essential anchor for all nongovernmental community groups, and they played major roles in public schools, as well. Men (such as T. McCants Stewart, Rufus L. Perry, and William F. Johnson) and women (such as Maritcha Lyons and Susan Smith Steward) emerged to shape Weeksville's unique identity as it moved into the twentieth century.

Political Developments

African American efforts to promote equal political rights took definable shape in October 1864, when 145 delegates from several northern states met in Syracuse, New York, to form the National Equal Rights League. In its Declaration of Rights and Wrongs, the convention acknowledged, "As a branch of the human family, we have for long ages been deeply and cruelly wronged," "we have been compelled, under pain of death, to submit to wrongs deeper and darker than the earth ever witnessed in the case of any other people; we have been forced to silence and inaction." Now was the time to speak. The objects of the league, read its constitution, were to "encourage sound morality, education, temperance, frugality, industry, and promote everything that pertains so well-ordered and dignified life; to obtain, by appeals to the minds and consciences of the American people, or by legal process when possible, a recognition of the rights of the colored people of the nation as American citizens." Established leaders such as Frederick Douglass, George Downing, and Henry Highland Garnet dominated the convention, but a younger generation also made its mark. J. Mercer Langston assumed the presidency of the national organization. George B. Vashon, first African American lawyer admitted to the bar in New York State (whose law office still stands in Syracuse), played a key role. Rev. R. H. Cain, pastor of the Bridge Street A.M.E. Church, attended from Brooklyn.[10]

State chapters were quickly organized throughout the North, Midwest, and South. By April 1865, Louisiana, North Carolina, Tennessee, Missouri, Michigan, Ohio, Pennsylvania, and Massachusetts all had affiliates. New York State organized its own chapter on March 16, 1865, in the Hamilton Street Baptist Church in Albany. The convention elected statewide officers. J. Sella Martin of New York City was elected president, and P. W. Ray of Brooklyn and Charles L. Reason of New York City served on the Executive Committee. But upstate activists dominated the rest of the board. W. M. H. Johnson of Albany, Jermain Loguen of Syracuse, and George Weir of Buffalo were elected vice-presidents. Secretaries were John Bosman from Troy and Robert Jackson from Albany, with Albany resident Adam Blake as treasurer. Along with Ray and Reasons, executive officers included Garrett Beyo from Hudson, William Rich of Troy, and William H. Berns from Rochester.[11]

Of these state organizations, Ohio, Massachusetts, and—most important—Pennsylvania assumed leadership roles. New York's Equal Rights League left few traces of its existence. And Weeksville residents played little role in this movement.

Instead, the movement for equal suffrage proceeded in Brooklyn on its own trajectory. By the mid-1860s, both Republican and Democratic politicians began to pay attention to African American men in Brooklyn as voters. Republicans, "working a new vein in this city," paid special attention to Weeksville, reported the *Brooklyn Eagle* in 1865. Brooklyn had three or four hundred African American voters—men who owned at last $250 worth of property and could vote under New York State's constitution. But Brooklyn's political organizations had generally ignored them. The Civil War changed that. In 1865, "local orators, white and colored, have taken the colored folks in hand." They began to hold meetings in Weeksville addressed by both African Americans and European Americans.[12]

Extensive national lobbying, petitions, speeches, and meetings with politicians (including President Johnson) led to few gains. The Fourteenth Amendment protected equal legal rights but made no mention of suffrage for northern free black men. In 1867, New York State again voted down a provision for equal male suffrage, as did every other state where this appeared on the ballot. By 1868, however, a mix of "idealism and pragmatism" led national Republican leaders, including presidential nominee Ulysses S. Grant, to coalesce around black male suffrage and the proposed Fifteenth Amendment. They did so partly because the amendment was extremely limited in scope. It did not give suffrage to anyone but only mandated that suffrage could not be denied "based on race, color, or previous condition of servitude." Notably, it made no mention of suffrage discrimination based on sex.[13]

Passage of the Fifteenth Amendment on February 3, 1870, meant that, now, at last, all African American men could vote on an equal basis with European American men. For the first time, black men in New York State and the nation could vote equally with white men.

In Brooklyn as elsewhere, attempts to woo African American voters assumed new urgency. Republicans seemed most likely to promote equal rights. Junius C. Morel and a committee of African American Republicans from Brooklyn and New York City addressed a meeting at the A.M.E. Church in Weeksville in May 1870, chaired by Reverend John D. Bagwell, a local African American minister. Morel advised everyone to conduct themselves as "upright and good citizens." P. W. White urged them to vote the straight Republican ticket: "The Republican party had many faults," he acknowledged, but the Democratic party "was always against them." R. F. Wake echoed these sentiments. The Republican party was not without its "political tricksters," and no one should allow himself to be "browbeaten." When Dr. Sidney, the only European American speaker, spoke to the audience as "fellow citizens," the audience greeted him enthusiastically. He was once a slave owner, he said, but was now "a Radical of the deepest kind." He displayed, to wild applause, a sample ballot and asked, "Who did all this for them?" "Was it the party that burned their school houses in 1863 and hung the colored people to the lampposts?" "No! No!" shouted the audience. The implication was obvious. African Americans owed their right to vote to the Republican Party, and the time had come to pay up.[14]

By the 1870s, African Americans ran for office themselves. In 1870, John Flamer, major Weeksville landowner and activist in the African Civilization Society, served as second vice-president for the Republican Central Committee in the Ninth Ward. Flamer was then fifty-five years old, a boot maker, born in Maryland, living by himself on Pacific Street near Troy Avenue, with property worth seven thousand dollars. In 1874, Flamer ran for the New York State Assembly on the Republican ticket.

In 1875, he ran for county representative, while his neighbor, Elijah Bundick, ran for the New York State Senate.[15]

African American voters organized a Republican General Committee, with Rev. Stansberry as president. In 1884, the *New York Globe* reported that Republicans in the Twenty-Fourth Ward held a torchlight parade on Schenectady Avenue, with a banner for Blaine and Logan "stretched to the breeze" and "a large representation of colored men and veterans." The Republican Party did not always treat its new black voters respectfully. At a campaign rally for Blaine in 1884, the only two African American politicians in the hall, Rev. T. T. B. Reed, a member of the national committee, and Charles B. Ray, one of the oldest African Americans in New York, were "ruthlessly crowded to the wall" by the sergeant-at-arms and two policemen, when they asked to go on the platform.[16]

Several African Americans did benefit, however, from Republican patronage when they received jobs in the custom house, post office, tax office, sheriff's office, or other federal or city departments. Peter Vogelsang, for example, a veteran of the Massachusetts Fifty-Fourth Regiment and a resident of Weeksville, was appointed messenger to the collector of the port.[17]

Votes in Brooklyn, as in many places, were often for sale. In 1883, the *Eagle* quoted a member of the Common Council who said that it was the habit of nearly all of the "colored voters" in his ward to sell their votes. "This, however, is by no means peculiar to the colored people," he acknowledged. "Out of the 1,500 votes in the ward I have no doubt that fully 600 are purchased every year. Why, I have had white men who own real estate come up and offer their votes to the highest bidder, and at times when they found no money was being used they refused to deposit their ballots at all." We do not know what ward the councilman represented or how accurately he assessed his constituents.[18]

Women's Activism

Leadership roles among African Americans, as among European American cultures, were in part defined by gender. By 1870, as men focused intensely on voting, women took different routes toward empowerment. Some worked within their own families to raise children as citizens;

some became professionals in schools and social welfare institutions; and some organized movements to promote rights for themselves in the larger world, both as African Americans and as women.

Beginning in the 1830s, African American women had begun to speak and write for a broad public audience. Their struggle as women ran parallel to and often intersected with the emerging women's rights movement dominated by European American women. In the 1840s, women's rights received considerable support from African American men as well. But passage of the Fugitive Slave Act shifted attention away from gender and toward race. With few exceptions (notably Frederick Douglass, Martin Delany, and Junius C. Morel), black male leaders abandoned women's rights in the 1850s. The Civil War changed all that, however, as black women took advantage of new openings in teaching, speaking, fund-raising, and support for soldiers and freed people to carve out new roles in the public world. Increasingly, women shared a political presence with men.

Because men—and not women—were identified with full political and legal power, men retained formal leadership roles in community institutions such as churches, schools, and orphanages. Women, however, carved out their own public spaces, sometimes working in similar roles as males (in public speaking, teaching, and musical performances, for example), sometimes creating alternative opportunities (in nursing and work for women's suffrage, for example). Often, as in the Brooklyn Literary Union and Howard Orphan Asylum, they worked with men in the same institutions. They also created separate female organizations, especially as the National Association of Colored Women's Clubs emerged on a national level after 1896. Developed during the Civil War and Reconstruction, this pattern formed the roots of the national Progressive movement. Linda Kerber has argued that women's concerns and organizations initiated Progressive reform. African American women, including women associated with Weeksville, were part of these origins.[19]

Women who worked within their own families built on a cultural legacy of African American women's importance as mothers. They also adopted the image of women as "republican mothers." As Linda Kerber suggested, women played a special role in the early Republic because they were responsible for passing on ideals of equality, liberty, and civic virtue to their children. This ideal of republican motherhood brought importance and respect to women. It also promoted female education. To educate their children well, supporters argued, women needed to be educated themselves.[20]

In their quest for independence and empowerment, African American male leaders held up respect for women as republican mothers as a major goal. In 1852, Martin Delany argued, "Let our young women have an education; let their minds be well informed." And why did women need an education? Because, he asserted, "they are to be the mothers of our children. As mothers are the first nurses and instructors of children; from them children consequently, get their first impressions, which being always the most lasting, should be the most correct. Raise the mothers above the level of degradation, and the offspring is elevated with them."[21]

When Delany and others organized the African Civilization Society, headquartered in Weeksville, they incorporated this ideal of African American womanhood. As Carol Faulkner suggested, the African Civilization Society "sought to promote a new black manhood sustained by a new black womanhood." Their main goal was not to promote the status of women in the public world but to define their own roles as independent African American men. As Faulkner argued, "Using gendered language," northern black [male] reformers "combined black nationalism and domesticity to create the image of a new black manhood." In the process, however, they worked to elevate the status of both men and women, espousing what some might call middle-class values as a way to bridge class lines between free people of color in the North and people newly liberated from slavery in the South. By emphasizing the importance of education, the African Civilization Society highlighted the skills of women as well as men, building on the role of women as mothers and teachers and ultimately transforming that role, to create a model of women as professionals in the public sphere.[22]

Reverend R. H. Cain, Brooklyn clergyman, leader of the African Civilization Society, and later congressman from South Carolina, argued this position in the *Christian Recorder*:

Negro gentlemen and ladies must become teachers, . . . teach them [freed people in the South] that though they be black, they are as good as any

other class whose skin is whiter than theirs; teach them that their com-
plexions may differ but man is man for all that. Finally, colored men in
the North have got to come to this doctrine, that black men must think
for themselves—act for themselves, and thus help our white friends to
elevate us by a proper recognition of our manhood.[23]

Black women's activism also built on another tradition, that of African American women speaking for themselves in the public sphere,
asserting their own rights as women of color. As Martha Jones argued,
this work of women defining their own central role in public culture
"occurred not within a distinct female sphere but in those spaces that
men and women shared: churches, political organizations, mutual
aid societies, and schools." It began in the 1830s, when women such
as Maria W. Stewart (Boston teacher, abolitionist, and member of the
African Meetinghouse) and Jarena Lee, African Methodist Episcopal
minister, began to address public audiences, both in person and in
print. Stewart published her *Religion and the Pure Principles of Morality* in 1831. Jarena Lee published *Life and Religious Experience of Jarena
Lee, a Coloured Lady* in 1836. African American women also organized
literary societies.[24]

By the late 1840s, key African American male leaders had embraced
the vision of African American women's rights. In September 1848,
the National Convention of Colored Freedmen, meeting in Cleveland, endorsed a resolution initiated by Frederick Douglass and Martin
Delany, asserting, "We fully believe in the equality of the sexes, therefore, Resolved, That we hereby invite females hereafter to take part in
our deliberations." Certainly, Douglass had been influenced by his presence at the first U.S. women's rights convention, held in Seneca Falls,
New York, earlier that summer. But, as Martha Jones argued, this resolution also reflected a decade-long discussion of women's rights in African American churches, fraternal orders, and political organizations,
as "female influence was giving way to women's rights." "Through this
lens," she suggested, "the Cleveland convention of 1848 looks typical
rather than novel."[25]

After 1850, passage of the Fugitive Slave Act refocused the attention
of African American male activists on race. Among black men, debates
over women's rights almost disappeared. "To advocate women's rights

in black politics was to champion a lame horse," noted Jones. A few stalwart women's rights activists continued to speak out, however. One of these was Frederick Douglass. In 1853, at the Colored National Convention held in Rochester, New York, he successfully promoted Mary Jeffrey from Syracuse as a delegate, the only woman so designated. In 1854, Jermain Loguen, the "king of the Underground Railroad" in Syracuse, gave a speech titled "Woman's Rights" at the New York State Council of Colored People. The chair, William Rich, ruled, however, that this entire question was "irrelevant." Notably, Junius C. Morel, from Weeksville, "warmly approved" of Loguen's speech. "Human Rights were not to be defined either by sex or by complexion," he asserted.[26]

Among African American male activists, women found considerable direct support from people advocating emigration. Martin Delany did not simply talk about women's rights. He implemented it. In the 1854, the same year that William Rich called women's rights "irrelevant," women made up one-third of the delegates at the Cleveland emigration convention.[27]

Women in Weeksville built on ideals of republican womanhood to shape their identities not only as mothers but also as professional women and activists in the public sphere. Debates over women's rights infused discussions in churches, schools, and benevolent institutions. In Weeksville, they focused on the A.M.E. Church, Public School No. 2 (which became P.S. 68 and later P.S. 83), the Howard Orphan Asylum, and Zion Home for the Aged. (Berean Baptist Church may also have been involved in this debate, but controversies over its minister, Simon Bundick, and lack of extant church records make it difficult to document gender issues.) By the late nineteenth century, two women associated with Weeksville—Maritcha Lyons, teacher, and Susan McKinney Steward, doctor—became nationally prominent. Through their work with the National Brooklyn Literary Union and the National Association of Colored Women's Clubs, they infused perspectives of African American women into the emerging national Progressive movement.

Weeksville's School

Debates over integrated schools in Weeksville mirrored similar conflicts elsewhere in the country, and they involved issues of gender as well as race. Proponents of full integration argued that integration was the only way to provide high-quality educational facilities for African American students. Nevertheless, they recognized the possible negative effects: students might be subjected to racial prejudice from white students or teachers; black teachers and administrators might well lose their jobs. Weeksville residents were at the forefront of this debate, which involved the whole city of Brooklyn. One result was that the Weeksville school became one of the first schools in the United States to hire both black and white teachers to teach both black and white students. Maritcha Lyons, assistant principal at P.S. 83 in Weeksville, became perhaps the first African American teacher in the country to supervise European American student teachers from many different ethnic backgrounds.[28]

The road to this pathbreaking decision was a long one. Beginning in the 1840s, Weeksville's children attended school in Carrsville. Not until 1853 did Weeksville have its own school, constructed on Troy Avenue near Dean Street, on what would become Weeksville's most important public block. As one of the main public institutions in Weeksville (and for African Americans generally in Brooklyn), this school became the focus of debates over race and gender, coming to a crescendo after the Civil War.

From the very beginning, Weeksville's school was unusual. Its principal and main teacher was Junius C. Morel. Morel was, noted the *Brooklyn Eagle*, "a gentleman of about the complexion of Fred Douglas—intelligent, unobtrusive, and highly thought of by the members of the Board of Education." Without intending to make an issue of it, Morel turned Weeksville's school into one of the earliest integrated public schools, not only in its student body but also in its teaching staff, in New York State. By 1851, twelve white children were among the forty students attending Colored School No. 2. People certainly noticed this, but no one complained, at least officially.[29]

About 1867, Weeksville's citizens appealed to the Board of Education to change the name of the school, and "Colored School No. 2" became "Public School 68." By 1869, after European Americans began to move into Weeksville in larger numbers, forty of Weeksville's eighty-nine schoolchildren were white. This time the Brooklyn School Board became upset. It was unhealthy, they claimed, for black and white students to have such an "intimate relationship." Even black students would suffer, they argued, since African American teachers would pay more attention to their white students. European American students would have to leave the Weeksville school, the school board ordered, and enroll in white schools elsewhere. Nevertheless, five years later, seventeen white students still remained in P.S. 68.[30]

The board's concern about mixing white and black students presaged the issue of hiring African American and European American staff members to work together. In Weeksville, principal Morel was assisted by an African American teacher, the wife of William F. Johnson. Neither the local school committee nor the Brooklyn School Board found her satisfactory, however. In 1869, they replaced her with Emma Prime, whom the *Brooklyn Eagle* labeled "a gentlewoman of the Caucasian race." The Brooklyn City Directory of 1872 listed "Emma C. Prime, teacher, 424 Herkimer Street." The U.S. census in 1870 listed her as living in a predominately European American neighborhood in the Twenty-First Ward. She was twenty-five years old, born in New York, living with John A. Colson, age forty-five, a sea captain; Vesta Colson, age thirty-five, with real property worth four thousand and personal property worth one thousand dollars; and their daughter Vesta A., age nine, all born in Maine.[31]

Weeksville's citizens divided over this appointment. Neither side hesitated to express their opinions. Because the issue is so important, and because the debate offers a rare opportunity to hear the words of Weeksville residents themselves, it is worth eavesdropping on the hearing held before a committee of the Brooklyn Board of Education on the afternoon of February 24, 1869. Reverend Simon Bundick, pastor of Berean Baptist Church, joined Reverend Rufus L. Perry, general agent of the African Civilization Society and editor of the *National Monitor*, a Baptist newspaper; William F. Johnson, whose wife had resigned from teaching at Colored School No. 2 (for reasons of health, she asserted); and others in condemning Miss Prime's appointment. She was appointed, they said, with "wanton disregard for the feelings of colored parents and tax-payers, and done in the spirit of the Dred Scott decision—that we have no rights white men are bound to respect." They asked the board to give "the white incumbent of this Ethiopian school a more congenial situation, and allow us to have a competent colored teacher, such as can be found by properly advertising." The board also received a second petition characterizing the objections made to the white teacher as "wicked and silly."[32]

There were essentially two objections to hiring a white teacher. The first was that a white teacher could not do the job as well as an African American. "She must necessarily lack sympathy with colored people and their children," said Rufus Perry. "She did not love any of them; would not nurse or fondle them; would not visit their homes, and become intimate with their parents." The second reason was that African American teachers could do the work as well and should have the opportunity. Reverend Bundick noted that "there were educated black ladies compelled to accept menial positions at six or eight dollars a month, while here was a position one of them ought to have, held by a white woman—earning forty-five dollars a month. The taxpayers of Weeksville—the colored folks—supported this school and they ought to have black teachers." Mr. Jenkins echoed this argument. What incentive had he to educate his children, he asked, "if all the avenues to the higher class of callings were closed to them? Was he expected to educate them to be bootblacks, whitewashers, cooks, and coachmen? Few respectable callings were open to them. Teaching in colored schools was one; he did not believe whites ought to be preferred there."[33]

Mr. Crump, an African American resident of Weeksville, represented parents and taxpayers who signed the petition supporting Prime's appointment. Their main goal, he said, was to have a good school. "The Board in its wisdom having selected a white teacher they were well satisfied with her, and to discharge her on account of her color simply, would place the colored folks in a strange position. She was laboring with success to instruct their children." Mr. Dryer, one of the local committee for Public School 68, echoed this sentiment. He had tried, he said, to find a competent colored teacher but did not succeed, and so he had "secured the services of a competent white lady and he believed in doing so he was sustained by the colored people whose chief desire was a good school for the instruction of their children."[34]

Junius Morel, principal of P.S. 68, noted,

> he had been a teacher in the locality for over twenty years. Two generations of his pupils lived around him. He said he had been treated with uniform kindness by the white people of Weeksville. In his school at

present there were forty white children. They had equal school facilities elsewhere, but they preferred to attend his school. While he said this he did not desire to be suspected of any lack of fidelity to his own people. In the trying times that are past, he stood with them, but he would bear true testimony if it cost him his place. He had aided the Committee but he had no application in his hand from a colored teacher that he had not submitted to the authorities of the Board. In answer to a question by Mr. Rhoads, the speaker said that his white assistant was giving satisfaction.

At the end of the hearing, Mr. Rhoads summed up the proceedings: "In view of the fact that efforts were made to secure a competent colored teacher, without success, and of the general [. . . ?] that there is no fault found with the lady [. . . ?] concerned, except that she is white, I am not prepared for one to supply her place as long as she chooses to remain. The Committee stands adjourned and will not require your further attendance."[35] The Board of Education discussed the question again on March 2, 1869, when a special subcommittee endorsed racial segregation and recommended that all forty of the white students move to another school. Two weeks later, William F. Johnson, who opposed hiring Miss Prime, printed handbills, three feet by four feet, inviting community members to a meeting in Weeksville itself:

> A public meeting of the citizens of Weeksville, Ninth Ward, Brooklyn, will be held on Thursday evening, March 25th, in the African Civilization Building, Dean street, near Troy avenue, at which the interest of the school question will be considered. All parents and guardians of adjacent neighborhoods, whose children attend school No. 2, are invited to attend. To commence precisely at 8 o'clock.
> S. Bundick,
> W. Ryerson,
> H. Almond,
> W.F. Johnson.[36]

Nothing more came of this matter, however, and Emma Prime remained at Colored School No. 2 until January 31, 1872.[37]

Questions about the quality of Weeksville's teachers were not new, nor would they end with the 1869 decision to keep Miss Prime. In 1865,

Simon Bundick, who had sent all five of his sons to Colored School No. 2, complained that Mr. Morel, "a neabour and a jentleman," gave his children only fifteen minutes to write. Bundick's sons, who were then in the U.S. Navy, could not write him a letter "fit to be seen." By 1873, Reverend Perry seemed to have reversed his opposition to white teachers and students in the Weeksville school, and he came out strongly for desegregation. "We do not ask that the colored public schools . . . shall be closed," he argued in an editorial in the *National Monitor*. "Not at all. What we reasonably demand is . . . that colored children be allowed to attend any of the public schools most convenient without regard to color." If a school is "not good enough for white children, then it is not good enough for black children," he asserted.[38]

In 1886, when John Q. Allen, African American, was principal of P.S. 68, a biracial teaching staff posed a different problem. Two white teachers assisted Allen. Their performance left much to be desired. Three different superintendents had reported that teachers in the higher grades spent much of their time bringing pupils who had studied with these teachers up to appropriate grade levels. When Philip A. White, African American member of the Brooklyn School Board, tried to have these teachers dismissed, a fellow board member charged him with "drawing the color line." The *New York Freeman*, always a staunch proponent of integrated schools, strongly defended Philip White. "If the white members of the School Board did not draw the color-line themselves," noted the *Freeman*, "there would be no colored schools in Brooklyn, and white and colored teachers and white and colored pupils would share alike the school facilities of Brooklyn." Furthermore, the *Freeman* went on, "the colored tax-payers of Brooklyn demand that these two white teachers be dismissed. They demand that this be done. The political wire pulling and dodging must give place to the superior power and interests of the people."[39]

A shortage of African American teachers continued to be a problem. In 1891, the *New York Age* reported, "The Brooklyn schools controlled by Afro-Americans are in prosperous condition. The great trouble is the lack of teachers. There is room on the list of available teachers for at least three or four young women." And two months later the *Age* noted, "The crying need in Brooklyn now is for more young women of the race to successfully undergo the teachers' examination."[40]

From the earliest years of the Weeksville school, children of European American background had attended along with African American children, without complaint from the people of Weeksville. Full integration of public schools in Weeksville and in Brooklyn generally, however, was a long and difficult process. In 1873, New York State passed a law providing that no citizen should be excluded because of race or color "from the full and equal enjoyment" of public facilities, including schools. In Weeksville, William F. Johnson, superintendent of the Howard Orphan Asylum, decided to test this law in 1875. He asked to have his son admitted to a white school. The Brooklyn Board of Education denied his appeal, and the New York State Supreme Court upheld the board's position, arguing that the 1873 law required only that student have access to equal facilities, not necessarily the same facilities. Johnson's case was one of four such cases in New York State in the 1870s. All of them lost.[41]

In the 1880s, a second court case, outside of Weeksville, challenged the Brooklyn Board of Education once again, and this time the outcome was different. When Theresa W. B. King tried to enter P.S. 5, at the corner of Johnson and Duffield Streets, the board initially denied her appeal. They argued that "the Fourteenth Amendment does not protect the colored people in the matter of school privileges; that they must rely solely on the laws of the State." "That is not discrimination against the colored child," they asserted, "because she can attend one of the colored schools if she pleases." Remarkably, however, the board changed its position and ended up requiring principals to admit African American children to schools on an equal basis with European American children.[42]

Brooklyn African Americans found allies on the Board of Education. Some were European American, but, beginning in 1883, Philip A. White became the first African American member of the school board. A druggist in lower Manhattan, White had been educated at the African Free School and eventually became a member both of the Academy of Sciences and the Metropolitan Museum of Art before Mayor Seth Low appointed him to the Brooklyn Board of Education in 1883. When White died in 1891, T. McCants Stewart, lawyer from South Carolina, became his successor on the school board. According to historian Carleton Mabee, Brooklyn was the only place in New York State to have African Americans on its school board in the nineteenth century.[43]

When the Brooklyn School Board proposed building a new school in Weeksville, Weeksville's citizens were poised to tackle the question of race head-on. T. McCants Stewart led them. In 1891, at Stewart's insistence, the Board of Education removed all reference to the word "colored," and Stewart became chair of schools 67, 68, and 69 and of the Howard Orphan Asylum. His tenacity in the face of tremendous obstacles eventually made Weeksville's P.S. 68 (then 83, and finally the current P.S. 243) a fully integrated public school.[44]

McCants Stewart was a brilliant leader, not only in education but also in religion, law, and community organizing. Born in Charleston, South Carolina, on December 28, 1854, he attended both Howard University and the College of South Carolina, graduating as valedictorian from this integrated school with a general college degree and a law degree. McCants Stewart became a successful lawyer in New York City and a well-known speaker and activist. As the *New York Age* noted, "Few men have greater influence over a popular assembly than he. His wit is unfailing; his familiarity with all phases of a question he undertakes to discuss truly remarkable; while the fullness of his information, the result of a life of studious, systematic study of the literary masters, together with his very pronounced originality, makes him a charming companion and an irresistible speaker."

McCants Stewart served as pastor of Bethel A.M.E. Church in New York City and also in Weeksville for two and a half years from 1880 to 1883, before going to Liberia. Stewart's biographer, Albert S. Broussard, titled the chapter dealing with this period in Stewart's life "A National Leader Emerges." He returned to Brooklyn to become a founder and president of the Brooklyn Literary Union, an active supporter of the Democratic Party, and a vocal and effective member of the Brooklyn School Board from 1891 to 1894. In this position, he helped to establish P.S. 83 in Weeksville as an official mixed-race school and the first public school in the country to include an African American (Maritcha Lyons) as supervisor of beginning teachers.[45]

Albert Broussard summarized Stewart's importance in the United States in the late nineteenth century:

T. McCants Stewarts was fundamentally a man of ideas. That fact allowed him to wear many hats during his long public career—minister,

T. M'CANTS STEWART.

T. McCants Stewart in William J. Simmons, *Men of Mark: Eminent, Progressive, and Rising* (Cleveland, Ohio: Geo. M. Rewell, 1887), 1056. General Research & Reference Division, Schomburg Center for Research in Black Culture, New York Public Library, Astor, Lenox, and Tilden Foundations.

professor, writer, racial activist, attorney, and Black Nationalist—and to
become an important African-American intellectual. The quality and
breadth of Stewart's mind earned him the respect of some of the fore-
most black thinkers of his generation. His ideas, disseminated through
some of the leading black newspapers and periodicals, allowed him to
challenge the ideas of competing African-American leaders. His association with prominent black leaders such as Booker T. Washington, Frederick Douglass, Bishop Alexander Payne, T. Thomas Fortune, Blanche K.
Bruce, Edward Blyden, Alexander Crummell, and Francis and Archibald
Grimke significantly enhanced his prestige as a major African-American
spokesman.[46]

In 1898, T. McCants Stewart left the United States for Hawaii, where he
spent seven years before going to London and then, in 1906, to Liberia, where he revised Liberia's legal code, helped establish the Liberian
National Bar Association, and, in 1911, became associate justice of its
supreme court. When he accused government officials of corruption,
however, he was removed from office. He returned to London in 1914,
where he lived until he moved with his second wife, Alice Franklin, and
children to St. Thomas in 1921. He became an active attorney, journalist,
and activist in St. Thomas until his sudden death in January 1923 at the age
of sixty-nine. At his request, he was buried wrapped in the Liberian flag.[47]

T. McCants Stewart published four books. In 1880, he published a
sermon *In Memory of Rev. James Morris Williams* (Philadelphia: A.M.E.
Book Rooms, 1880). His most famous work was *Liberia: the Americo-
African Republic: Being Some Impressions of the Climate, Resources, and
People, Resulting from Personal Observations and Experiences in West
Africa* (New York: E.O. Jenkins' Sons, 1886), which students in Brooklyn
schools used for recitations. With Rufus L. Perry, Weeksville editor and
former president of the African Civilization Society, McCants Stewart
also published *The Cushite; or, The Children of Ham (the Negro Race) as
Seen by the Ancient Historians and Poets: A Paper* (New York: African
Islamic Publications, 1988, 1887). Finally, McCants Stewart worked on
the *Revised Statutes of the Republic of Liberia: Being a Revision of the
Statutes from the Organization of the Government in 1848 to and Including the Acts of the Legislature of 1910–1911* (Paris: Etablissements Busson,
1928), published after his death.[48]

Conflict over the Weeksville school emerged powerfully in 1890, when the board purchased property at the corner of Bergen Street and Schenectady Avenue to build the new P.S. 68. "Some queer white residents of the neighborhood have sent a petition to the Board opposing the location of the school there on the ground that as it will be attended by colored children it will depreciate the surrounding property," noted the *New York Age*. Why residents should object was questionable, since the proposed new school was only one block south of the old one. African Americans, not to be outdone, organized a mass protest meeting at the Bridge Street A.M.E. Church. A delegation of European Americans, led by John Croger (most likely English-born John W. Croger, born about 1849, who worked in 1880 as a clerk in the gas company), and another of African Americans, led by W. F. Johnson and Rufus Perry, complete with legal counsel for both sides, met before the Board of Education in an "exhaustive session." They ended by agreeing that they wanted a building large enough to hold all of Weeksville's children, regardless of color. "The white representatives," noted T. McCants Stewart, "said that they had no objection to colored teachers, as some of them had been taught in this very public school No. 68 by colored teachers."[49]

With twenty-four classrooms, the new school would hold about 720 students. It would be a mixed-race school for both students and teachers, and it would retain its old name of P.S. 68. In October 1891, the *New York Age* reported that the Brooklyn Board of Education adopted the following resolution, presented by T. McCants Stewart:

> Whereas, the new school house on Bergen street and Schenectady avenue, was built for the relief of Public School number 68, and upon the joint request of certain white and colored citizens, was made large enough to accommodate all the children residing in the vicinity of said school, with the understanding that Public School No. 68, as now organized, would occupy the entire new school house, and that the pupils and any additional teachers needed therein would be classified and employed without regard to race or color; and
>
> Whereas, it is the intention of this board to comply with the request of the said citizens; and
>
> Whereas the number 83 has been placed upon the said school house instead of the number 68; therefore

> Resolved, That the Committee on School Houses is hereby authorized and directed to remove the number 83 from the said new school house and put in its place and stead the number 68.[50]

As Carleton Mabee noted in *Black Education in New York State*, "It was indeed a daring plan. It is doubtful that any plan like it had ever been carried out in any public school in the nation. Although there had been rare, isolated instances of a lone black teaching in a predominantly white public school in Northern states, including New York, this was a much more threatening attempt to mix a considerable proportion of both black teachers and black children into a predominantly white school."[51] The story did not end there, however. Caesar Simis, one of the three members of the local school committee for P.S. 68 on the Board of Education, convinced the board to change its mind yet again. P.S. 68, with African American children, would occupy the first floor until a new school could be built on the Troy Avenue site. European American children would attend school on the second floor, officially called P.S. 83. T. McCants Stewart was disgusted. "Under some circumstances American race prejudice is stronger than its sense of justice," he concluded.[52]

For a year, this plan was put into effect. P.S. 68, with five African American teachers and about 150 children, moved into the first floor. P.S. 83, with 500 students (including about 50 African American children) and all European American teachers, moved into the second floor.[53]

The next summer, led by T. McCants Stewart, African American parents in Weeksville developed a daring plan to circumvent this new requirement. Nothing in Brooklyn's law required black and white student to attend different schools. What if African American students in Weeksville all registered to attend P.S. 83, officially the white school? They could effectively create a biracial school in spite of the board's decision.[54]

This plan, plus some solid homework of his own about integrated schools in New York City and Columbus, Ohio, changed Caesar Simis's mind. "At the outset," he explained,

> he had been controlled by class prejudice against the negro which was based upon the knowledge of their former servile condition. In the

P.S. 83, Weeksville, built 1891. Courtesy Weeksville Heritage Center.

course of his experience with school No. 83, where a number of colored pupils are enrolled, he found them clean, tidy and studious. He also saw the injustice that has been done the pupils of school No. 68, in that the teachers who have charge of them are required in two cases to teach four grades and in no case less than two grades, while the rules of the board of education set out one grade as a teacher's work load. . . . In school No. 83 . . . the majority of the pupils who stood highest at the last examination were colored children.[55]

Simis's support, together with that of T. McCants Stewart, meant that two out of three of the local school committee endorsed a mixed-race school. "This means that the school will have a single organization of teachers white and colored, and that the white and colored children will have to sit together unless the board interferes," noted the *Brooklyn Eagle*. "Undoubtedly there is a bitter contest in store."[56]

Indeed there was. Several European American parents appeared before the board to declare, "The development of the neighborhood assures an immediately useful future for the school if it be devoted to the use of the white children alone." But Caesar Simis and T. McCants Stewart, with the support of the teachers' committee, carried the day. Caesar Simis asked dramatically, "What is there harmful in a little colored child? I confess that I am heartily ashamed of the opinions I expressed on the other side of this question several months ago." T. McCants Stewart gave a long speech, often interrupted by noise throughout the room. He concluded by saying,

> I favor the consolidation of the two schools because it will be a natural solution of the present difficulty. The two schools are now together without the slightest friction. I see children, white and colored, arm in arm together up there. They play leap frog, they shoot marbles together. The white and colored boys alike, the white and colored girls alike, mingle and commingle, innocent of the feelings of prejudice, which are fanned into flame by the older people who have kept up the unfortunate agitation, which has been so hurtful to the entire school district and to both school organizations. . . . I appeal to you, gentlemen of the Board, on behalf of the most patient and long suffering portion of our constituency, a people who long have borne wrongs and still do bear them, to make your judgment this day an honored landmark, so that Brooklyn in this, as in other progressive matters, may have a fresh title to the grateful regard of mankind and be an example of progress and liberality unto other cities throughout the nation.[57]

Professor Hooper reported that he had visited P.S. 83 several times and found that "a majority of the best scholars were colored" and "the children are good friends." "I am surprised," he said, "that a deliberative body like this so far north of the Potomac should hesitate so long to do what is manifestly the right things to do." The board voted seventeen to eleven to consolidate the two schools.[58]

When P.S. 83 held its closing exercises in June 1893, students sang "Hail Columbia" and other songs, recited parts of the Declaration of Independence and several poems, and received their diplomas. All three members of the local school committee—Caesar Simis, T. McCants Stewart, and Ebon Miller, the dissenting member on the mixed schools issue—attended, but no one made any mention of the traumatic debates of recent months. The best tribute to the success of this experiment was that P.S. 83 functioned like any other school.[59]

Brooklyn was one of the last public school districts in New York State formally to integrate its student body. New York City and most upstate cities had done so earlier. But Weeksville's P.S. 68 and 83 was first or among the first in the nation to integrate its teaching staff. In many places throughout the country, European American teachers taught both white and black students. But in Weeksville, for the first time in U.S. history, African American teachers taught European American students on a regular basis, as part of the normal curriculum. And Brooklyn's story, centered in Weeksville, was particularly dramatic and particularly well documented.

By every measure, the experiment was a success. In 1897, a committee of the board reported, "The school had demonstrated that black teachers could successfully teach white children." By 1899, more than seventeen hundred children attended the Weeksville school, including Italian, Jewish, and African American children.[60]

For African American women as for European American women, school teaching offered one of the few available professions. Georgiana V. Putnam, who had been assistant principal of Colored School No. 1, became principal of P.S. 68. When that merged with P.S. 83, she became head of a department. Maritcha Lyons, who had worked with Miss Putnam in School No. 1, eventually became assistant principal in P.S. 83. There she was responsible for supervising student teachers, many of whom later became permanent teachers in that school. As Carleton Mabee noted, "In a dramatic reversal of the usual roles, a black teacher was helping to educate white teachers."[61]

"During my twenty years in this sort of service," remembered Lyons,

I learned to know and to have an affectionate regard for very many young persons representing all the various nationalities to be found in a cosmopolitan city. My recollections of these "my girls" as I think of them are among my cherished memories. I may safely state we did each other much good and no evil . . . how tender are the ties among persons working together where no pernicious caste feeling tarnishes the lustre of affectionate regard. "Love knows no burdens and often has no bounds." . . . All who desired to teach were required to stand the same tests; all appointments were contingent upon ratings received as the result of such examinations. I have lived to see the reasonableness of the practical application of the axiomatic principle upon which the stability of a democracy depends, "No race, sex, creed or color discrimination, in civil affairs."[62]

Maritcha Lyons (1848–1929) became assistant principal of P.S. 83 in Weeksville in the 1890s. At the same time, she joined the new National Association of Colored Women's Clubs. In this position, she became nationally known for her work for the rights of African Americans and women.

Lyons was born to a family that included African, Dutch, English, Venezuelan, and Native American ancestry. Her mother's father purchased land in Seneca Village, which later became part of Central Park. Her father, Albro Lyons, kept the Seaman's Home in New York City.

From childhood, Lyons was surrounded with African American leaders. She attended St. Philip's Episcopal Church, home of the famous Rev. Peter Williams. Her godfather, Dr. James McCune Smith, was the first African American to be awarded a medical degree. Lyons attended school under professor Charles L. Reason, who had taught at the mixed-race New York Central College and set up Philadelphia's Institute for Colored Youth. The Lyons home was also a center of Underground Railroad activity. Her father estimated that his family had helped one thousand people escape from slavery.

Driven out of New York City by the draft riots of 1863, the family took refuge first in New England, then in the Williamsburgh section of Brooklyn, then in Providence, Rhode Island. In Providence, the family fought a legal battle to get their children enrolled in the public schools, and Maritcha, at sixteen years old, made her first public speech, an appeal to the Rhode Island state legislature to open the public schools to everyone equally. She won her case and enrolled in Providence High School.

In 1869, Maritcha Lyons began to teach in Colored School No. 1 in Brooklyn. Although only a high school graduate, she took advantage of every opportunity for further learning, and there were many. "The Teachers' Association, Public Library, the Institute, all were accessible and furnished every facility for information, instruction, research and recreation of the varied and valuable sort," she remembered. She

Maritcha Lyons. Harry A. Williams Photograph Collection, General Research & Reference Division, Schomburg Center for Research in Black Culture, New York Public Library, Astor, Lenox, and Tilden Foundations.

took classes in elocution, arithmetic, geometry, voice culture and oral reading, and psychology (under Nicholas Murray Butler). She went to classes four or five evenings a week, and on Saturday mornings she studied at the Natural History Museum. "It was the era of a revolution in ideas regarding the aims, work and management of schools," she recalled. "Into all this I plunged with zest and assiduity."

When she became assistant principal of P.S. 83 in the 1890s, she assumed responsibility for supervising student teachers, including European Americans. She stayed at P.S. 83 until her retirement in 1918 after forty-eight years of teaching.

By 1892, Maritcha Lyons lived in Brooklyn with her father and mother (ages seventy-eight and seventy-seven) and her brother, thirty-four-year-old Albro Lyons, Jr. Albro listed his occupation in the census as musician, but he also kept a store for teas, coffees, and spices at 51 St. Felix Street, Brooklyn. Maritcha Lyons continued to live in Brooklyn until her death, first with her brother until his death and then with her nephews Harry Williamson and the Kingsland brothers, and finally with nephew James L. Kingsland and his family.[63]

Lyons took an active role in public advocacy for African Americans and especially for African American women. She became well known as an orator, beginning with a recitation in 1870, at a celebration for the Fifteenth Amendment in Brooklyn. She later spoke in Carnegie Hall, the Academy of Music, the A.M.E. Church in Manhattan, and elsewhere, always on behalf of African American rights. She also became a writer. She contributed eight biographical sketches for Hallie Q. Brown's *Homespun Heroines and Other Women of Distinction* (1926). She counted as friends Sarah Smith Garnet and Susan McKinney Steward, sisters whose father had purchased land in Weeksville, as well as Ida Wells Barnett (leader of the antilynching campaign) and Mary Talbert, president of the National Association of Colored Women.[64]

At her death in January 1928, Maritcha Lyons was widely eulogized. The *New York Age* published an obituary with her photograph on the front page, headlined "Miss Maritcha Lyons: For 48 Years Teaching in Brooklyn Schools, and a Militant Fighter for Women, Is Dead." The *Brooklyn and Long Island News* called her "one of the best known women in Brooklyn."[65]

Women and Churches in Weeksville

Lines between secular and religious public life were blurred in most African American communities. Barred from formally voting in the secular world, African American women sought to vote and hold office in churches instead. The 1870s were the key turning point, and the A.M.E. Church was at the forefront of the debate. Evidence for debates about women's rights in the A.M.E. Church comes not from Weeksville's local congregation (for which no local records have survived) but from debates at national A.M.E. conferences, which surely affected local congregations. In 1872, Rev. Thomas Henderson from Missouri proposed "the word 'male' wherever it occurs as a qualification of electors be struck from the Discipline." With almost no debate, women gained equal voting rights in the A.M.E. Church, which included the Weeksville congregation. The battle for equal rights on a practical level was not easily won, however. At the same 1872 meeting, the church conference created the office of stewardess, and women also served in missionary societies. In all of this work, however, they worked essentially as ladies' auxiliaries. The issue of women's rights had been introduced and formally accepted. In the ensuing decades, it would be constantly negotiated.[66]

Brooklyn Literary Union

In addition to politics and schools, benevolent institutions became a strong focus of African American life after the Civil War. Rooted in individual churches, they formed an interdenominational network, knitting Weeksville into larger communities in Brooklyn, New York State, and the nation. In the process, they involved women as well as men, African Americans as well as European Americans, and poor as well as well-to-do citizens, creating part of the grassroots origins of the nationwide Progressive movement.

The earliest known benevolent society associated with Weeksville was a women's group, the Abyssinian Benevolent Daughters of Esther. Men may have joined one or another lodge of Prince Hall Masons, but no documentary evidence has been found to support that.

After the Civil War, the Brooklyn Literary Union provided the main African American anchor for intellectual discussion and social reform. Organized in March 1886 by Rev. W. H. Dickerson and T. McCants Stewart, it counted two hundred members by the end of the year. In November 1886, the Brooklyn Eagle noted, "the union is in all respects a success." Stewart was first president and permanent lecturer, delivering a public talk every month. As lawyer, school board member, activist, and pastor of the A.M.E. Church in Weeksville, Stewart connected Weeksville citizens to African American intellectual and social leaders throughout Brooklyn. Reverend Rufus L. Perry was also a leading member and lecturer. Although the Brooklyn Literary Union met primarily at Siloam Presbyterian Church (and sometimes also Nazarene Congregational Church), it was a nonsectarian, independent organization.

It sponsored lectures on topics relating to race, sex, class, and culture, including "The Past Grandeur of the Dark Race," "Labor and Capital," "Woman's Suffrage," "Music," "Prohibition," "Grumbling and Grumblers," "The Race Problem," "Phases of the Industrial Problem as Affecting the Colored People in the North States," and "The Negro Problem."[67]

Women and men both joined the Brooklyn Literary Union, and Maritcha Lyons, assistant principal of P.S. 83 in Weeksville, was first vice president of the union in the early 1890s. Women also spoke regularly at meetings of the Brooklyn Literary Union. In May 1890, Elizabeth Frazier, a graduate of the Normal College in New York, spoke in a "bright, graceful way," before a standing room only audience. "The advancement of colored women toward the elevation of their race, both morally and intellectually . . . has been wonderfully rapid," she argued. As examples, she highlighted Sarah Smith Tompkins Garnet, who spent her life as a teacher in Brooklyn schools, and her sister Susan Smith McKinney Steward, one of the country's first women doctors, "a lady of whom we are all proud." (Their father, Sylvanus Smith, had been one of Weeksville's early landowners.) In 1892, Frances Ellen Watkins Harper spoke at the Union on "Enlightened Motherhood." Another of their topics was woman suffrage.[68]

Benevolent Institutions

Members of the Brooklyn Literary Union were also active in social reforms. The Howard Orphan Asylum and Zion Home for the Aged, later called the Brooklyn Home for Colored People, tied the Brooklyn Literary Union directly to Weeksville, as a logical location for these benevolent institutions. Not only did Weeksville highlight black empowerment. It was also located among hills and woodlands, which nineteenth-century reformers considered not only picturesque but also healthy. They were the preferred location for institutions such as cemeteries, orphanages, homes for the elderly, and even penitentiaries. One observer noted that the Weeksville area, "on account of its extreme healthfulness, is better adapted for hospital purposes than any other in the city."[69]

Other benevolent institutions, designed by and for European Americans, were also located among the hills and woodlands of eastern

Brooklyn. Locally, the Brooklyn penitentiary, built in 1846, stood in Crown Heights (an adaptation of the name Crow Hill) just southwest of Weeksville; a truant house for homeless children was built nearby in 1857; a Roman Catholic orphanage for boys stood just south of Weeksville, beginning in 1867; the Brooklyn Orphan Asylum was built at Kingston and Atlantic Avenues in 1872; and several hospitals, schools, and other public institutions dotted the surrounding area.[70]

These new institutions offered an opportunity for women as well as men to shape public dialogue. Women did much of the fund-raising that kept these institutions going, working with women's groups, primarily church-based, throughout Brooklyn. In turn, these institutions provided career opportunities for women as teachers, lecturers, matrons, and nurses. Just as they provided opportunities for women to create middle-class roles for themselves, they also crossed class lines. In some cases, including the work of the King's Daughters with Zion Home for the Aged, they crossed racial boundaries as well.

Howard Orphan Asylum

Founded in 1866 to meet the needs of freed women of color and their children who poured into Brooklyn from the South, Howard Orphan Asylum was located on the same block as Colored School No. 2 and the African Civilization Society, on the southwest corner of Troy Avenue and Dean Street.

During the draft riots of 1863, the Colored Orphan Asylum in New York City, operated by Quaker women, had been burned. The asylum remained without a building, so Sarah A. Tillman, widow of a black minister, took twenty children into her Manhattan home at 104 East Thirteenth Street. Mrs. Tillman's obituary reported that, acting on the advice of General Oliver Howard, head of the federal Freedmen's Bureau, and Rev. C. H. Howard, his brother, she moved her group to Weeksville. In 1868, assisted by Henry M. Wilson, secretary of the African Civilization Society, with funding from the Freedman's Bureau, the asylum incorporated as the Howard Orphan Asylum and moved into the headquarters of the African Civilization Society. The *Brooklyn Eagle* noted sarcastically that "Howard took the institution named after him into his special favor, and a part of the Freedmen's Bureau funds extorted from Brooklyn taxpayers found their way back here, as a government appropriation in aid of the labors of Brothers Wilson and Perry at Weeksville."[71] In 1891, when Mrs. Tillman (later Mrs. Collier) died in Providence, Rhode Island, Weeksville remembered her with a special ceremony at the Orphan Asylum.[72]

Two more orphanages were established nearby. The Roman Catholic Orphanage for boys was built between 1865 and 1868 just south of the Howard Orphan Asylum. The 1870 census listed 201 boys as residents in the Roman Catholic orphanage. They ranged in age from two to fifteen years old. Most either had been born in Ireland or had parents who were foreign-born. All were white. None were listed as attending school. (Perhaps the orphanage itself maintained a school internally.) A staff of twenty women—most likely nuns—operated the orphanage. All were Irish-born except two (one from New York and one from Maryland).[73]

A second small orphanage housed five African American boys, ages four to eleven. Sophia Searby, matron, and her husband Henry J. Searby, architect, both born in England, operated this from their home. Mary Lewis, a domestic servant born in Virginia, aided them, and her young daughter Sarah (only eight months old) lived in the same household.[74]

The Howard Orphan Asylum in Weeksville remained the major institution for African American children in Brooklyn, however. In 1870, thirty-seven children, both boys and girls, lived there. Most of them (twenty-three, or 62 percent) had been born in New York State. Nine, however, were southern-born: four from Virginia, four from Maryland, and one from South Carolina. Three more were from other northern states, one each from New Jersey, Maine, and Pennsylvania. Two more had an illegible birthplace (perhaps Haiti). Children ranged in age from two to eighteen. All children eleven years old and older (but none younger than that age) attended school. Many sibling groups shared this home, including the Henderson, Wilson, Smith, Roberts, and Pollard families. Five adults also lived in this building, including New Jersey–born Annie C. Pollard, matron, forty years old; Harriet Strange, teacher, age thirty-eight, born in Virginia; Robert Johnson, superintendent, age sixty-seven, born in Virginia; Adeline Tillman (perhaps related to founder Sarah Tillman), age seventy, born in New

York; and Vacilla Emery, laundress, one hundred years old, born in Maryland.

Until 1902, the board and staff of the Howard Orphan Asylum were composed entirely of African Americans. Unlike the New York Orphan Asylum, which hired primarily a white staff, those who operated the Howard Orphan Asylum, from the superintendent on down, were all African American. William F. Johnson, a blind African American minister (perhaps related to Robert Johnson, listed as superintendent in the 1870 census), took over the asylum's management in 1870 and maintained it under black control for thirty-two years.

Born free in Baltimore, Maryland, William F. Johnson was related to America's first African American poet, Phyllis Wheatley. He was raised in Ithaca, New York, and studied at the Institute for the Blind in New York City during the 1850s. He became a popular antislavery lecturer, appearing with such well-known speakers as Henry Ward Beecher and Henry Highland Garnet. He also gave "magic lantern exhibitions." In 1870, he lived with his wife Mary A. Johnson, age forty-three, born in Bath, Maine, and their children, William H. M., age eighteen, and Florence A., age four. Cousin Caroline Haley, age fifty-seven, born in Baltimore, also lived with them, and Agnes Smith, age fifteen, was a domestic servant in the household. The 1880 census listed William F. Johnson as living on Herkimer Street (the 1880 city directory listed him at 605 Herkimer Street).[75]

As superintendent of the Howard Orphan Asylum, Johnson supervised staff, helped in the care of hundreds of children, promoted the construction of two new buildings, and managed to pay off the institution's mortgage for their new building. His family gave him considerable help in writing letters, keeping the books, and traveling on asylum business. Johnson attributed his longevity as superintendent of the orphanage to "an element of love, hope, and stick."[76]

Johnson also worked tirelessly for civil rights. When the Brooklyn Board of Education refused to admit his son to an all-white school in 1874, he took them to court. Although he lost that case, he enrolled his daughter in a formerly all-white school a decade later, when the board reversed its decision. He supported T. Thomas Fortune's Afro-American League, which promoted equal rights for African Americans, giving a lecture to its state convention on African Americans in Egypt. The

New York Age said that Johnson "does more and better work than any man of the race in Brooklyn. . . . He is into every race effort, with voice and pen and purse."[77]

Like the New York Orphan Asylum (which had an all-female board until 1940), the board and staff of the Howard Asylum were dominated by women. Although the superintendent was male, women made up the rest of the board. In 1886, officers included Rev. William F. Johnson, superintendent; Mrs. L. A. Cooper, first directress; Miss H. E. Thompson, second directress; Mrs. G. Groves, recording secretary; Mrs. M. Augusta Johnson, treasurer and corresponding secretary; and Rev. R. H. Johnson, traveling agent. Trustees were W. F. Johnson, S. A. Thompson, G. M. Drayton, M. Richards, and I. J. Bolden. Officers were remarkably stable. Four years later, the same group still held office, except that Mrs. Sylvania R. Thompson was now second directress and Mrs. S. E. Brown was now corresponding secretary. This group met monthly throughout the whole existence of the Howard Orphan Asylum in Weeksville.[78]

By March 1883, reported Superintendent William F. Johnson to the *New York Globe*, thirty-four girls and fifty-six boys lived at the orphanage. They ranged from two to twelve years in age, and they were all half orphans (with only one parent living) or destitute children. The great need, reported Johnson, was a new building. M. Augusta Johnson took on the challenge. Treasurer of the Asylum for many years, she became in 1883 the major fund-raiser for a new building and in fact suggested its design. In July, workmen broke ground for the new structure, a three-story brick building, forty-five by fifty-six feet on Dean Street, near the corner of Troy Avenue. The cornerstone was officially laid on October 18, 1883, with a program of distinguished ministers, refreshments organized by the "Lady Managers and their chosen assistants," and an opportunity in the evening for anyone who wished to speak to give "a free expression of their feelings."[79]

Finances remained a problem. In 1884, the orphanage owned ten city lots that, with their new building, were worth $45,000. But they owed the builder $7,000, and they had a mortgage of $14,500.[80] Constant efforts to raise money—including fairs, community concerts by the orphans, and dinners given in their honor—helped maintain their financial health. Citizens in New York and the larger Brooklyn community, both African American and European American, contributed

Howard Orphan Asylum, 1883. Courtesy Brooklyn Public Library, Brooklyn Collection.

to the building fund, as well. Alanson Trask, a retired merchant who lived during the 1870s at 28 Monroe Place, gave $10,000 from the Marquand Fund to support the institution, and in 1886 he added another $4,500 toward canceling the mortgage. The mortgage was finally paid off in September 1891. The board gave its congratulations to superintendent Johnson, "the Moses who had led them through the Red Sea of indebtedness." Now the asylum needed to raise only $600 per month to pay its expenses.[81]

The new building allowed the asylum to take in several more children each year. In 1890, between 116 and 130 orphans lived there. When a reporter for the *New York Times* visited the Howard Orphan Asylum in 1894, he reported that almost 150 children lived there in "comfortable and spacious quarters" with "excellent care and teaching."[82]

The Howard Orphan Asylum, like the New York Asylum, adopted a system of indentures, at which children from about twelve to twenty-one would be put to work with families who would care for them, teach them a trade, and pay them a small sum, which would be put in the bank for them. Sometimes pupils at the asylum returned to work there. Mary J. Wilson came to the asylum when she was three years old and did so well academically that she was sent to the Robinson Female Seminary in Exeter, New Hampshire, under the guardianship of a former matron, Mrs. Davis, who had married and moved to Exeter. At Exeter, Mary Wilson "distinguished herself for scholarship [and] gained a promotion on each commencement day." In 1884, she returned to the Howard Orphan Asylum "filled with joy because of her ability to take a position in the institution and repay the managers for the long continued interest they have taken in her welfare."[83]

The Howard Orphan Asylum sustained itself through a very active network of community volunteers. Annually, women met twice a week in a fall sewing circle, converting donated material into usable items for sale at a Thanksgiving fair. These sewing circles involved women not only from Weeksville but also all over Brooklyn. Regularly, the asylum presented concerts and programs for the community, both to raise money and to demonstrate how much the students had learned. In July 1889, for example, the children showed "marked progress" in their "recitations, dialogues, and singing," so as "to elicit the admiration of the large audience." Two weeks later, they invited the community to their first lawn and garden party, complete with large decorated tents, including a gypsy tent, with music supplied by the boys' drum corps of the William Lloyd Garrison Post, as well as an Italian band.[84]

Perhaps the asylum held the lawn and garden party, with its Italian band and gypsy tent, as a way to create kindly relationships with a growing Irish, German, and Italian population in Weeksville. They had recently endured a "brutal assault" from Irishman James Heny, who jumped on the asylum fence and threw a "large stone," striking a ten-year-old boy. Superintendent Johnson brought a complaint against James Heny. The judge heard testimony from three little boys and their teacher, Miss Miles, and sentenced Heny to twenty days in jail or a twenty-dollar fine.[85]

By the 1890s, Howard, as well as the New York Asylum, began to emphasize industrial education on the model of Tuskegee Institute. In 1894, Howard built an annex for an industrial school. This was a two-story frame building, with a dormitory on the top floor that held about sixty children. In 1898, they lobbied unsuccessfully for funds from the New York legislature to build another industrial school building, since there were "no shops where colored children could be instructed in the different trades."[86]

From 1906 to 1910, one of the most famous people at Howard was Ota Benga, an Mbuti rescued from enslavement in Africa and brought to the United States, where he lived first in the African exhibit at the Louisiana Purchase Exposition in St. Louis in 1904; then he became an exhibit at the Museum of Natural History in New York City and the Bronx Zoo. Protests by African American clergyman, including Rev. James H. Gordon, superintendent at Howard Orphan Asylum, led to his move to Howard, where he remained four years.[87]

In 1910, the New York State Board of Charities declared that the Weeksville building was overcrowded and unsafe. The board sold its Weeksville property to the Nassau Railroad Company and moved the orphanage to a model farm and industrial school they had purchased in 1906 at St. James, Suffolk County, Long Island (Indian Head Farm), with Rev. Gordon, a graduate from Tuskegee, in charge. The *Brooklyn Daily Eagle* called Gordon "one of the most eloquent Negroes in the country," and Gordon's eloquence brought considerable support for his effort to make Howard into "one of the greatest projects to benefit the Negro in the North . . . since the Emancipation." As part of its attempt to create a national model of professionalism, Howard hired Mary Eliza Mahoney as superintendent of nurses. A graduate of the New England Hospital for Women and Children, Mahoney was the first professional African American nurse in the United States and a founder of the National Association of Colored Graduate Nurses, which still gives an award in her name.[88]

The renamed Howard Orphanage and Industrial School began teaching cooking, shoe repair, shop, farming, and other vocational skills. To meet new financial burdens, the board chose a new president in 1913, a European American Quaker named L. Hollingsworth Wood, who also became president of the National Urban League. Two Quaker women were added to the board, which included five African Americans and eleven European Americans. Residential cottages housed no more than thirty children each. When Booker T. Washington visited the Howard

Orphan Asylum in 1913, he commented that he was most pleased "to note the natural bearing of the children; they had nothing of the 'institutional' atmosphere. A natural relation seemed to exist between them and their instructors."[89]

The Howard Orphan Asylum held a farewell reception at its old building on Dean Street, near Troy Avenue on May 10 and 11, 1911. "Many prominent citizens, both white and colored, were among the callers," reported the *New York Age*. "The rooms on the first floor presented a gala scene, decorated with American flags, palms, plants and cut flowers. There are at present 240 children in the asylum, all of whom present a hale, hearty appearance, evidencing good care is taken of them." Two months later, the old building, one of Brooklyn's landmarks for forty-five years, was entirely vacated.[90]

Zion Home for the Aged (Brooklyn Home for Aged Colored People)

The presence of Howard Orphan Asylum and the earlier African Civilization Society brought regional and national attention to Weeksville. It was the logical place to create a home for the aged. In the process, more opportunities opened for women to work as staff in the home. As usual, women became the main fund-raisers. In this case, both African American and European American women joined to support the new home.

On December 7, 1869, members of the Zion African Methodist Episcopal Church on Bleecker and West Tenth Streets, New York City, organized the Zion Aged Relief Association. Five years later, on December 21, 1874, they opened a home, Zion Home for the Aged, on Dean Street near Troy Avenue, on the same block as the Howard Orphan Asylum, the African Civilization Society, and Colored School No. 2. "It is a plain three story and basement frame structure," reported the *Brooklyn Eagle*, "and has all the appearance of a factory from the outside." By 1875, more than fifty people, both men and women, lived in the home, with Mrs. E. Cox as matron and Rev. Jacob Thomas as spiritual advisor. People of many denominations supported it.[91]

By 1887, the home had only twenty-nine residents and was having trouble raising money to sustain itself. Rev. Richard Penfield, city missionary for "destitute colored people," organized a benefit, and "every seat in the chapel of the home was filled last evening with both white and colored people." "Three colored ladies," members of the King's Daughters, presided over the refreshment table, while "the entertainment was given by the Dorcas Juvenile Missionary Society, composed of thirty pretty white misses, whose ages range from 12 to 18 years, and who are being trained for practical missionary work by Mr. Penfield and his amiable wife."[92]

The financial situation grew worse in the next few years. Although each resident paid $150 to become a life member of the home, their care was minimal, and they were virtually starving. By 1890, the matron, a resident herself, had not been paid in two years. The twenty-four residents lived on minimal provisions sent by board members from New York City but paid for by contributions from the people of Brooklyn. Dr. Ross Sidney, who donated his medical services, told the *Brooklyn Eagle* that

> the place should be investigated, and the public would be astonished at the results. Why it's a sin to see those poor folks treated as they are. . . . The fact is, they are half starved, and they would be altogether if it weren't for Brooklyn people. As it is, they have only half enough to eat. Since I was asked to become a visiting physician, I have never seen any accounting or report made. The money as fast as it comes in is gobbled up by the New York contingent and that's the end of it. . . . I have known the matron, Mrs. Blake, to take a basket and go begging for something to eat.

Day in and day out, all year long, reported one resident, they ate oatmeal or hominy, molasses, bread, and tea for breakfast; corned beef or pork, potatoes or turnips ("when we have them") for dinner; and bread and tea for supper.[93]

The building itself was dark and crowded. A reporter for the *Brooklyn Eagle* described three stories, with the upper two divided into sleeping rooms, more like closets, since they were only about six by eight feet, "dark and uninviting," with an iron bedstead, chair, and washstand. If people could afford it, they had rag rugs on the floor. The chapel, with a red and black ingrain carpet, was on the first floor; the dining room was in the basement. "The whole story," concluded the reporter, "is that Brooklyn people are not only supporting an institution controlled by persons not residents of this city, but the money they give to charity does not reach the parties for whom it is intended." Holes in the ceiling let rain fall on residents' beds. Racial issues brought extra problems. In June, the cook assaulted one resident, who charged that, because she was born in England, "a strong feeling of dislike has sprung up against her among the Southern negroes, led by Cook Johnson, in the home." Attempts to track down the managers of the home proved fruitless. They seemed to be working people, unable to handle the burden of the home, in some cases taking contributions from the people of Brooklyn and not returning them fully to the residents of the home. The *Eagle's* exposé, noted one letter to the editor, was "the hope of all the inmates and friends to the home, and all rest their hope on it."[94]

Faced with this desperate situation, a new network of supporters emerged. Margaret McDonald Bottome, a European American Methodist from New York City, founded the King's Daughters in 1886. Organized as an interdenominational "sisterhood of service," the King's Daughters formed circles in churches, both European American and African American, throughout Brooklyn, the nation, and the world, using the motto "not to be ministered unto, but to minister." Each circle chose its own project. By 1896, King's Daughters had organized in twenty-six states, as well as Japan, China, Syria, India, and most European countries.[95]

In 1890, several of these circles organized visits and fund-raising efforts on behalf of Zion Home for the Aged, both to support the current residents and to raise money for a new building. The Lower Lights Circle of the King's Daughters of the white-dominated Washington Avenue Baptist Church started the effort with an entertainment in May 1890. They were a group of ten determined young women, and they quickly enlisted aid from other circles. In December, they held a mass meeting of 250 circles of King's Daughters from several denominations, apparently both African American and European American, probably bringing in groups from far beyond Brooklyn. Reverend Dixon, of Concord Baptist Church, opened with prayer, but women officers of the King's Daughters conducted the meeting itself. President Margaret Bottome welcomed the group: "We have never met with such opportunities of doing Christ like work in view, as we now have a grand chance of helping our sisters in need. These woman inmates of the home are

our friends in black, and to devise means for caring for them is our purpose in coming together tonight. I want to associate with this meeting
the passage from Hebrews, 'remember them that are in bonds as bound
with them.'" Mrs. Isabella Davis, the corresponding secretary, noted,

> Our order claims to break down all barriers of race, creed and condition,
> teaching the fatherhood of God and the brotherhood of man. And I am
> thankful to see that the young daughters in Brooklyn are moving along
> in this broad path. . . . I trust we can make the last days of these old per-
> sons their best and happiest days. Remember how much their dear bod-
> ies need your comforting and helping. We are not pleading for a home
> that shall be worthy of them, but a home for Him, who centuries ago
> knew what it was to be homeless. . . . The dream of ages has been the
> unity of the church of God; a wider dream is the brotherhood of the race,
> and by making this real our order has achieved its high prosperity.

Reverend Walters of African Methodist Episcopal Zion Church then
spoke. He himself had been in bondage but a few years ago, he said.
"These hands were shackled, these feet not my own. My voice was not
recognized in the courts of this land; for no outrage against me could I
get redress. The highest tribunal denied me the rights of a citizen, and
in the land where I was born they refused to grant me the means of
reading the Bible." He explained why Zion Church was no longer able
to support the home, and asked for help in maintaining the institution.
The leaders collected one thousand dollars that evening, resolved to
raise money for a new building, and appointed a committee to supervise fund-raising.[96]

By April, they had incorporated and appointed officers, an advisory
board (which included African American members such as Rev. William T. Dixon from Concord Baptist Church and Charles A. Dorsey,
principal of P.S. 67), and a Board of Managers (which included African American members such as Mrs. Philip A. White and Dr. Susan
McKinney Steward). At a mass meeting in the Hanson Place Methodist
Episcopal Church, they reported the results of their work so far. They
had spent $125 to clean the home. Residents now had clean clothes and
three good meals each day. Rev. Dixon noted that "I stepped in its door
the other day and O, what a change was there. New mattresses were on

the beds, the walls were newly papered and calcimined. I looked with glad surprises. New life was stamped on the faces of the old ladies. One of these said: 'Do you notice anything? Isn't it grand? The white ladies (Pardon me for using the term. I am quoting an old lady who is behind the times), These white ladies have been so kind.'" "You cannot converse with these old women at the home without having an inspiration," said Reverend Dixon. "One of them is 92 years old. She is a queenly woman. She is black. When you meet her you feel, first, that there is a woman; second, that there is a lady, and, third, that there is a Christian. . . . These are my people. It brings tears to my eyes and my heart glows with pride when I think of their records. God bless the King's daughters, in whom I have much confidence. In His name a new building for the aged colored people will be erected." Dr. R. S. Storrs echoed Reverend Dixon. "There is nothing so hard to kill in Brooklyn," he said, "as an institution in which women have got themselves interested."[97]

One of the most important of these women of Brooklyn was Susan Smith McKinney Steward. Born in 1847, McKinney Steward became the first African American woman medical doctor in New York State and the third in the nation. Her father, Sylvanus Smith, owned a pork farm in Carrsville/Weeksville and hog business in downtown Brooklyn. While city directories list the family's address as downtown Brooklyn, the Smiths may well have spent time in the Weeksville area. Susan Smith graduated from New York Medical College for Women and practiced in Brooklyn from 1870 to 1895. In 1876, she gave one of her earliest public lectures to the New York Conference of the A.M.E. Church. She spoke on ventilation and its effect on the human body and created a sensation when she mentioned the negative effects of tight corseting on women. She was a founder of the Women's Hospital and Dispensary (Myrtle and Grand Avenues), which later moved to 808 Prospect Place and became the Memorial Hospital for Women and Children. In 1891, the *New York Age* called her "one of the medical institutions of Brooklyn." She was the organist of Bridge Street A.M.E. Church for twenty-eight years. In 1891, she became a member of the Board of Managers of Zion Home for the Aged in Weeksville and served as one of its physicians.[98]

In 1874, she married Reverend William McKinney, an Episcopal minister. They had two children. After his death, she married Reverend Theophilus Gould Steward, a U.S. Army chaplain. With him, she

Dr. Susan Smith McKinney Steward. General Research & Reference Division, Schomburg Center for Research in Black Culture, New York Public Library, Astor, Lenox, and Tilden Foundations.

traveled extensively throughout the West. She was active in the temperance and woman suffrage movements and spoke on "Colored Women in America" at the 1911 Interracial Conference in London, England. W. E. B. Du Bois eulogized her on her death in 1918. She was buried in Greenwood Cemetery.[99]

The King's Daughters kept their pledge to Zion Home. Throughout the 1890s, they continued to hold fund-raising fairs, strawberry festivals, musical entertainments, donation parties, and plays. In 1892, they moved residents of the home to a new building at 1888 Atlantic Avenue, corner of Utica Avenue. Private contributions averaged about $3,000 a year in cash, with $1,200 in donations of food and clothing and an annual contribution from the city of $2,500. Mrs. P. A. White contributed generously. So did the Fruit and Flower Mission of Manhattan and several Brooklyn churches. The home paid no salaries, only room and board for help.[100]

Such personal interest brought its own rewards. One observer noted that "this is one of the most Christianly managed institutions with which I am acquainted. There is not a happier set of people in the country than these aged colored people. The home seems like heaven to them. It is more a family home than a public institution, and the patrons and managers are looked upon by these old people as personal friends."[101]

One of the most famous residents of the home was Aunt Jane Brown, president of the King's Daughters Circle of the Home, whose birthday was the featured entertainment of the year, celebrated with a reception and bazaar. Aunt Jane was 103 years old in 1896. Although she was blind, she continued to spend most of her day sewing quilts and hemming towels for sale in the bazaar, to raise money for the new building. Aunt Jane died in 1898, aged 105, mentally alert to the last.[102]

The secretary of the King's Daughters Circle was Aunty Serrington, born enslaved in the Burdette family in Fort Lee. When she was eight years old, she moved to New York City with a daughter of the family. Freed at twenty-one, she married a Methodist minister, who died in California at the time of the gold rush, leaving her with four children to support. She had recently visited her birthplace in Fort Lee and had "a delightful visit with the oldest member of her master's family, Mrs. Catherine Burdette, aged 84 years." She died in April 1895, aged ninety-four.[103]

By 1897, the corporation had acquired land at the corner of Kingston Avenue and Douglass Street (now St. John's Place). Two years later, they laid the cornerstone for the new building. It was to be a three-story brick structure with gray limestone trim, costing $25,000, heated by steam, with the most up-to-date plumbing and ventilation, three dining rooms (one on each floor), a chapel, and extensive fire escapes. It was built to hold fifty people, twice the number that occupied the Atlantic Avenue site. The builder, George Stone, furnished the plans, and offered his services as superintendent free of charge. George Stone's son was the architect. Cranford Brothers, plumbers, also donated their services. Several individuals, churches, and circles of the King's Daughters furnished the rooms. The managers already had $12,000 in cash, equity in the Atlantic Avenue property of $3,000 to $3,500, and a promise of $1,000 in cash from George Peabody. "It is expected," noted the *Eagle*,

Brooklyn Home for the Aged, 1095 St. John's Place. Photo by Megan Goins Diouf, October 2013.

"that the new structure will be dedicated upon its completion entirely free of debt." That expectation was not realized, however, and the board took out a $15,000 mortgage.[104]

Both men and women, African Americans and European Americans, were leaders in supporting the home. In 1899, the officers of Zion Home, now called Brooklyn Home for the Colored Aged, were all women. At least one of them, Mrs. Philip A. White, was African American. All except one of the Advisory Board were male. At least three them, W. T. Dixon, C. W. Dorsey, and the only woman, Dr. Verina Morton, were African American. Reverend William Dixon, pastor of the African American Concord Baptist Church, presided at the ceremonies laying the cornerstone, while Reverend Horace F. Porter, assistant pastor of Plymouth Church, and Reverend Dr. Braislin, former pastor of Washington Avenue Baptist Church, both predominately European American churches, gave addresses.[105]

The new home was dedicated on January 25, 1900. Twenty-four residents, ranging in age from sixty to ninety years old, had already moved in. Reverend Dixon of Concord Baptist Church presided. Six "sweet-voiced children" from the Howard Orphan Asylum sang several hymns, and one of them sang a solo. Reverend Horace Porter of Plymouth Church reminded the audience, many of whom were African

American, that "completion of the home was an evidence of the inherent strength, ability, tact and intellectual resources of the American girl and the Brooklynite in particular." Never losing an opportunity to raise money for the cause, the managers opened the building for a reception and sale after the ceremony.[106]

Financial support for the home became increasingly difficult after the city of Brooklyn withdrew its support from seventeen charities, including the Brooklyn home. The Board of Managers continued to hold regular fund-raisers, including picnics, musicales, donation parties, and fairs. Many of these featured African cultural events, such as Jeanette Robinson Murphy's musical lecture on "African Music and Voodoism in America" in April 1902.[107]

Zion Home is an exceptionally well-documented case study of what was happening in many urban areas across the country in the late nineteenth and early twentieth centuries, as people—motivated primarily by religious values—came together across lines of class, race, age, and sex to create institutions that would care for everyone in the community. Cumulatively, these movements merged to create what became known as Progressive reform. But this national movement began in local places such as Brooklyn, with grassroots efforts such as that of the King's Daughters and Brooklyn Home for the Aged. People across Brooklyn took the lead in organizing support for Zion Home, but the focus of this effort was on the institution in Weeksville. Support for this home reflected the emerging power of women as social reformers.

As Weeksville's African American residents confronted the dynamic world of post–Civil War America, they were no longer living in a relatively independent black community. They had been engulfed by the city of Brooklyn.

5

"Cut Through and Gridironed by Streets"

Physical Changes, 1860–1880

In the 1860s, Weeksville, with its steep hills, woods, and deep hollows, remained a pocket of rural life, with "the most uneven land in the city, where hollows of fifty feet or more alternate," surrounded by the city on its north and west sides.[1] From the hills of Weeksville, visitors could look east for a "magnificent view" of Jamaica Bay. They could look west to see the "roofs and spires" of Brooklyn. Gazing north, they could see "dimly outlined hills of New England" across Long Island Sound.[2]

The Brooklyn City Railroad Company completed rail service along Fulton Avenue to East New York, just north of Weeksville, in 1857. The new railroad gave Weeksville yet another connection to downtown Brooklyn and then to Manhattan via the Fulton or Atlantic ferries. But Weeksville itself remained relatively rural and relatively intact. As the *Brooklyn Eagle* noted in 1868, "To talk of Weeksville, where our colored brethren congregate and pray . . . , is to speak of a *terra incognita* to most of the people of Brooklyn.[3]

This stable neighborhood was about to change. Renewed debates about emigration in the 1850s and the cataclysm of the Civil War in the 1860s embroiled Weeksville's citizens directly in national events. Meanwhile, at home, the village of Weeksville reflected major demographic changes. In the 1860s, partly as a result of increased access to transportation, European Americans began to move in large numbers into Weeksville. Population in the Ninth Ward mushroomed. So did the need for affordable housing. And so did opportunities for making money from land investments. Major physical changes altered Weeksville's landscape forever, as urban development flattened hills, filled in valleys, and brought a new street grid system to overlay the old roads that meandered over the hills.

The process of Weeksville's absorption into the city of Brooklyn took at least forty years, but it was steady and inexorable. It had begun before the Civil War. In 1840, Weeksville's population was 82.3 percent African American, and it remained essentially the same (82.1 percent) in 1850. By 1855, however, although its African American population had risen by 42 percent (from 366 to 521), its European American population had increased more than threefold (from 79 to 334). African Americans in 1855 still remained a majority of Weeksville's population, 60.9 percent, but they lost that majority by 1860, when African Americans numbered only 458 out of 1,240 people in Weeksville (36.9 percent of the population). Five years later, in 1865, Weeksville's population had risen to 1,424, but African Americans formed only 32.7 percent of the total. African Americans remained more concentrated in Weeksville than they were in the surrounding area, but European Americans were rapidly flooding into the area.[4]

The boundaries of Weeksville never matched ward boundaries, so printed census records do not give us a very good idea of population changes within Weeksville itself. We do know, however, that in 1865, 687 African Americans lived in the Ninth Ward, where Weeksville was located, forming 2.9 percent of the total population of 23,443. After 1874, Weeksville was in the Twenty-Fourth Ward. By 1900, the total population of the Twenty-Fourth Ward had grown to 31,767, while the African American population had grown to 1,937, or 6.1 percent of the total population.[5]

For several years, Weeksville remained a community whose inhabitants, the *Eagle* noted in 1873, were "principally colored people." That same year, however, a retired policeman (European American) named Hanft, recalled, "there is as many whites as blacks" in Weeksville. The 1870 manuscript census confirmed his observation, as the census taker listed African Americans and European Americans living throughout Weeksville sometimes side by side, sometimes clustered in racially distinct areas.[6]

In 1873, the *Eagle* showed remarkable interest in Weeksville because it offered so obvious an opportunity for development. All around it, Brooklyn was a bustling city. Weeksville, hilly and relatively rural, had been bypassed by earlier urban growth. All that was about to change. In 1868, Brooklyn began a massive program of street development. Eastern Parkway intersected Hunterfly Road seven blocks south of Bergen Street, and the city had plans for four more huge parkways. One of them was supposed to run right through Weeksville itself, "from Prospect Park, across the hills and valleys . . . and on across Crow Hill, through the negro settlement at Weeksville, and the wild district beyond, at Carsville, to the city line at East New York."[7]

In 1873, the *Brooklyn Eagle* noted that Crow Hill, including Weeksville, "is now cut through and gridironed by streets." Another observer noted the same year that Weeksville was "all intersected with streets and built up with houses." City services accompanied house construction. In 1867, for example, the Brooklyn Common Council authorized the street commissioner to "set gas lamp posts and lanterns" on Schenectady between Herkimer Street and Fulton Avenue, as well as along Fulton Avenue to Rochester Avenue. In 1868, the city constructed a well and pump near the corner of Rochester Avenue and DeGraw Street. In 1869, the city issued bonds to install drains in Rochester Avenue and elsewhere. In 1873, the city graded and paved Buffalo Avenue from St. Mark's to the city line and Rochester Avenue from Atlantic Avenue to Herkimer Street. They added flagging (presumably sidewalks) on Rochester between Fulton and Atlantic Avenues. The following year, they added sewers along Herkimer Street from Utica to Rochester Avenues.[8]

As late as 1888, however, Weeksville had still not filled in as rapidly as the surrounding areas. An article in the *Brooklyn Eagle* noted that the Bedford Hills, which included Weeksville, had not "grown so rapidly as those parts along the highways," but "is now being filled up." The Sanborn insurance map of that year revealed many houses in Weeksville still located at angles to the grid. Some of them still sat in the middle of streets that had been surveyed, if not built. As late as 1896, these sand hills had not yet been cleared away. As Howard Place (two blocks east of Buffalo Avenue) was extended, a fifteen-foot-high sand embankment at the corner of Prospect Avenue collapsed and killed a thirteen-year-old Hunterfly Road resident.[9]

As the grid expanded, two old colonial roads survived. West of Weeksville, part of Clove Road still led south from Bedford, while Hunterfly Road marked Weeksville's eastern end. In 1863, an enterprising

German American carpenter named Ferdinand (sometimes noted as Frederick) Volckening bought a piece of land on the west side of Hunterfly Road, just south of Bergen Street. He purchased these lots from Samuel Bouton, who in 1839 had bought them from the estate of Samuel Garrittsen. He eventually moved four houses onto these lots. They survived into the late twentieth century (and three of them survived into the twenty-first century) as mute reminders of the changing world of Weeksville. These are the houses now owned by the Weeksville Heritage Society.

Some of the changes in Weeksville in the 1860s and 1870s were not positive ones. Former policeman Hanft remembered in 1873 that, as increasing numbers of whites moved into Weeksville, so did crime. Hanft remembered "gambling shops," "dirty dens," "draw poker," robberies, and "one or two murders." Fights occurred frequently among "common white people, who gradually mixed in and settled with the darkies," but the "darkies always fought with razors or clubs." "Policy shops," places in which people could bet on random numbers, also came for the first time to Weeksville. Hanfft thought they encouraged people to be "lazy and confirmed gamblers." Finally, the increasing population, mixed white and black, led to "gin mills of the lowest character and houses of ill fame," called "Amalgamation Houses," "where on Saturday nights the Devil himself would be to pay."[10]

A decade later, however, two other police officers had a very different view of Weeksville. Charles Bedell, with nine years experience in the Crow Hill area, thought that residents had a "wholesome respect" for the law. Captain Folk noted that "out of 674 arrests made in the precinct last year, only 55 were those of colored persons, and these were principally for petty offenses. Among the colored people living up here there is, of course a great deal of degradation, and still there are a good many worthy, industrious, and, I think, intelligent persons, who make worthy citizens." A reporter from the Eagle noted, "The percentage of arrests by the police of persons of African descent is considerably below the average of the whole number of captures."[11]

In 1883, Rev. Amos N. Freeman, pastor of Siloam Presbyterian Church on Prince Street, who had come to Brooklyn in 1852, described African American occupations in Brooklyn generally. "The great ambition of those who are working for a living," Freeman noted, "is to own

the houses in which they live, and quite a number have progressed that
far. The occupations of the colored folks are varied, and it is a fact that
the women do more than half the work." Several people were worth
ten thousand to fifty thousand dollars. The richest African American
in Brooklyn was a woman, Elizabeth Gloucester, wife of Rev. Gloucester, an activist for African American rights (and a supporter of John
Brown). She made her money herself, keeping a boarding house for
European Americans at the old Long Island Club at the corner of Clinton Street and Remsen. When she died in 1883, people believed that she
was the richest African American in the country.[12]

Most men worked in service occupations "as caterers, coachmen,
calciminers, drivers and porters." The few who worked in skilled trades
were generally carpenters and masons from the South. One man from
South Carolina, who lived in the Eastern District (most likely Weeksville), was a machinist who owned his own business. A few men became
druggists. Two or three were physicians. Thomas Fortune and Rufus L.
Perry (from Weeksville) were editors, one of the *New York Globe* and
the other of the *National Monitor*, published in Brooklyn. Women generally worked as seamstresses, laundresses, maids, housekeepers, or
boardinghouse operators. More than two-thirds of African Americans
in Brooklyn worked in New York City.[13]

Some people in the Twenty-Fourth Ward (the old Ninth Ward, which
included Weeksville) were not doing well. On Atlantic Avenue, in a
place called Chicago Row, sixty families, all but three African American, crowded into six houses. An *Eagle* reporter, in an early example of
what would become the muckraking tradition of reform newspapers in
the Progressive Era, described the home of one such family:

A very old lamp stood unsteadily upon the wooden mantel, reflecting
a dismal light upon a scene of abject poverty. There was no carpet on
the seamed and blackened floor. The walls were darkened with the grime
of generations. The ceiling had lost its usefulness to such an extent that
much of it had disappeared, exposing the bare and broken laths. A stove,
hardly larger than those that are sold in the toy shops for doll houses,
and old enough to have served from the foundation of the row, stood
beneath the mantel, holding within its fractured frame a few cinders that
had burned once and were seemingly trying to burn themselves over

again. Upon the wall, in a rude frame, hung a certificate of membership in the African Methodist Church; a campaign lithograph of James A. Garfield and two or three cheap advertising chromos flanked the illuminated programme of a recent cake walk. By the feeble rays of the lamp an aged colored man was making a determined effort to fashion himself a pair of mittens out of a few wretched rags; and his youngest son, a lad of 14, was also engaged in the manufacture of some rude hand covering. The room was not more than twelve feet long by eight in width, and yet beneath its smoked and broken ceiling five people nightly find shelter. The head of the establishment, whose name is Bailey, said that he found it a very uncomfortable place, but it was the best they could do on $3 a month, and he supposed they would have to stand it.[14]

This man was, the reporter noted, "one of the most respectable colored men in the precinct," but he was forced to live on what work he could find, shoveling coal or doing other odd jobs.[15]

The 1880 census, however, gave a very different picture for African Americans in Weeksville. Enumeration District 241 covered most of Weeksville. In terms of the poorest people, the census taker in 1880 did list several families in this general area as "squatters." All but one of these families were labeled "white," however, suggesting either that the racial balance in the neighborhood changed dramatically between 1880 and 1883, or that the census taker simply ignored many poor European American families.

Although the 1880 census did not give the value of houses or list home ownership, we can tell something about the relative economic stability of the community by analyzing the occupations of its residents. A profile of African American families from the 1880 census who lived in the area between Albany, Troy, and Schenectady Avenues and from Atlantic through Pacific, Dean, Bergen, St. Mark's, and Park Place reveals that almost every adult had some kind of employment. It also suggests an emerging class of female skilled and professional workers. Of the 138 workers, 99 were men and 39 were women, working in a total of 44 different occupations.

Of the eighty-seven adult men who listed an occupation, only one, a gardener, worked in agriculture. Fifteen (17.2 percent) worked in manufacturing, including three "segar makers," three tailors, two carpenters, and one each who worked as a basket maker, brick mason, cooper, cutler, shoemaker, boot maker, and stonemason. Forty-two (48.3 percent) worked in some area of service or professional work, including nineteen waiters, five coachmen or coach drivers, five who worked in a store, four porters, three janitors, two barbers, two school teachers, two truck men, two ministers, two sailors (one in the U.S. Navy), and one each who was a bell boy, china packer, clerk, dealer in furniture, editor, "flour inspection," life insurance agent, herb doctor, hostler, news dealer, office boy, painter, pedlar, sweep, watchman. Twenty-six (29.9 percent) listed their occupation only as laborer. Three (3.4 percent) were unknown, including "House of Refuge," "phot?," and "fudler?" One was in prison.

We can also categorize occupations by relative status, whether they were high white-collar/professional jobs, proprietary occupations, skilled artisan work, or unskilled labor. Of the males, five, or 5.1 percent (two ministers, two teachers, and a newspaper editor), were white-collar or professional workers. Six more men, or 6.1 percent (the two barbers, the furniture dealer, the life insurance agent, perhaps the herb doctor, and the news dealer), can be classed as proprietary. Seventeen more, or 17.2 percent of the male workforce (the basket maker, brick mason, carpenters, cooper, cutler, segar makers, shoemaker, boot maker, stonemason, and tailors), were skilled artisans. The rest (71.7 percent) were relatively unskilled workers, either those who had some training, such as coachmen, or those who worked at odd jobs, perhaps by the day, and listed their work simply as "laborers" (26).

Most adult women were married, and they worked at keeping house. Eighty-nine women were listed with this occupation. Thirty-nine women worked at paid employment. Of these, fifteen worked as laundresses, ten were dressmakers, three worked as nurses, two more were music teachers, two were house cleaners, and one each was a seamstress, a servant, an organist, a steward, a teacher at the Orphan Asylum, a cook at the Orphan Asylum, and a matron and assistant matron at the Orphan Asylum.

Compared to the male workers, a higher percentage of women worked as professionals or skilled workers. Counting the teachers, nurses, organist, and matrons as professionals, nine of the thirty-nine (or 23.1 percent) were professionally employed (compared to 5.1 percent of the men). Twelve (the dressmakers, seamstress, and cook) or 30.8 percent were skilled workers (compared to 17.2 percent of the men). Almost half (46.2 percent) worked at unskilled jobs (compared to 71.7 percent of the men). No women were listed as proprietors, however (compared to 6.1 percent of the men.)

Most of Weeksville's African American residents were fully employed, with steady jobs, living in two-parent families with children. More than one-third (35.5 percent) were skilled artisans, proprietors, or white-collar and professional workers. This is a very different picture from the destitution reported by the *Brooklyn Eagle* on Crow Hill three years later. Undoubtedly, the *Eagle*'s portrait was a reasonably accurate one for those places that the reporter visited, but his dramatic anecdotal account certainly did not characterize Weeksville as a whole.

This occupational profile suggests an economic prosperity that many African American communities lacked. In Smithtown, Long Island, for example, the position of African American landowners in the mid-nineteenth century was precarious. Bradley Harris noted that several black landowners in 1860 were all listed as renters in the 1900 census. Restricted to work as laborers or servants, they were apparently unable to hold on to the small property holdings they had won after emancipation.[16]

Similarly, Ira Berlin noted for New York city that "during the 1830s, the growing number of newly arrived Irish and German immigrants began to muscle free Negroes out of many of the low-paying trades they controlled. . . . In 1855, nearly 90 percent of all New York City blacks worked at menial, unskilled jobs." Jane H. Pease and William H. Pease concluded in *They Who Would Be Free*, "By 1861, Northern blacks had gained little, except in race pride and organization, beyond what they had in 1830. In some cases, they had lost ground." "In one word," they suggested, "black America was powerless."[17]

Other historians painted a more hopeful picture, however. Graham Hodges suggested that, in Monmouth County, New Jersey, "the census of 1860 shows for the first time the full emergence of an economically independent black population in Monmouth." African Americans in 1860 could be impressed "by how far free blacks had advanced their position in the course of a generation. Land ownership, organization of churches and schools, and the rise of a small middle class all heralded the arrival of a people of substance."[18] Weeksville's population reflected this more optimistic picture, "of a people of substance."

Hunterfly Road

Hunterfly Road marked Weeksville's eastern boundary after the Civil War, as it had from the beginning. In 1860, the LeGrant family still lived in their old neighborhood. All five people in the LeGrant (now listed as "Grant") household remained together. Ann Simmons, Lydia LeGrant's mother, fifty-six years old, born in Columbia (i.e., Washington, D.C.) was listed as household head. Lydia (now called Mary Ann) was forty years old and listed her birthplace as Pennsylvania. James was thirty-two years old. He listed his birthplace as North Carolina (instead of the earlier South Carolina), but Edward Butler, age forty-two, still noted his birthplace as South Carolina. Ann E. Dixon, Lydia LeGrant's daughter, born in New York, was now thirteen years old. James Grant and Edward Butler were no longer listed as carpenter and shoemaker. They had taken to sea, James as a sailor and Edward as a rigger. Neither they nor Ann Simmons and Mary Ann Grant were listed as owning property (although we know from deeds that LeGrant did), and Ann Dixon was not attending school.

The LeGrant family now lived in a single-family house instead of the two-family house they had occupied in 1850 and 1855. Since James LeGrant and Edward Butler inherited life use and income from Graham's properties, they may have moved after court decisions confirmed the validity of Graham's will in 1857. It is possible that, by 1860, the LeGrants had built a new house, leaving Butler in their old one.

In 1865, the census taker omitted everyone in the Hunterfly Road neighborhood, including the LeGrant-Butler families. By 1870, however, the LeGrant-Simmons family appeared again, living in a single-family dwelling. Lydia LeGrant was listed as head of household, born in Pennsylvania, age forty-six, with property worth one thousand dollars. Her mother Ann Simons (*sic*) was born in Washington, D.C., age seventy-two. Ann Dixon, Lydia's daughter, was twenty-two years old. James LeGrant, born in South Carolina, was forty years old. Lydia LeGrant listed her occupation as a dressmaker, while James LeGrant had left the sea to resume his old work as a carpenter.[19]

In 1870, Edward Butler, age fifty, was back to working at his former occupation as a shoemaker after his seafaring days during the Civil War. He was now married to Mary, an Irish-born woman, aged fifty-two. They lived in a separate house next door to the LeGrant family. City directories generally listed this as 117 Rochester Avenue. In 1869, the first year that Butler appeared in the city directory, he was listed at Bergen n. Rochester Avenue. In 1871, he was listed at Rochester Avenue c. of Bergen. Beginning in 1871, he was listed at 117 Rochester Avenue, although in 1876, he was listed at 119 Rochester Avenue, with his business in "boots and shoes" at 117 Rochester Avenue. City directories for 1878, 1879, and 1880 continued to Butler at 117 Rochester Avenue. After 1880, he did not appear in city directories.[20]

Lydia Simmons LeGrant continued to pay taxes on a one-and-a-half-story house and lot on the east side of Rochester Avenue, valued at four hundred dollars, from 1869 (the first year that assessment records were kept) through 1874. If assessment records are accurate, however, she left the neighborhood by 1875. Perhaps she died. Coinciding with the probable final settlement of Francis P. Graham's estate, Edward Butler sold one lot on this block to John Flamer, on September 1, 1875. On September 9, 1875, Butler and James LeGrant sold another lot to Emma Campbell. This may have been Lydia LeGrant's house, where Campbell continued to reside with LeGrant's daughter Ann Dixon until 1880. On March 3, 1879, the heir of Henry Dixon (most likely Anne Dixon) sold a lot on this block to George O. and Clarissa Birch, both from Virginia.

By 1870, Lydia LeGrant's neighborhood was a multicultural mixture of African Americans (from Virginia, South Carolina, Washington, Pennsylvania, Spain, and South America) and European Americans (from Ireland, Prussia and Baden—in what is now Germany, France, and New York State). In 1870, Irish-born grocer John McMurn lived north of the LeGrant-Campbell-Dixon household, for example, on the corner of Dean Street and Rochester Avenue. McMurn had recently moved here from the corner of Butler and Franklin, where he worked as a liquor dealer. In 1868, he purchased a small two-story frame house with a broad piazza on two sides at the corner of Dean Street and Rochester Avenue (later listed as 99 Rochester Avenue) from Sarah Corprew and her children. On July 3, 1875, the *Eagle* interviewed McMurn at his house for his work as a juror in the famous trial of Henry Ward Beecher, pastor of Plymouth Church in Brooklyn. Beecher, perhaps the most famous preacher in the United States, had been accused of adultery, but the jury—with McMurn included—acquitted him. On August 4, 1876, McMurn became a U.S. citizen. From 1879 to 1881, the city directory listed him as "real estate," living on 186 Buffalo Avenue, where he died of apoplexy in January 1880.[21]

In 1880, the census listed Edward and Mary Butler as living at 119 Rochester Avenue, with Anne Dixon (Lydia LeGrant's daughter), age twenty-eight, living at 117 Rochester Avenue as the adopted daughter of fifty-eight-year-old Emma Campbell, born in South Carolina. The Birch family lived three doors away. After 1880, the LeGrant-Butler-Dixon families disappeared from extant historical records.[22]

Today, Kingsborough housing occupies the LeGrant-Butler block. South of this block, the Weeksville Heritage Society owns three small original houses (and one replica of a house that burned in the 1980s) along Hunterfly Road, mute reminders of the original Weeksville community. A complex mosaic of detailed evidence from a wide variety of sources suggests that these houses were built before the Civil War, perhaps by James LeGrant for his uncle Francis P. Graham or perhaps on land near Citizens' Union Cemetery. They were moved to their current site by Ferdinand F. Volckening, a German-American builder who purchased this property in 1863 and moved at least three rental houses there by 1874 and perhaps one more about 1883.

At first glance, evidence about these houses from architectural details seems to conflict with evidence from written records and archaeological material. On the one hand, architectural evidence convincingly suggests that the Hunterfly Road houses were built before the Civil War. In terms of both style and physical features, these houses reflected earlier construction styles, common to pre–Civil War buildings. All of them were built with their roof ridges parallel to the street, for example. After the 1830s, urban builders in the northeast more typically constructed either row houses or individual buildings with their gable ends to the street, reflecting new Greek Revival form and saving space on crowded urban blocks.

All of the Hunterfly Road houses were also constructed with heavy timber framing, using posts and beams. Beginning in the 1830s, urban houses were typically constructed with lightweight studs and balloon framing. Use of heavy timber framing on Hunterfly Road may have reflected relatively easy access to woods and relatively difficult access to sawn lumber. These construction techniques strongly suggest a pre–Civil War building date, however.[23]

Two of the Hunterfly Road houses—1700 and 1702–04—contain interior fireplaces. Again, beginning in the 1830s, wood stoves were more commonly used in residential construction. Fireplaces might be included in new construction for upscale houses, but as an amenity for evening relaxation rather than as a primary source of heat.

These Hunterfly Road houses reflect various vernacular forms, suggesting that they may have been built over time, rather than all at once. Each is a different design. One, at 1698 Bergen Street, is a hall and parlor plan, common to many houses, urban and rural, throughout the United States. The second, 1700 Bergen Street, is a three-bay house, broad side to the street, story and a half, with a chimney at the gable end of the house. And 1702–04 Bergen Street is a single-story double house, with a central chimney that gives access to interior fireplaces for apartments on each side. (The residence at 1706–08 Bergen Street was another double house, two stories, with a central chimney. The original burned about 1980. The current building on that site is a reconstruction, so it is not considered here.)

Using such architectural evidence, Loring McMillen dated these houses as early as 1830 for the New York City Landmarks Preservation Commission. Archaeologist Roselle Henn supported this conclusion, suggesting that 1702–04 Bergen Street, the one-story two-family house, appeared to date to the first half of the nineteenth century. In 2004, Neil Larson reached a similar conclusion, arguing, "The form and design of the double house on Hunterfly Road [1702–04] clearly associates it to vernacular architecture of the second quarter of the nineteenth century. This determination is supported by the physical presence of hewn framing members and the dimension of sawn rafters typical of this period." If these houses had been built on this site before 1850, as some have argued, they would have been constructed for one of two owners. As Neil Larson suggested, they may have been used as farm tenant houses while the land was owned by Samuel Garrittsen. Alternatively, they may have been built by or for Samuel Bouton, who purchased this land from the Garrittsen estate in 1839.[24]

Samuel Bouton, a "wealthy resident" of Brooklyn, most likely used this area for dairy farming. He was a longtime Democratic politician from Brooklyn's Seventh Ward, and he made much of his considerable income (more than ten thousand dollars in 1849) from real estate investments. City directories, however, called him a milkman or a dairyman. He was one of those farmers who sold swill milk from cows fed on slop. He also owned a small garden farm of about sixteen acres known as the Beelman farm, south of Weeksville, "about half a mile east of the county poorhouse" in Flatbush. Throughout 1844 and the first half of 1845, Bouton advertised this farm for sale for three thousand dollars. It had, he reported, "a good two-story house, with wings at the ends, large columns in front, and piazza in the rear—also a good barn; and a well of excellent water is near the door." There were "pleasant woodlands on the east, west, and north sides." It is quite possible that Bouton purchased his Weeksville property in 1839 as an adjunct to this farm. Perhaps also he bought it on speculation, hoping to increase his investment by selling his lots to developers as the city moved east.[25]

Either way, these houses would have been oriented toward Hunterfly Road, a main pathway leading to the salt marshes at Jamaica Bay. A tavern (listed as owned by John Vanderveer at Keuter's Hook on Sidney's 1849 map but later known as Wohlke's tavern) stood just south of the current site of these houses. By the 1850s and perhaps earlier, picnic grounds along Hunterfly Road south of the tavern attracted large parties of both European Americans and African Americans from all over Brooklyn. High on the hill, a bit farther toward Jamaica Bay, Citizens' Union Cemetery was organized in 1851. Travelers to the tavern, picnic grounds, and cemetery would have passed directly in front of the Hunterfly Road houses, making Hunterfly Road a major thoroughfare, not a backwater.

A pre-1850 construction date for these houses fits the architectural evidence. It would also be consistent with the first major period of settlement of the area. Between 1840 and 1850, Weeksville's population expanded rapidly. In each of these years, census data show that more than 80 percent of the population was African American. Therefore, if these houses were built before 1850, it is likely that they were built by and for African Americans.[26]

The pre-1850 construction date for these houses receives support not only from the physical evidence of the houses themselves but also from the very first map that mentioned the village of Weeksville. In 1849, J. C. Sidney published *Sidney's Map of Twelve Miles around New York*, which presented a regional view of the whole New York City area. In the area just east of the city of Brooklyn, Sidney drew a collection of houses just south of the Long Island Railroad, and he labeled this "Weeksville." East of Weeksville stood Suydam's Pond, and just east of the pond, along the line of the railroad, stood the home of Maria Suydam, widow of Moses Suydam. South of Weeksville, a long hill ran east and west. On top of the hill, on its west side above Weeksville, stood another small collection of houses that Sidney labeled "Crow Hill." From Maria Suydam's house, Hunterfly Road ran south over the middle of the hill. On the south side of this hill, Sidney showed three houses along the west side of Hunter-fly Road, in almost the exact location of the current Weeksville houses. The center house is noted as wider than the other two, much as the current double house at 1702–04 Bergen Street is wider than its neighbors.

Some of Sidney's drawing makes us doubt its accuracy as a detailed picture of Weeksville's built environment, however. Deeds from the 1840s and census records in 1850 suggest that many people—including the LeGrant, Butler, and Graham families—lived in the neighborhood south of the Suydam house and north of the current Hunterfly Road houses, but Sidney showed no buildings here on his map. Nor is it likely that the houses in the area that Sidney labeled Weeksville were not arranged in such a regular way. These inaccuracies suggest that Sidney may have taken artistic license with his drawing.

In fact, at least four other sources—a map, a collection of artifacts, a newspaper article, and tax assessment records—offer compelling evidence that the Hunterfly Road houses now owned by the Weeksville Heritage Center did not exist on their current site until after the Civil War, most likely not until the early 1870s. They suggest either that Sidney placed the Hunterfly Road houses in the wrong location in 1849 or that he drew houses that stood for only a few years.

In 1869, Matthew Dripps published *Map of the City of Brooklyn*. Dripps's map was a remarkably detailed record of land patterns and houses throughout Brooklyn, including the village of Weeksville. Like Sidney, Dripps indicated the location of individual houses. These included the houses owned by the LeGrant, Butler, and Graham families on Hunterfly Road on block 1350, just north of the current site of the Weeksville houses. Dripps did not, however, show any houses on the current site of the Hunterfly Road houses.

Dripps documented landscape and buildings sometime after 1865, since his map included the new Roman Catholic Orphanage for boys. Construction on this building began in 1865, and one wing of it opened in the fall of 1868. This was a three-story stone building, 170 feet across the front with 170-foot wings on either end, built on the block bounded by Troy and Albany Streets and Wyckoff and Warren Avenues. Operated by the Sisters of St. Joseph, it was designed to accommodate twelve hundred boys. Although Dripps's map identified this orphanage, the map was not current in all its information. It listed S. Bouton as owner of the current site of the Weeksville houses, although Bouton's estate sold this property in 1863.

It could be, of course, that Dripps's map was wrong and that Sidney's map was correct. But three other sources—archaeological evidence, a list of Samuel Bouton's real estate sold at auction in 1863, and assessment records—support the accuracy of Matthew Dripps's map in terms of its depiction of the current site of the Hunterfly Road houses.

One historian—Robert Swan—and several archaeologists found no evidence of human habitation on the current site of the Hunterfly Road houses before the Civil War. In 1978, based on evidence from the 1849 Sidney map (which is ambiguous about possible houses on the Hunterfly Road site) and city directories, Robert Swan suggested that "these houses were not built until after 1863, probably after the Civil War."[27]

Between 1978 and 1982, archaeology students from the City University of New York worked on the Weeksville site. From 2000 to 2003, Wank, Adam, Slavin Architects (WASA) conducted further archaeological studies, as part of the Weeksville Heritage Society's Master Plan for restoration and interpretation of these structures. One of the earliest artifacts recovered from archaeological digs was a bottle manufactured between 1857 and 1870 under the cellar of 1698 Bergen Street, suggesting that no house could have been located earlier on that site. Most artifacts date to the 1870s and later. In 2000, WASA found this archival and archaeological evidence compelling and concluded that the houses were all built after the Civil War. They did not find "any document that supports the existence of the houses before ca. 1869." In 2001, by using census records, city directories, and assessment records to augment maps and deeds, Joan H. Geismar placed possible human settlement here a bit earlier, arguing that "this house cluster may have been established by about 1865." In 2009, Geismar issued a report on the total collection of artifacts assembled from various archaeological digs from 1978 to 1982 and from 2000 to 2003. Based on cataloging and analysis of 8,314 mostly fragmentary artifacts and 3,690 faunal specimens, Geismar suggested "that the houses probably were first occupied in the early- to mid-1860s."[28]

Assuming that both Dripps's map and the archaeological evidence are accurate, we can reasonably hypothesize that no houses existed on this property before the 1860s. Neither the Garrittsen family nor Samuel Bouton built any houses—at least any permanent houses—on that site.

This hypothesis receives strong support from a list of Samuel Bouton's real estate sold at auction in 1863. Samuel Bouton died in 1862. When his estate—"mostly located in East Brooklyn"—went up for auction in May 1863, the Brooklyn Eagle published a list of properties sold. "The prices brought are good," noted the Eagle, "as good in fact as in peace times. Much of it was bought for permanent investments and some for speculative purposes." The list included eight properties listed as "house and lot," with an average price of $2,720. The auction also included nineteen listings of forty-eight separate lots, without houses. These lots were all located along or near Hunterfly Road, on Rochester and Buffalo Avenues and Bergen and Wyckoff Streets. They were almost all 25 feet wide by about 128 feet deep, and they ranged in price from $75 for ordinary lots to $150 and $155 for corner lots (one on the southwest corner of Rochester and Bergen and one on the northeast corner of Rochester and Wyckoff). Among these lots were several on Hunterfly Road, between Wyckoff (later St. Marks) and Bergen Streets, on the current site of the Weeksville Heritage houses.[29]

Most likely, Bouton's lots were hilly and relatively wild, typical of other undeveloped land in the area. The Brooklyn Eagle described this territory in 1868: "Midway between Weeksville and East New York, there is a territory, half a mile in breadth from Atlantic avenue to the city line at East New York avenue, and more than a mile in length from East New York to Weeksville, on which are scarcely any houses, and where the primitive forest and the tangled underbrush still retain unchallenged occupancy of the soil." In 1868, the *Eagle* highlighted the difficulty of developing this virtual wilderness. Walking "from Atlantic Avenue to the city line, along the old Hunterfly road" revealed "the vast extent of the waste spaces which yet exist within the city limits, on grades inaccessible to city streets and improvements, involving vast alternations of elevation and depression, and requiring fabulous expenditures of money before they can be made fairly habitable by the overflow of our city population." The land was cheap, noted the *Eagle*, "$300 per lot, whole blocks at a bargain," so people bought it "for speculative purposes, in hope of what the grand 9th Ward boulevards may effect in bringing that part of the city into the real estate market, rather than in any sober expectancy of immediate occupation of the land for building purposes."[30]

Ferdinand F. Volckening, German-born carpenter, builder, and architect, was one of those speculators who purchased lots in these "waste spaces." Volckening had been born about 1827 in Hanover, Germany, and became a naturalized U.S. citizen on March 28, 1854, joining Gustav Volckening, perhaps a brother, emigrating from Hamburg, whose naturalization was recorded on March 10, 1854. By the 1860s, Ferdinand may have joined Gustav in the grocery business, since the 1862 and 1863 directories listed "Frederick F. Volckening" and "F. F. Volckening" as a grocer. Gustav continued in the grocery business, but from 1870 to 1890 city directories listed Ferdinand Volckening (sometimes noted as Frederick K. Volckening) as a builder, located at 19 Columbus Place. In 1890, the directory listed him as an architect. In 1873, Ferdinand Volckening had a brief fling with politics, when he ran for the Democratic General Committee from the Twenty-Fifth Ward. Interestingly, Ferdinand Volckening never appeared in census records, although Gustav Volckening did. Ferdinand Volckening died on December 17, 1898, at age seventy-one.[31]

On May 14, 1863, Volckening paid $445 to John W. Hunter and Henry N. Conklin, executors of Samuel Bouton's estate, for lots 2, 3, 4, 41, 42, and 43 on block 1885 (presumably surveyed from Garrittsen's original lot 21). According to the list of Bouton's real estate at auction, these were undeveloped lots without houses. Lots 2, 3, and 4 faced Hunterfly Road, while lots 41, 42, and 43 faced Wyckoff Street. Eleven years later, Volckening purchased another nearby lot, on the corner of Herkimer Street and Buffalo Avenue, from J. Fassoscht.[32]

Table 5.1.Assessed Valuation, F. F. Volckening, Wards 9 and 24, Brooklyn, 1869–90

Ward	# on Ward Map	Block	Location	Name	Year	Assessed Value (1870s Dollars)
9		592	Wyckoff St. north side	Volckening, F. F.	1869	400
9		592	Wyckoff St. north side	Volckening, F. F.	1870	400
9		592	Wyckoff St. north side	Volckening, F. F.	1870	400
9		592	Wyckoff St. north side	Volckening, F. F.	1871	400
9		592	Wyckoff St. north side	Volckening, F. F.	1872	400
24	4B	592	St. Mark's Ave. north side	Volckening, F. F.	1873	400
24	4B	592	St. Mark's Ave. north side	Volckening, F. F.	1874	1,800
24	18	185	Bergen St. south side	Volckening, F. F.	1881	1,800
24	115	185	St. Mark's Ave. north side	Volckening, F. F.	1881	1,800
24	18	185	Bergen St. south side	Volckening, F. F.	1882	1,800
24	115	185	St. Mark's Ave. north side	Volckening, F. F.	1882	250
24	115	185	St. Mark's Ave. north side	Volckening, F. F.	1883	1,800 (crossed out)
24	18	185	Bergen St. south side	Volckening, F. F.	1884	600
24	115	185	St. Mark's Ave. north side	Volckening, F. F.	1884	250
24	18	185	Bergen St. south side	Volckening, F. F.	1885	995
24	115	185	St. Mark's Ave. north side	Volckening, F. F.	1885	250
24	115	185	Bergen St. south side	Volckening, F. F.	1886	250
24	115	185	St. Mark's Ave. north side	Volckening, F. F.	1886	1,000 (plus?)
24	18	185	Bergen St. south side	Volckening, F. F.	1886	1,400 (crossed out)
24	18	185	Bergen St. south side	Volckening, F. F.	1887	250
24	18	185	Bergen St. south side	Volckening, F. F.	1888	2,000
24	18	185	Bergen St. south side	Volckening, F. F.	1889	250
24	18	185	Bergen St. south side	Volckening, F. F.	1890	2,000

Source: New York City Municipal Archives.

Volckening purchased these lots because he saw an opportunity to develop rental properties on Hunterfly Road for working-class families. He made a wise choice. For more than one hundred years, Volckening and his heirs owned this property, until the Society for the Preservation of Weeksville and Bedford-Stuyvesant bought it in 1968.

Assessment records for Volckening support the assertion that no houses existed on either the Hunterfly Road or Wyckoff lots when Volckening purchased them in 1863. Furthermore, they indicate that no houses existed here until 1874. Tax assessments for this area began in

1869. From 1869 to 1873, Volckening's assessment was four hundred dollars, consistent with the price of empty lots. Beginning in 1874, however, his assessments rose to eighteen hundred, suggesting that houses now stood on this location.

In sum, archaeological material, the 1863 list of Bouton's properties, Dripps's 1869 map, and assessment records for Ferdinand Volckening provide compelling evidence that no houses existed on the Hunterfly Road site before at least the mid-1860s and most likely not until 1873–74. Archaeological studies revealed no traces of habitation before the mid-1860s, at the earliest. The *Eagle*'s list of Bouton's property showed only empty lots on Hunterfly Road in 1863. Volckening's 1863 purchase price—$445 for six lots—was extremely low compared to the *Eagle*'s 1868 estimate of $300 per lot, supporting the idea that his land included "primitive forest" and "tangled underbrush," unadorned by buildings. No structure appeared on this site on the detailed Dripps's map of 1869. And Volckening was not assessed for houses on these lots until 1874.

How can we reconcile the seeming contradiction between architectural evidence, which strongly suggests that these houses were constructed before the Civil War, and evidence from Dripps's 1869 map, archaeological studies, newspapers, and assessment records that clearly indicate that these lots had no houses on them before the 1860s at the earliest? Understanding Volckening's development plan helps us reconcile this conflicting data. Volckening cut costs by buying older houses from nearby lots, moving them to his new property, and fixing them up as rental units. These houses were constructed before the Civil War, but Volckening moved them to Hunterfly Road only after the Civil War. This hypothesis allows us to respect both architectural evidence—compelling in its indication that the Hunterfly Road houses were built before the Civil War—and archaeological, map, newspaper, and assessment sources, which overwhelmingly argue that no houses stood on this site until the mid-1860s, at the earliest, and probably not until the early 1870s. At least by 1874, however, Ferdinand Volckening had moved at least three houses onto his Hunterfly Road property.[33]

Evidence is not conclusive, but it is possible that 1700 Bergen Street, standing between 1698 Bergen Street (facing the main road) and the double family house at 1702–04, may not have been placed on these lots until the early 1880s. A building permit dated December

11, 1883, apparently referred to 1700 Bergen Street, noting that it had a "mortice & tenoned" framing structure. As Edward Chappell has pointed out, this might be compared with other building permits from the 1880s to see whether other houses of the period were commonly mortised and tenoned. If, however, building permits were routinely used for structures that were moved as well as for those that were constructed in situ, this might not give an accurate portrayal of either new construction techniques or date of construction for 1700 Bergen Street. To add to the confusion, in 1883 Volckening spent $350 on one more piece of property, a twenty-five-foot strip of land extending from Bergen Street to St. Mark's Avenue, adjoining his Hunterfly Road lots on the west side.[34]

These Hunterfly Road houses do share certain similarities—most obviously their interior woodworking and windows. If Volckening did indeed move these houses from nearby lots to Hunterfly Road, he undoubtedly used his skills as a professional builder to fix them up, perhaps making his own woodwork or purchasing materials for two or three houses at the same time, from the same source. As Neil Larson has suggested, fireplace surrounds that are very similar to those located in the Hunterfly Road houses were readily available through local builders' supply companies. It is even possible that Volckening purchased much of this material at auction from the sale of a carpenter shop on Bergen Street, close to downtown, in 1873.[35]

Evidence is circumstantial, but Volckening may have purchased at least one of these houses from the estate of Francis P. Graham. Graham had died in 1853. Not until 1857, however, did the court confirm the validity of Graham's will, leaving life income from all his property to James LeGrant and Edward Butler but giving all his real and personal property to his lawyer and friend N. Bergasse La Bau.[36]

In 1862, just a year before Volckening's purchase, Francis Graham's will was finally probated, and N. Bergasse La Bau sold much of Graham's land to Daniel H. McDonnell. In the decade that followed, Graham's lands changed hands rapidly. There are forty-four transfers of land between June 1862 and November 1873, most if not all recording a transition from African American ownership to European American owners.[37]

On block 1350, just north of the Weeksville houses, much of the land changed hands in the 1860s. In 1860, James and Jane Moody sold their small piece to Patrick Heney, European American philanthropist, who gave much of his estate to the Roman Catholic Orphan Asylum. John Flamer, an African American who owned several pieces of land in Weeksville, sold his lots on block 1350 to John Peterson and Frederick Klem in 1864. Sarah Corprew, widow of Doxie Corprew, sold their land on Rochester Avenue to John McMurn in 1868. Charles and Millie Lewis also sold their land to John McMurn in 1868. Nathan C. B. Thomas and Henrietta Thomas sold their land to Jane Smith in 1868. "Widow of Francis P. Graham" (who could be either Graham's first wife or his last wife) sold her remaining land to David R. Brown, John and Mary McGrand, Patrick Heney, and Caroline R. Ritter in 1871. For the most part, new owners retained the historic buildings. All but one of these buildings were still marked on the Sanborn insurance map in 1888.[38]

The rest of Graham's land in Weeksville was tied up in legal limbo until it was sold in 1871 and 1872, just about the time that houses appeared on Volckening's Hunterfly Road property. Daniel H. McDonnell purchased four acres on the east side of Hunterfly Road in 1862 and sold them at public auction in March 1871, as part of a foreclosure. Almost certainly, this plot was undeveloped, since it was located among the strips of woodlots parceled out to several different owners. The rest of Graham's land, however, likely contained several rental houses, and it was the subject of a lengthy court action settled finally in 1872.[39]

The saga of legal action, as befits Francis P. Graham's life, was complicated. In 1821, at the time of Graham's deportation to Africa for his supposed role in the Denmark Vesey rebellion, Graham's first wife, Sarah, had stayed in Charleston. When Sarah refused to join Graham in New York, he married at least twice more. In the early 1870s, Sarah Graham was still living in Charleston. But she was not about to give up her rights in Graham's estate. She brought several suits against N. B. La Bau, executor of Graham's will and inheritor of his estate, arguing that she should have dower rights in Graham's property. In January 1872, she finally won her case for twenty-six lots on Albany, Troy, and Rochester Avenues in Weeksville. In February, she brought another suit against

La Bau to recover dower rights in an additional five acres on the boulevard. When she won these cases, she sold much of her land on October 23, 1872, to John Flamer, a major African American landholder and Republican politician in Weeksville.[40]

By the terms of Graham's will, the LeGrant and Butler families had received life interest in all of Graham's estate, and this 1872 verdict in favor of Sarah Graham must have cut significantly into their regular income. The case was not yet closed, however. In 1877, the *Eagle* reported on a new action regarding Graham's estate, most likely brought by Graham's executor N. B. La Bau, whose own wife Mary, daughter of Commodore Vanderbilt, was then involved in contesting her father's will. "The case promises to be one of considerable litigation, and will no doubt be food for much gossip among the legal fraternity," noted the *Eagle*. But the *Eagle* printed no further reports of this case.[41]

Did Volckening take advantage of the turnover of properties from Graham's estate in the early 1870s to purchase buildings from Graham's estate and move them to his own lots on Hunterfly Road? The timing suggests that this was quite possible. It is also possible that Volckening bought houses located on property owned by the Mount Pleasant Cemetery (formerly Citizens' Union Cemetery). Original investors in the cemetery purchased the property in 1851, but when they could not pay the mortgage, it reverted to the original owner. In 1865, ten African Americans formed a new corporation, the Mount Pleasant Cemetery, to repurchase this property. When the corporation sold the cemetery five years later, in 1870, most of the bodies were reburied in Greenwood Cemetery. In 1869, just before the sale, Matthew Dripps recorded at least six houses on or near the property, including the large home of Alexander Duncan and his family. The Duncan house remained on site at least until 1887. A second house was still standing in 1923. The other four houses, however, may well have been moved in the early 1870s to other locations.[42]

Whether or not the Hunterfly Road houses were located originally on land owned by Francis P. Graham, on former Citizens' Union Cemetery land, or on land owned by Lydia LeGrant or Edward Butler, they may have been constructed by James LeGrant, Francis P. Graham's nephew and the only carpenter—either African American or European American—listed in census records for Weeksville in 1850.[43]

In 1850 and 1855, the census listed LeGrant as living in a two-family home with his wife Lydia Simmons LeGrant and shoemaker Edward Butler, another one of Graham's protégés. It is possible, even likely, that LeGrant built both his own house and many other houses in Weeksville, including perhaps the house at the northeast corner of Rochester Avenue and Bergen Street. It would not be unusual if Graham hired LeGrant to build rental housing in the late 1840s and 1850s on lots that Graham owned elsewhere in Weeksville.[44]

The possibility that the Hunterfly Road houses were built by James LeGrant, a South Carolina-born carpenter, gains credence from the form of the houses themselves. Features of both 1700 and 1702–04 hint at a builder with southern origins. The chimney at the gable end of 1700 is a common characteristic of houses along the eastern seaboard, from the Chesapeake area on south. The structure at 1702–04 is even more intriguing. Down bracing in the corner of its framing structure is unusual in northern areas. As Bernard Herman has noted, such down bracing is more common in southern building traditions, at least in the mid-Atlantic areas of Virginia, Maryland, and Delaware.

As a double house with a central chimney, 1702–04 might reflect New England models. It also suggests housing designed and built for working people, both enslaved and free. In particular, it bears a striking resemblance to cabins built for enslaved people by a Yankee-born plantation owner in South Carolina, described by Frederick Law Olmsted in 1852. The building at 1702–04 is a single-story structure with a central chimney and two front doors. It is 21 by 43 feet, designed to hold two families. (An attached back shed was probably added in the 1880s.) Each family had three rooms. The front door opened to a main room, 10 feet 7.5 inches to 10 feet 11.5 inches wide by 15 feet 3.5 inches deep, with a fireplace on the side facing the center and a closet between the fireplace and rear wall. Two bedrooms, the front one 9 feet 4.5 inches wide by 8 feet 10 inches deep and the rear one 9 feet 4.5 inches wide by 6 feet deep, were on the outside walls, each with a window at the front or rear.[45]

In December 1852, Frederick Law Olmsted, best known for his work as a landscape architect, designer of Central Park in New York and later of Prospect Park in Brooklyn, toured the southern U.S. to observe slavery firsthand. In the course of his travels, he visited a South Carolina

Down bracing in the corner, 1704 Bergen Street, December 2003. Photo by author.

plantation and described housing that almost exactly duplicated the house on Hunterfly Road:

> Each cabin was a framed building, the walls boarded and whitewashed on the outside, lathed and plastered within, the roof shingled; forty-two feet long, twenty-one feet wide, divided into two family tenements, each twenty-one by twenty-one, each tenement divided into three rooms—one, the common household apartment, twenty-one by ten; each of the others (bed-rooms) ten by ten. There was a brick fireplace in the middle of the long side of each living room, the chimneys rising in one, in the middle of the roof. Besides these rooms, each tenement had a cock—entered by steps from the household room. Each tenement is occupied, on an average, by five persons. There were in them closets, with locks and keys, and a varying quantity of rude furniture. . . . Each cabin has a front and back door, and each room a window, closed by a wooden shutter, swinging outward, on hinges.[46]

Similarity, as Edward Chappell has pointed out, is suggestive but does not by itself prove derivation:

> While the form of 1702/04 Bergen Street is quite similar to what were in the 1840s and '50s considered model housing for enslaved Low Country workers, the Weeksville pair is not necessarily *derived* from them, or from slave quarters in general. Duplexes were a relatively economical means of building houses, and center-chimney pairs were built for both black and white mill workers in cities like Savannah, Georgia and Petersburg, Virginia, through the second half of the 19th century.[47]

Although the houses that Olmsted described were built specifically for people in slavery, they may also have reflected up-to-date plans for workers' houses, whether North or South. Olmsted noted that the plantation owner was a Yankee, a New England farmer's son, and a former merchant and manufacturer, whose wife had grown up on the plantation. He operated his holdings efficiently, with a "practical talent" common to New Englanders. His lands included a large barn with a steam engine to thresh the rice, and he was also very likely up-to-date on model workers' housing.

Whatever patterns these South Carolina houses followed, whether they were indigenous to the region or an extension of New England workers' housing, they were undoubtedly constructed by African American carpenters. Mr. X was proud of the blacksmiths, carpenters, and mechanics, all enslaved, who worked on his plantation, and he noted that "they exercised as much ingenuity and skill as the ordinary mechanics that he used to employ in New England." Mr. X "pointed out to me," noted Olmsted, "some carpenter's work, a part of which had been executed by a New England mechanic, and a part by one of his own hands, which indicated that the latter was much the best workman."[48]

The building at 1702–04 was a double family house built with post-and-beam construction and was identical in plan to at least one example of South Carolina low country African American housing. The fact that James LeGrant, the only local carpenter in Weeksville in 1850, was born in South Carolina and lived in a two-family house himself lends credence to the hypothesis that LeGrant may have constructed 1702–04 before the Civil War, perhaps as rental housing for his uncle Francis

P. Graham or perhaps as his own house on his new wife's property. At least ten houses in Weeksville were listed in the 1850 census as two-family dwellings. It seems likely that Ferdinand Volckening moved one or more (1702–04 and 1706–08 were both double houses) of these two-family houses to his new lots on Hunterfly Road after the Civil War, certainly by 1874.

Hunterfly Road, Social Context, 1870s

In 1870, we can trace people in the general neighborhood of Hunterfly Road by identifying the approximate route of the census taker. Frederick Kammen, a German-born grocery and liquor dealer, owned a tavern at the corner of Buffalo Avenue and Wyckoff Street. The census taker listed several other families nearby, most likely living in the "old houses" mentioned in a description of this area in the *Eagle* in 1887. Two doors away on one side lived a Virginia-born African American who listed his occupation as "doctor's servant." Two doors down on the other side lived an Irish couple who kept a furniture store.

Six families with a total of seventeen people (all but one of them listed as Black or Mulatto) lived in the neighborhood of Hunterfly Road, probably near the corner of Buffalo Avenue and Wyckoff Street rather than in the current Hunterfly Road houses. With the exception of two boarders, these were all nuclear family units. Four of the six families included only husbands and wives. Of the two families with children, one family had one child at home and the other had two children.[49]

Charles Tillman, a fifty-eight-year-old seaman, born in New York, lived with his Pennsylvania-born wife, Mary Ann Tillman, age forty-seven, and their daughter Josephine, age twenty-six, in one of the duplexes. John Till, forty-two years old, a cook in a hotel, and his wife, Rachel, thirty-five years old, born in Pennsylvania, who "works on Steamboat," shared the double house with the Tillmans.

Three of the workers—Jacob Pearson, musician; Rebecca Pearson, teacher; and Alfred Cornish, cabinetmaker—worked in skilled trades or professions. Jacob and Rachel Pearson, musician and teacher, aged forty-seven and forty-three, both born in New York, lived in a separate house (probably 1700), befitting their slightly higher occupational status. Alfred Cornish (aged twenty-eight), cabinetmaker, and his wife

Isbella (twenty-five), lived on "Rochester Avenue, near Bergen," according to the 1870 census. They had two small children, Frances (aged two) and William (aged six months). Isbella took in a boarder, Thomas Taylor, a twenty-five-year-old tobacconist, born in Virginia, to help with expenses. She also took care of a seven-year-old boy, Samuel Bailey.

Richard Carman (hostler) and Louisa Carman, aged forty-three and fifty-two, shared a duplex with William H. Porter (expressman) and Hortence Porter, aged twenty-eight and twenty-one. All but Louisa had been born in New York State. Louisa was European American, born in France.

Except for Rachel Till's work on a steamboat and Rebecca Pearson's teaching, all the women were listed as "keeping house," or "at home." All the adults were literate except for Isbella Cornish and Thomas Taylor, who could read but not write, and Richard Carman, who could neither read nor write. None of the children were of school age. Both the Cornish children were too young (an infant and a toddler); Josephine Tillman was twenty-six. Nearby, perhaps across the street in a farm carved out of former woodlands, Irish-born James Smith kept a dairy with his New York–born wife, Susan.

In 1873, physical changes in the neighborhood certainly had some impact on developing the Hunterfly Road house sites. In the winter, Suydam's Pond, a large spring-fed pond with no apparent outlet, flooded. It extended from Utica Avenue to Hunterfly Road, and its flooding left many Weeksville residents with "three to four feet of solid ice in their cellars for more than two months. When the thaw came the result was even worse . . . the water made itself at home in several parlors and refused to leave until the Spring months had almost passed away." Some of this flooding may have resulted from construction projects along Rochester Avenue, where the city was installing a new sewer line as well as a railroad, connecting with the Broadway line of cars. These new urban amenities may well have encouraged Ferdinand Volckening to move forward with developing his rental properties.[50]

Although almost all the families on Hunterfly Road were people of color, they lived in a racially mixed neighborhood. Fifteen years before, Weeksville had been almost entirely African American. Now, people of many colors and various places of birth increasingly lived next door to each other. Newcomers often had different occupations from Weeksville residents in the old days, too. Now people were often farmers and store-keepers or even inventors. People from England, Scotland, and Minnesota joined those from Hanover, Wurtenburg, and Hesse Darmstadt. Weeksville would never again be the rural enclave that had sheltered African Americans for so many years. Now the residents of Hunterfly Road were part of a world that included whites as well as blacks, immigrants as well as native-born people, and people who spoke many different languages.

Partly, the Civil War itself caused the change. Alfred Cornish, for example, lived in various houses in the Hunterfly Road area from at least 1870 until his death. He had grown up in Binghamton, New York. He was working as a painter when the war broke out, and he might well have stayed content with life in his hometown had he not felt called to greater duty. On April 8, 1863, when he was only eighteen years old, he joined Company F of the Massachusetts Fifty-Fourth Colored Volunteers in Boston under the command of colonel Robert Shaw, and he fought in South Carolina at the ill-fated battle of Fort Wagner. When the war was over, he was discharged in Charleston, South Carolina, on August 20, 1865. He lived briefly in New Jersey before settling first on "Rochester Avenue n. Bergen" and then at various other nearby locations, with his wife and two small children.

Cornish came to Brooklyn having experienced more of life and the world than most young men had thought possible before the war. He came with knowledge and hope, knowledge that he had helped to end slavery and hope that he could live freely as a full American citizen—with self-respect, respect from others, safety, and economic opportunity for himself and his family. He lived to see the transformation of his old neighborhood into a vibrant and ethnically diverse part of Brooklyn, poised to meet the dramatic changes of the twentieth century.[51]

6

"Part of This Magically Growing City"

Weeksville's Growth and Disappearance, 1880–1910

By the 1880s, Weeksville was clearly integrated into the city of Brooklyn.[1] A decade earlier, in 1874, the "whole district lying east of Bedford avenue was cultivated as farmlands and market gardens," with separate settlements surrounded by "old farm houses, with corn fields, meadows, and gardens," noted the *Brooklyn Eagle*. By 1884, all that had changed. The *Eagle* rejoiced that Bedford, Crow Hill, Weeksville, New Brooklyn, East Brooklyn, and Brownville were all "merged into the common city, and all distinctive lines have been obliterated." Along Fulton, Flatbush, and Atlantic Avenues, "brown stone stores and Philadelphia bricks have been erected by whole blocks, and now extend out to Rochester avenue, a distance of four miles from the Court House, and are nearly all occupied for business purposes," patronized by neighborhood residents.[2]

Such expansion was propelled by the completion of Eastern Parkway between 1870 and 1874. Designed by Frederick Law Olmsted and Calvert Vaux as the world's first parkway for pleasure travel, Eastern Parkway carried traffic from the Grand Army Plaza in downtown Brooklyn to Ralph Avenue, just west of Weeksville, and then to Evergreen Cemetery. It was also enhanced by completion of elevated railroads, which shortened travel time to downtown ferries.[3]

Expansion escalated after 1883, when the Brooklyn Bridge allowed foot and vehicle traffic to go directly from Brooklyn to New York City. Suddenly the hills of Bedford, Flatbush, Weeksville, and East New York became much easier to reach, and real estate developers eyed them eagerly for homes for middle-class families. In Flatbush, John Lefferts put more than five hundred lots of the old family farm up for auction in June 1887, to be developed as single-family homes. "The absurdity of devoting lands so desirable, central, and valuable to raising corn and potatoes," noted the auctioneer, "has finally induced the owner to part with lots." Lefferts's sale would result in the gradual loss of colonial Dutch farmhouses, to be replaced by individual frame houses and elegant brownstones.[4]

The effect of all this development was to flatten the hills, fill in the valleys, and create a large grid of streets across the landscape. "Eastern Parkway," noted one observer in 1888, "swept through the Bedford Hills—and leveled a great portion of them; gradually the great banks are being cut away and the hollows are being filled; the hill east of Bedford is almost gone; the remainder of the Clove road down about Malboneville is being obliterated; Crow Hill is losing its crown, and streets are being out through it; the hill is being dumped into the hollow and there is a general leveling going on."[5] This process went right through the middle of Weeksville, just as it did Bedford and Flatbush. By the early twentieth century, Weeksville still retained some of its mid-nineteenth century frame houses, but small townhouses and larger brownstones dominated the landscape.

The old Hunterfly Road remained an exception to this grid expansion. In the midst of all the new construction, Hunterfly Road reflected an earlier time. In October 1887, H. J. S. walked along the old road and described his trip for the *Brooklyn Eagle*. Hunterfly Road began "near to where Stuyvesant avenue crosses Fulton street." It ran "through the woods toward Canarsie and Flatlands and passed through the place known as Crow hill, a settlement of colored people that had an unenviable reputation for a long time. To-day the place is built up with good residences, stores, etc., and the neighborhood considered very nice in every way."

The road began about fifty feet west of Reid Avenue and Bainbridge Street and led south across a vacant lot toward Fulton Street. Past the carpenter shop of J. King, between Herkimer Street and Atlantic Avenue, Hunterfly Road remained open, with "half a dozen houses" along it. South of Atlantic Avenue, Hunterfly Road dipped down to a lower level, passing between "a very old farmhouse and stable on the west side" and "two other houses, doomed soon to disappear." Families listed on Hunterfly Road in the 1880 census were located on this northern section of the road.

South of where Pacific Street would have crossed had it been completed, Hunterfly Road led to the corner of Dean Street and Rochester Avenue. There the road turned east and was "being fast filled up." The east side of Rochester Avenue was leveled up, along with Dean Street and Utica Avenue, both "filled and graded, with houses built along Utica Avenue." All these street renovations created a dam confining Suydam's pond to one-eighth of a mile in length by about two hundred feet wide, one-third of its former size. The old Moses Suydam farm still stood opposite the pond, on the east side of Rochester Avenue near Dean Street. Census records for 1880 are ambiguous for homes and families in this area. The census taker either counted existing Hunterfly Road houses as listed on different streets or simply ignored the area that now includes the Kingsborough housing units and the block owned by the Weeksville Heritage Society.

South of the corner of Dean Street and Rochester Avenue, "several old houses" still stood along Hunterfly Road, most likely those built by Francis P. Graham and his neighbors in the late 1840s and 1850s. "A couple of hundred feet from the corner," the road turned south, diagonally across the block, along a hill then being leveled. It climbed the hill across Bergen Street to the corner of Buffalo and St. Marks Avenues, also "high ground, which is being cut down." Although H. J. S. mentioned no houses on this last block, this is the current site of the Weeksville Heritage Society houses. The road across both of these blocks was closed by 1887. In the first block, Hunterfly Road had been filled in. In the second block, it was closed off by Bosch's grocery store on the corner of St. Marks and Buffalo Avenues, both graded streets.

Before it was blocked off, Hunterfly Road had crossed the corner of St. Marks and Buffalo Avenue "diagonally to the southeast," H. J. S. explained. As it had been for many years, this corner formed a small neighborhood of homes and businesses, dominated by German families. Bosch's grocery store stood at the corner of St. Marks and Buffalo avenues (most likely on the northwest corner). On the northeast corner of that intersection stood Kohler's blacksmith and wheelwright shop. The 1880 census listed Charles Kohler, born in Saxony, age thirty-one, as a blacksmith, living with his wife Lena, age twenty-nine, also from

Saxony, their two children (Barbary, age two, and Lena, eight months) and boarder Charles Stinson, age fifty-nine, also a blacksmith, born in Schleswig, Germany. The Kohlers shared a house with the family of Devereux Bilyn (age thirty) and Kate Bilyn (age twenty-six) and their daughter Kate (age three), all born in New York. Devereux was a wheelwright. With them lived Elizabeth Gobel, a dressmaker, age twenty-four; Annie Gobel, age twenty-two, and Herman Gobel, age ten. This building was once known as Fred Cameron's, and it did "a thriving trade with farmers who passed over the Hunter fly to market, or those who traveled down that way for pleasure to Carstein Schriefer's Rising Sun tavern and on down to Canarsie." Some old houses stood beyond that, and six large willow trees stood in front of the shop and these houses. Four houses, "two of which are quite old," stood northeast of the corner of Buffalo Avenue and St. Mark's.[6]

On the southeast corner of Buffalo and St. Mark's stood Wohlke's Hotel. This most likely belonged to Fred Wohlke, listed in the 1880 census as age thirty-one, liquor dealer, born in Hanover, Germany. He lived with his wife Geismar, age twenty-nine, also from Hanover, and their one-year-old son William. Next door, a two-family house held the Cornelius and Amanda Coleman family, with their daughter Maria. The Colemans were African American, and both parents listed their birthplaces as Virginia.[7]

From St. Marks to Douglass Street, Hunterfly Road remained open, passing the ropewalk of Otto Morrison. Otto Morrison, age twenty-eight, had worked with his father John Morrison in their ropewalk at the southeast corner of Troy and Warren Streets, kitty corner from the new Roman Catholic orphanage. By 1869, this ropewalk was operated by R. & R. Barth, and Otto Morrison had started his own operation between Butler Street on the north and Douglas on the south, on the east side of Weeksville. In the 1870 census, Otto Morrison listed his occupation as "rope manufacturer," with real property worth three thousand and personal property worth five hundred dollars. Southeast of the ropewalk (between streets marked on the grid as Prospect and Park Places and Patchen and Howard Avenues) were the "old picnic grounds familiar to a large portion of the inhabitants of Brooklyn."[8]

South of the picnic grounds and west of Hunterfly Road stood a high hill along Butler Street, on top of which was "a two-story frame house

with wings, and a cupola in which are Gothic windows of stained glass."
This was Alexander Duncan's old home. Duncan had been an undertaker and caretaker of Citizens' Union Cemetery. From here, the Duncan family had "a magnificent view" all the way to Jamaica Bay.[9]

"The spirit of improvement," noted H. J. S., "like democracy, is a great
leveler, and the pass of the Aander Vly road will, ere another ten years
have fled into the misty past, have joined the Jamaica pass as a memory, and the Aander Vly road, which is still struggling for recognition
among the new made streets and against the . . . gentlemen with carts
and shovels who do what is called filling, will join the Cripplebush, the
old Clove, the King's Highway and other roads as a misty memory of
Brooklyn's early days."[10] A year later, in 1888, the *Eagle* noted both with
nostalgia and optimism, "Now is positively the last exhibition of those
different localities in anything like their natural form, for the level, the
compass and the carts are at work." "Within the next five years," pre-
dicted the *Eagle*, "the Bedford Hills will have nearly disappeared, and
inside of ten years there will be nothing left of them, and where they
stood will be graded streets and thousands of dwellings, a part of this
magically growing city."[11]

This prediction proved true, and Weeksville became part of this
transformation, with "an almost complete metamorphosis." In 1888, the
same year that the *Eagle* recorded "the last exhibition of those different
localities," the Sanborn Insurance Company published a detailed map of
the Weeksville area. Between then and 1904, when Sanborn published
its next area map, Weeksville experienced major building, demolition,
and rebuilding of its physical fabric. Developers constructed blocks and
blocks of frame Italianate row houses. In 1893, the *Eagle* reported, "The
old Hunterfly Road, as far as East New York, [had] nothing but farm
lands and cow pastures, all open, with a few dilapidated shanties and
cow sheds. All this has entirely disappeared. Fine streets, avenues, and
blocks of fine dwellings have taken their place."[12]

On Weeksville's eastern border, block 1350 provides a typical example. Block 1350 included the land where Francis P. Graham, Lydia Simmons, James LeGrant, Edward Butler, Nathan Thomas, Sarah Corprew,
James Moody, and others had created such a cosmopolitan neighborhood in the 1840s. After 1888, pre–Civil War structures on this block
were either demolished or moved. By 1904, they had been replaced on

north, east, and south sides of the block by Italianate frame row houses. On the south side of the block, facing the Hunterfly Road houses across Bergen Street, stood a series of frame residences, both one-story and two-story structures.

On the east side of block 1350 (on the west side of Buffalo Avenue, between Bergen and Dean Streets), a row of residences had been constructed before 1888. After 1888, similar residences filled in the block along Dean Street between Buffalo and Rochester Avenues.

Brooklyn's growth—and Weeksville's disappearance—brought terrible disruption to those of Weeksville's citizens who did not have clear title to their lands. Many of them lived near the old penitentiary, raising pigs and living peacefully in "odd little shanties," made of tin and boards, with a living/sleeping room, kitchen/storage area, and open windows on all four sides. In 1912, the *New York Herald* reported that only about a dozen squatter families remained. Many, like Bob Mitchell, the "lonely squatter of old Weeksville," had a hard time leaving. Mitchell's home at the corner of Rochester Avenue and Lincoln Place was torn down in 1910, to be replaced by new two-family row houses. Mitchell told one of the wreckers that "since I lost Mary Ann, it don't make much difference was becomes of me now, but if she were living to-day, not a mother's son of you would dare put an ax to that old shanty." After the wreckers tore down the house, threw the debris into their cart, and drove away, Mitchell leaned down to speak to all he had left, his old shaggy black spaniel dog. "Come Boy," he said. "You an' I are not going to part. We'll manage to pick up supper somehow tonight and find a bed of straw someplace. We are not much on porcelain bathtubs and janitors, or steam heat, are we, Boy? Or noisy squabbling tenants and rafts of children and landlords and the like? Not much." With that, local children who were his friends looked on in silence as he and his dog disappeared over the hill.[13]

Weeksville, Early Twentieth Century

In the late nineteenth century, Weeksville's institutions—churches, school, orphanage, and home for the aged—brought regional and national attention to the village. By the early twentieth century, however, both Zion Home for the Aged and the Howard Orphan Asylum

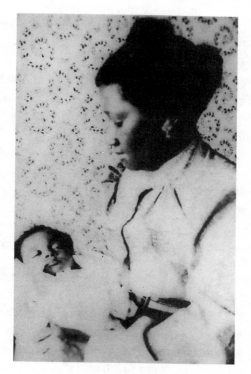

Katharine Harris Moore and child. Courtesy Weeksville Heritage Society, Percy Moore Collection.

had left Weeksville (the first in 1900 and the second in 1910). The people of Weeksville—many African Americans but increasing numbers of first-generation immigrants from Germany and Ireland—focused on day-to-day living in their urban neighborhood.

At first glance, Weeksville's twentieth-century residents seem to have lost some of the economic independence that had characterized the community as late as 1880. A sample of seventy families and 325 people on the east side of Weeksville in 1910, along Bergen Street, Hunterfly Road, Rochester Avenue, and Dean Street, revealed that only one family owned its own home. William J. Simpson was a retail merchant, owner of a grocery store, born in South Carolina, age fifty-two. Sixty-seven families rented their homes, including two families who were boarders.

Almost every adult in this sample of Weeksville's residents was literate. Only 3 adults out of 116 reported that they were unable to read or write. One of these was born in the West Indies and worked as a book-binder in a publisher's office.

Occupational opportunities and status seem to have declined since 1880, however. One hundred thirty-two residents in this area of Weeks-ville engaged in a total of forty different occupations, fewer than the fifty they had worked at in 1880. Unlike the 1880 census, the 1910 cen-sus listed the occupation of women who worked at home as "none." Women who worked for pay were laundresses, dressmakers, and mil-liners. Only ten people (two women and eight men) reported that they were out of work on April 15, 1901. Ninety-seven people reported that they were employed on that day.

Manufacturing jobs declined from 17.2 percent in the 1880 sample to 10.6 percent of the 1910 sample. In 1910, only fourteen people worked in manufacturing jobs. Except for one bookbinder and one machinist, all of these worked in the clothing trades: eight dressmakers, one fit-ter, two milliners, and one tailor. Of the 117 people (89.4 percent) who worked in service jobs, the most common were laundress (16), wagon driver (15), porter (12), servant (11), cook (9), and waiter/waitress (8). Others worked as actor/actress (2), boot black (1), butcher (1), chauffeur (1), chef (2), clerk (3), coachman (4), handler (2), housework (2), jani-tor/janitress (4), laborer (7), longshoreman (2), nurse (1), painter (1), plasterer (2), proprietor (1), retail grocer (1), salesman (1), selector in a cigar factory (1), sexton in a church (1), station agent for the railroad (1), stenographer (1), stevedore (2), steward in a club house (1), and store repairer (1).

In terms of status, workers in 1910 seem to have experienced a gen-eral decline from Weeksville workers in 1880. None were working at professional jobs, compared to 5.7 percent in 1880. Only two (1.5 per-cent), the proprietor and grocer, were owners/proprietors, down from 6.9 percent of the 1880 workforce. Twenty-one (15.9 percent), including actors, bookbinder, dressmakers, machinist, milliners, nurse, tailors, butcher, station agent, and stenographer, were skilled workers, down from 19.5 percent in 1880. The rest, 82.6 percent, were mostly unskilled workers, although plastering and painting demanded some training.

Differences in the proportion of Weeksville's population in various types of jobs may reflect differences in the samples themselves, since

Weeksville residents enjoying an evening of music, ca. 1900. Courtesy Weeksville Heritage Society, Percy Moore Collection.

the 1880 sample reflected Weeksville's western residents and the 1910 sample was of the eastern section. Without closer investigation of both neighborhoods, we cannot tell whether these data suggest a general change over time for all of Weeksville or whether they reflect the different character of areas within Weeksville itself.

Hunterfly Road, Social Context, 1890s–1910

By the 1890s, Hunterfly Road had become part of Brooklyn, but it remained a semirural neighborhood. "Bergen Street," noted the *Eagle* in 1893, "is very dark and lonely. Patches of sidewalk are few and so are the gas lamps." It is "the loneliest part of Crow Hill." Mary Jane Betts and Sarah Samuels, sisters, lived at 1698 Bergen Street (now one of the Weeksville Heritage Center houses). One November night in 1893, they walked to the Cosmopolitan Mission on Atlantic Avenue, near the corner of Stone Avenue, to hear Rev. J. Johnson, a preacher in the A.M.E. Church. Sarah Samuels carried a pistol, left from her days as a steward on a steamboat, while Mary Jane Betts armed herself with a whip, a foot and a half long and heavily loaded at the butt. Before she reached her meeting, Sarah collapsed and died, most likely from a heart attack.[14]

The 1900 U.S. census listed Mary Betts (forty-seven years old, born in Louisiana) as still living at 1698 Bergen Street. Her husband Abijah (sixty-one years old, born in New Jersey, working as a day laborer) and their eighteen-year-old daughter Beatrice (born in Washington, D.C.) lived with her.

The Cornish family shared this house with the Betts family. Alfred Cornish was a Civil War veteran, cabinetmaker, finisher, and plasterer. He and his family lived in various places in Weeksville from at least 1870. By 1892, he had moved to Hunterfly Road. His first wife, Isabella, had died. Perhaps he married a second time, for his pension record noted that his wife Katherine Brown Cornish died November 5, 1894. In 1898, Alfred Cornish married Frances, born in Washington, D.C. In 1900, Alfred and Frances Cornish lived at 1698 Bergen Street with their nine-year-old granddaughter, Fannie Trippen. Alfred Cornish was now a day laborer.[15]

Neighbors of the Cornish and Betts families in 1900 included both European Americans (born in Ireland, Austria, Germany, and New York State) and African Americans (born in New York State, New Jersey, Maryland, Virginia, and Bermuda). These families lived in the houses as they appeared in a photograph taken between 1900 and 1904. A similar view, taken in 1923, also showed the back of 1698 Bergen Street, the Cornish family home.

At 3 Hunterfly Road, Thomas Burke, born in Ireland, lived with his wife, Kate, born in New York of Irish parents. Both were thirty-seven years old. They had four children, ranging in age from seven to fourteen years old.

Julia and William Holtz, both forty-nine years old, lived at 5 Hunterfly Road. William was a day laborer, born in New York of German parents. Julia was European American, born in Connecticut.

The Johnson family, an African American family with nine children, lived at 1 Hunterfly Road (now 1700 Bergen Street). William H. Johnson was forty-four years old, a truck man, born in New Jersey. Susan Johnson was forty-five years old, born in Bermuda, a resident of the United

Weeksville houses, ca. 1923. Courtesy Brooklyn Historical Society.

States since 1868. Their children ranged in age from twenty-five-year-old Margaret to eight-year-old Corina. One grandson, four-year-old William, also lived with them.

Another African American family lived at 7 Hunterfly Road. William Mitchell, a plasterer, forty-nine years old, born in Maryland, shared this house with his wife Emma, thirty-two, born in Virginia, and their three children, Silvia, ten, Charles, eight, and Ellen, five.

At 9 Hunterfly Road, Michael, a day laborer, and Julia Bilelah, born in Austria and Germany, lived with their two children, Mariah and Julia, six and five.[16]

By 1910, the Cornish family was still at 1698 Bergen Street. Alfred Cornish now listed his occupation as plasterer. They shared the house with Frances's grown daughter (Alfred's step-daughter), Mary E. King (aged thirty-eight and a dressmaker), two granddaughters (Eva Trippet, aged fourteen, and Fannie Hunter, aged eighteen, a dressmaker), and one grandson (Edward Trippet, aged thirteen). A second family lived in the house with them. Mary J. Betts, aged fifty-seven, born in Louisiana, still lived here, taking care of her adopted daughter, Margaret Betts, aged seven, and two boarders (Edith Lattimore, aged seventeen, and Dorothy J. Lattimore, aged four months).[17]

Next door to the Cornish-Betts's household, William and Susan Johnson continued to live at 1 Hunterfly Road (1700 Bergen Street), now with six grown children and one granddaughter, in 1910. At this time William, aged sixty-three, born in New Jersey, was a wagon driver for a trucking company. Susan, sixty-two, was a housekeeper. Their son Charles E., forty-three, was a laborer. John S., twenty-three, was a machinist in a garage. Clarence, twenty-two, worked as a wagon driver for a furniture company. Arthur, twenty-one, was a clerk in a hotel. Albert E., twenty-three, worked as a tailor in a store, and Walter, twenty-eight, stayed at home, along with granddaughter, Corinne.

In 1910, William H. Smith, aged thirty-four, a waiter for a private family, and Hannah Smith lived at 1702 Bergen Street with their six children, Helen, twelve, Martha, ten, Lillian, seven, William, four, Eva, two, and Florence, two months. This seems like a very small house, with only two small bedrooms, for such a large family, but it fits the order of the dwellings listed in the census.

In 1910, August Mischler, thirty-six-year-old laborer for a contractor, and his wife, Ella Mischler, thirty-three years old, lived at 5 Hunterfly Road (now 1704 Bergen Street), with their two children, Louisa, ten, and Annie, eight. They headed one of only two European American families on Hunterfly Road. They shared their household with Ella's brother Emmanuel Kestly, thirty-one, a driver for a lumber company, and his son Edgar, three. Perhaps Louisa Mosler (who lived here in 1905) was related to August and Ella Mischler, since the names are similar. Again, the Mischler family is very large to have occupied one-half of this very small duplex, but the order of the household numbered in the census fits the order of the house on the street.

In 1910, the Davis family, all African Americans born in Virginia, lived at 1706 Bergen Street, then called 7 Hunterfly Road. George W. Davis was sixty-five, a sexton in a church. His wife, Sarah B. Davis, fifty-seven, stayed at home with their daughters, Eliza E., twenty-seven, Laura

H., twenty-five (a dressmaker), and their sons George W., twenty-three, and Harvey B., twenty-one, a wagon driver for an express company.

In 1910, Louis and Barbara Huber lived next door, at 1708 Hunterfly Road, in the other apartment of this two-family house. With the Mischlers, they were one of two European American families in this neighborhood in 1910. Louis Huber was forty-five. He was born in Germany and had come to this country in 1883. He worked in a butcher shop. Barbara Huber had emigrated from Germany in 1885.[18]

This neighborhood remained racially mixed in 1910, but, except for the Huber family, everyone had been born in the United States. Of those born in the United States, only William Johnson had been born outside New York State. All wives remained at home as housekeepers, but far more grown children lived at home with their parents, and most of these, including the women, were in the workforce. If Louis Huber owned his butcher shop, he would have been of higher status, in terms of class, than his neighbors. Alfred Cornish, plasterer; Mary King, Fanny Hunter, and Laura Davis, dressmakers; Albert Johnson, tailor; and John Johnson, machinist, would be skilled laborers. Arthur Johnson, clerk in a hotel, George Davis, sexton in a church, and William Smith, waiter, might be classified as having low white-collar jobs. The others were unskilled laborers. Although it is difficult to tell from the census description exactly what these jobs entailed, perhaps ten out of the fifteen workers who listed specific occupations had some kind of skilled work. Certainly most of these families survived in part by sharing their homes with grown children or taking in boarders.

Frances Cornish died at 1698 Bergen Street on May 3, 1910. Alfred Cornish continued to live there until at least 1912. By 1915, he had moved to 1673 Atlantic Avenue. He had become completely blind and afflicted by rheumatism, and for the last nine years of his life he relied on his granddaughter, Fannie Hunter, and after her death his grandson, Walter Trippet, for his care, sustained by his veteran pension of seventy-two dollars per month. He died on June 10, 1924.[19]

By 1900, Weeksville had changed a great deal from the isolated rural settlement of 144 African Americans in the Ninth Ward in 1840 (83.2 percent of the population) to the 1,937 African Americans in the Twenty-Fourth Ward in 1900 (6.1 percent of the population), mixed in

Muriel Williams Brown at 1698 Bergen Street, August 1964. Brown lived here for fifty-two years. Courtesy Weeksville Heritage Center.

with Irish, Germans, Italians, and French-Canadians. Weeksville had lost its independence as a separate African American community. It was no longer a wooded area of hollows and hills and dusty lanes. It had become a dynamic mixed-race neighborhood, with paved streets at right angles to each other and houses all in rows.

At the same time, parts of old Weeksville remained. Its institutions continued to set it apart. Although Howard Orphan Asylum and Zion Home for the Aged had moved out of Weeksville proper, P.S. 83 (later 243) remained. Weeksville's churches—African Methodist Episcopal and Berean Baptist—continued to serve the neighborhood, with the addition of St. Philip's Episcopal church, as well as a Catholic church and a Seventh-day Adventist church. Berean Baptist remained a cornerstone of Weeksville in the twenty-first century, representing continuity between past and present, as the community developed a new awareness of itself and its historic past. Some of Weeksville's older homes, including the four houses on Hunterfly Road and at least four other frame houses from the nineteenth century, continued to serve its residents. The last of the houses on Hunterfly Road remained occupied by private families until the Williams family left 1698 Bergen Street in 1968 after fifty-two years of residence.[20]

The history of Weeksville—as a separate African American community, established as a place of safety, economic independence, social respect, and political power—would be largely forgotten for more than half a century.

7

"A Seemingly Viable Neighborhood That No Longer Exists"

Weeksville, Lost and Found, 1910–2010

In the early twentieth century, two significant developments, both relating to transportation, added new elements to the landscape. One was the continued growth of rail transport, creating the iconic elevated trains that ran along the historic route of the Long Island Railroad on Atlantic Avenue. The second change was the automobile. To accommodate new gas-powered cars and trucks, people in Weeksville

Atlantic Avenue under the Elevated from Rochester to Buffalo Avenue. Photo taken July 11, 1939. New York City Housing Authority, LaGuardia-Wagner Archives, LaGuardia Community College.

"A seemingly viable neighborhood that no longer exists in Bedford-Stuyvesant, Brooklyn," noted the New York City Housing Authority on this photograph taken on July 11, 1939, of the two blocks looking north along Rochester Avenue past Dean and Pacific Streets. Two entire blocks on the right were razed to build the Kingsborough houses, including buildings constructed on the homesites of Lydia and James LeGrant and Edward and Mary Butler, at the corner of Rochester and Bergen (where the one-story and three-story stores stand in this photo). New York City Housing Authority, LaGuardia-Wagner Archives, LaGuardia Community College.

constructed dozens of one-story garages all over their neighborhoods. Many of these still stood in the early twenty-first century.

Otherwise, most of Weeksville's built environment—blocks and blocks of Italianate-inspired row houses and commercial structures—reflected its nineteenth-century expansion. Many of these buildings were maintained and often remodeled to serve succeeding generations of Weeksville residents and still stood in the early twenty-first century.

In 1941, however, eastern Weeksville was hit with a major change, when the New York City Housing Authority replaced all the buildings on block 1350, site of Francis P. Graham's early land investment, with the Kingsborough housing project.

Completed on October 31, 1941, Kingsborough housing complex was the New York Housing Authority's third public housing project in Brooklyn (and tenth in New York City). It sat on four blocks bounded by Ralph Avenue, Bergen Street, Rochester Avenue, and Pacific Street, directly across from the houses currently owned by the Weeksville Heritage Society. With sixteen six-story buildings, the complex included 1,148 apartments. In 1966, a new twenty-five story extension opened.[1]

A sixty-foot cast concrete frieze called *Green Pastures: Walls of Jericho* stood in the middle of the block. Sculpted in 1937–38 by noted African American artist Richmond Barthe (1901–89), it contained only figures of African Americans. Barthe designed it originally for the Harlem River Houses, built in 1937, but it was installed instead in the Kingsborough complex in 1941.[2]

The Kingsborough housing complex was the second rebuilding on these blocks, where Francis P. Graham had created such a cosmopolitan neighborhood before the Civil War. The first occurred in the 1880s and 1890s, when the spread of Brooklyn's grid pattern led to construction of Italianate row houses and commercial blocks and wiped out pre–Civil

Richmond Barthe, *Green Pastures: Walls of Jericho*, sculpted 1937–38, photo ca. 1944. New York City Housing Authority, LaGuardia-Wagner Archives, LaGuardia Community College.

Older Italianate residential blocks faced the new Kingsborough housing units across the street. New York City Housing Authority, LaGuardia-Wagner Archives, LaGuardia Community College.

War individual frame houses. Construction of the Kingsborough houses in turn destroyed this late nineteenth-century urban environment. Through both of these major reconstructions, Ferdinand Volckening's estate maintained control of the four houses on Hunterfly Road, and they survived the demolition that erased much of the surrounding neighborhood.

It is fitting that Weeksville should have been rediscovered in the 1960s, a decade that witnessed powerful grassroots movements for the very ideals that Weeksville embodied. From the civil rights movement to black power, Americans—led by black Americans—confronted issues of equality and justice and forced the world to explore the basic meaning of democratic ideals.

In the late 1960s, in a national context of turmoil and hope, James Hurley, formerly an aerial photographer with the U.S. Navy and Vice Consul to Pakistan, was giving tours of New York City neighborhoods. Called "Adventures on a Shoestring," these were sponsored through the

Museum of the City of New York. Building on this experience, Hurley offered in 1968 a noncredit workshop called "Exploring Bedford-Stuyvesant and New York City" through the Pratt Institute Department of Community Development. One group, including McCullough (court reporter) and Patricia Johnson (who worked in the New York City Office of Rent Control), focused on Weeksville. This group identified the location of the old Hunterfly Road from maps. They also met Joseph Haynes, an engineer for the Transit Authority and a professional pilot. As a lifelong resident of the area, Haynes had already seen the Hunterfly Road houses, but he knew little about them. When Haynes took Hurley on a low-altitude flight over Weeksville, they could see the old houses and road from the air. The *New York Times* did an article on the Haynes-Hurley flyover, and several other newspapers and television channels picked up the story from there. This was the beginning of the rediscovery of Weeksville.[3]

Ironically, threatened demolition of more historic buildings propelled awareness of Weeksville's historic importance. In 1969, when the New York Housing Authority, under its Model Cities program, decided to demolish houses in the block bounded by Troy Avenue, Pacific Street, Schenectady Avenue, and Dean Street, local residents saw an opportunity. James Hurley remembered sending the mayor a telegram late one night saying that "there might be something in those antiquated wooden houses that might be of value." Model Cities appropriated five hundred dollars for a community effort to explore the buildings and yards, to see what they could find about Weeksville's history. James Hurley and William "Dewey" Harley (a longtime Brooklyn resident born in 1898) organized a dig that yielded many artifacts, including a cannonball dating to the American Revolution and the tintype of the Weeksville Lady. They were assisted by Dolores McCullough; Wilson Williams, a neighborhood resident who brought his troop 342 of Boy Scouts; Elizabeth Welch, who got children from P.S. 243 involved; Elmira Coursey of Brooklyn Community College; Timothy Vincent, leader of Youth Leadership Institute of Bedford-Stuyvesant Youth in Action; Willie Jones and Les Campbell (later known as Jitu Weusi), of the Campaign Culture Program at Pratt; and many community volunteers, working as part of the newly formed Project Weeksville. Model

In 1969, Wilson A. Williams, in cap, and William Harley supervised Boy Scouts from Troop 342 as they dug in Weeksville near Troy and Dean Streets. Courtesy Weeksville Heritage Center.

Cities and the National Science Foundation also helped this project. In April 1974, after the dig, Weeksville Gardens (two buildings of four and five stories with 257 apartments housing 790 people) was completed on this site.[4]

Project Weeksville, with offices at New York Community College and later Medgar Evers College, conducted further research. Led by Barbara Jackson, schoolchildren studied Weeksville; many people gave oral histories about the Weeksville community; and Robert Swan produced the first historical reports on Weeksville. In 1970, Weeksville students successfully petitioned the New York City Landmarks Commission to declare the Hunterfly Road houses local landmarks. Boy Scouts "appeared in their uniforms," Hurley remembered, "carrying things that had been found—old boots and stuff—and it was quite picturesque and appealing to have these ten-year-old kids show up."[5]

In 1971, local people formed the Society for the Preservation of Weeksville and Bedford-Stuyvesant History, usually called simply the Weeksville Society. They organized in the apartment of Judge O. D. Williams, who had grown up in Weeksville and was then the first African American Supreme Court justice in Kings County. "He was always very helpful in getting us going," noted Hurley, "and he found a lawyer to do the incorporation. He knew some of the old-timers, and he brought some of them into the group." Initially, everyone thought of the society, remembered Hurley, "as a sort of Board of Directors of what was merely a project, a salvage archeology project." In 2005, this group changed its name to the Weeksville Heritage Center.[6]

James Hurley became first director of Project Weeksville and also the first president of the Weeksville Society. Tension developed as some project members, including Barbara Jackson and Robert Swan, believed that Hurley, a European American, should be replaced by an African American. Since the group was receiving federal funds, they petitioned Shirley Chisholm, then a congresswoman, to have Hurley ousted. Chisholm reviewed the evidence and concluded that Hurley should remain as president. Since he had been duly elected by the society, she had no interest in removing him. She also remembered, noted Hurley, that "I was the one walking the streets and telling the history of the people when no one else was doing that."[7]

Beginning in the early 1970s, the name of Joan Maynard, a Crown Heights resident, became virtually synonymous with that of Weeksville itself. Maynard, born in 1928, was a commercial artist for many years and the keeper of the legacy of her father John W. Cooper, a noted ventriloquist. Maynard herself became a founding member of the Society for the Preservation of Weeksville and Bedford-Stuyvesant History, and she served as president for two years (1972–74) before becoming executive director. She was a one-woman dynamo. She gave slide shows to local schoolchildren and community groups, directed tours, and organized programs. Most of all, she raised money, continually. She supported early work with her own savings, and also solicited money from donors as varied as schoolchildren giving pennies, private corporations (New York Landmarks Conservancy, Downtown Brooklyn Association, Mary Flagler Cary Trust, Sheffield Rehabilitation Corporation, Vincent

Astor Foundation, National Trust for Historic Preservation, Goldman Sachs, and others), and government (Borough of Brooklyn, City of New York, Save America's Treasures, and other agencies).[8]

In 1973, the Weeksville Society asked the Bedford-Stuyvesant Restoration Corporation to help purchase the historic Hunterfly Road houses from Ferdinand Volckening's estate. Schoolchildren from P.S. 243 raised the first eight hundred dollars toward the purchase of these houses. Through the assistance of several private and public funders, the Weeksville Society purchased three of the four houses. The fourth house was purchased with funds from the New York State Historic Preservation Office, matched with private donations. Under Maynard's leadership, these were restored in the early 1980s, with the help of architect William Cary. In 2000, Joan Maynard began a master plan, working with Wank, Adam, Slavin Architects (WASA). She also supervised several archaeological studies of the Hunterfly Road area.[9]

Throughout, Maynard and the board of the Weeksville Society faced extraordinary challenges. Violence threatened to disrupt restoration efforts for many years, and the Weeksville Society was forced to erect a chain-link fence around the property and to keep guard dogs there at night. In 1980, the last house on Hunterfly Road, 1706–08, burned. It was rebuilt in 1990–91, under the direction of Li/Saltzman, Architects. In December 1990, vandalism left one house looted and flooded. Devastated, the Weeksville Society rebounded. "Out of evil comes good," said Maynard. Again, students from P.S. 243 donated pennies, and local citizens came to the rescue. Joseph Haynes paid for plumbing repairs out of his own pocket.[10]

Loss of much federal funding after 1973 led to a scramble for new funds, including annual fund-raising dinners. In 1977, Alex Haley came as guest speaker. Reinstituted in 2000, these dinners continued to be a major source of financial support. By the time Maynard officially retired in 2001, the Weeksville houses were well on their way to restoration, and the Weeksville project had become nationally significant as an African American historic preservation project.

Pamela Green succeeded Joan Maynard as executive director. With a background in banking, computer programming, and administration (of a food bank and *Sesame Street*), Green brought extensive experience to her new position. Under Green's leadership, Weeksville placed a major emphasis on continued restoration, documentation, and community outreach, both to the local community and to heritage tourists. "After everything we've gone through," Green noted, "we don't want to just restore the houses and then have no one come here. Weeksville has to be made relevant for the 13-year-old across the street and the person visiting New York from across the country." "For some people, coming to Brooklyn is like going to Mars," Green noted. But she also recognized that Weeksville "will attract the tourist who is interested in something offbeat."[11]

In 2001, Weeksville received a four hundred thousand dollar grant from Save America's Treasures for preservation and documentation. They used these funds in part to create an entirely new nomination of the Hunterfly Road houses to the National Register of Historic Places, with research by Historical New York Research Associates and others. The National Register accepted the Hunterfly Road Historic District on March 22, 2006. Green also continued work with WASA on restoring the historic structures. In October 2003, Weeksville officially broke ground for restoration work. The restored houses were officially opened to the public on June 5, 2005, the culmination of thirty-five years of work.[12]

Building on these successes, Weeksville turned to the construction of a new cultural center. In June 2008, New York City Mayor Michael Bloomberg, Brooklyn Borough President Marty Markowitz, Pam Green and the Weeksville Heritage Center, and others proudly announced the groundbreaking. "This is an exciting time for Weeksville," said Green. "We are on the verge of becoming the premier African American cultural institution in Brooklyn and one of the largest African American institutions in New York. Weeksville has infinite potential as long as we stay true to our mission and vision, the heart of which is making sure the world knows our true history."[13]

Weeksville's work continued in the context of larger awareness of the importance of African American life and abolitionism in greater Brooklyn. The city of New York renamed Duffield Street, the center of much abolitionist activity in Brooklyn, as Abolitionist Place. A grant from the National Endowment for the Humanities combined resources from the Weeksville Heritage Center, Brooklyn Historical

Society, and the Irondale Ensemble Project to create "In Pursuit of Freedom," a multifaceted research and education project. Prithi Kanakamedala wrote a detailed overview of slavery and freedom about African Americans in nineteenth-century Brooklyn. And, in April 2012, the Irondale Ensemble Project produced a new play, *Color Between the Lines*, based on characters developed from historical documents.[14]

In 2013, the Weeksville Heritage Center celebrated the completion of its nineteen-thousand-square-foot Education and Cultural Arts building. Funded in cooperation with the New York City Council and the Brooklyn Borough President's office, this building was designed by Caples Jefferson Architects with landscape plans by Elizabeth Kennedy Landscape Architects. It is certified as a LEED Gold Sustainable structure. In keeping with Green's vision of Weeksville as a major center for arts and education as well as nationally significant historic site, the new education complex incorporates seventeen hundred square feet of exhibition space, a two-hundred-seat performance area, a resource center to promote research on Weeksville and African American history, and plenty of outside open space for a microfarm, heritage-based botanic collection, farmers' market, community gatherings, and concerts. At a gala awards benefit, "Save the Memories of Self," on June 11, 2013, two hundred people gathered for a tour. "We have much to celebrate tonight," said Pam Green. With this new building, Weeksville "will continue growing as a unique and important historical center." On December 11, 2013, Brooklyn Borough President Markowitz held a ribbon-cutting ceremony for this new complex, dedicated to "interpreting 175 years of freedom, agency, self determination, and creativity in Central Brooklyn and beyond."[15]

The Weeksville project is a remarkable example of historic preservation in the service of a larger cause. Completed under immense odds, Weeksville's restoration contributed to an emerging national awareness about the importance of preserving and interpreting African American historic sites. Parallel efforts included the reinterpretation of Colonial Williamsburg's past; the development of African American walking tours of Manhattan, Washington, D.C., and Boston; the National Park Service's creation of the Afro-American History Museum in the 1806 African Meeting House on Beacon Hill in Boston;

the development of Freedmen's Village in Houston, Texas; preserving the African Burial Ground and the site of Medgar Evers's assassination in New York City; and the Underground Railroad Network to Freedom administered by the National Park Service. Weeksville led the way in this movement because strong leaders—both African American and European American—from within the local community moved it forward with a strong ethic of community involvement and education as well as preservation.

A few people historically associated with Weeksville—Junius Morel, Maritcha Lyons, Henry Highland Garnet, T. McCants Stewart, Susan McKinney Steward—became nationally important figures. Most of Weeksville citizens, however, lived out their daily lives without leaving written records. But they did leave traces. Some were written (census records, directories, deeds, maps, court records, newspaper articles). Most powerful, however, were traces on the landscape.

In the early twenty-first century, Hunterfly Road marked, as it always had, Weeksville's eastern boundary. Visitors could still see that odd angle of Hunterfly Road that crossed the block between St. Marks and Bergen Streets, Buffalo and Rochester Avenues. They could still look at those four frame houses that stood silently beside it, witnesses

Architect's rendering of the new Weeksville Heritage Center block. Hunterfly Road houses are at right. Courtesy Weeksville Heritage Center.

Houses on Hunterfly Road owned by the Weeksville Heritage Society, 2005. Photo by
Stephen Barker.

to Weeksville's origins as an independent African American community founded on ideals of economic independence, social respect, and
political self-determination. At least four more frame houses scattered throughout the community also reflected this first period of
settlement. Blocks and blocks of intact row houses, both frame and
brick, told the story of Weeksville's development in the late nineteenth
century.

Many of Weeksville's early institutions were gone, including the
Howard Orphan Asylum, the African Civilization Society, the original Colored School No. 2, P.S. 68, P.S. 83, the original Zion Home for
the Aged, and the original A.M.E. and Berean Baptist church buildings. The Metropolitan Transportation Authority (MTA) had long
housed railway cars and stables on the western half of the historic

block that contained the Howard Orphan Asylum, Colored School No. 2, the African Civilization Society, and Zion Home for the Aged. When Howard Orphan Asylum left in 1911, the Nassau Railroad Company, precursor of the Metropolitan Transit Authority, purchased the entire block. In the early twenty-first century, the MTA still owned this block, walled off with high barriers topped with razor-sharp wire. Only one small Italianate structure, across the street from this historic block, remained to remind people of Weeksville's nineteenth-century development.

Other structures remained elsewhere in this historic community, however, including the 1894 Berean Baptist Church and the "new" Zion Home for the Aged, built in 1900.

Conclusion

African Americans who formed independent communities before the Civil War had several major goals. Chief among them were physical safety, economic sustainability, and political power. Those who invested in Weeksville were idealists as well as businesspeople. They used entrepreneurship to create a haven of freedom. As pioneers, they created a community where people could live in safety, where they could own land, vote, and prosper, with a sense of pride in themselves and a hope for a future that was better than the past. They chose to do this by creating a place where African Americans could escape constant pressures from the dominant society.

In many ways (including the development of community institutions, property ownership, and occupational opportunities for both men and women), Weeksville realized the dreams of its founders. As a conscious alternative, created by African Americans themselves, to Liberian emigration, it became one of America's first black suburbs and the largest independent African American community in the pre–Civil War United States, except for one (Carthagena, Ohio). Weeksville residents had a higher rate of property ownership than African Americans in any of fifteen other U.S. cities, North or South. Of the men in Weeksville aged twenty-one or older, 27 percent owned $250 worth of property or more, enough to qualify them to vote. Weeksville also had the highest percentage of artisans and the highest rate of occupational opportunity for African Americans of any of ten northern U.S. cities, increasing rather than decreasing up to 1880. Women as well as men found a variety of occupational opportunities in Weeksville. In 1880, 23.1 percent of the employed women in Weeksville were professionals, and 30.8 percent were skilled workers.

From the 1830s to the early twentieth century, Weeksville's residents also participated in every major effort to destroy slavery and affirm the rights of free people of color. Several nationally significant people (including Junius C. Morel, Susan McKinney Steward, Maritcha Lyons, Rufus Perry, and T. McCants Stewart) were associated with abolitionism, the Underground Railroad, education, community building, and social reform in Weeksville.

Finally, Weeksville successfully made the transition from an independent African American community before the Civil War to a racially mixed Brooklyn neighborhood after the Civil War. As Weeksville gradually lost its independent existence, it retained its public identity at least until the 1890s, but newspaper references to Weeksville and Crow Hill disappeared after that decade. Zion Home for the Aged moved a few blocks south to St. John's Place in 1900, and the Howard Orphan Asylum moved farther east on Long Island in 1911.

As an independent community, established by and for African Americans, Weeksville formed a remarkable experiment in American democracy. Its success—measured by home ownership, education, and occupational opportunity—invites us to consider the complex tension between integration and separatism—whether based on race, ethnicity, sexual preference, religion, culture, or age—as tools to ensure physical safety, economic independence, mutual respect, and equal rights for all people.

But how fragile is historical memory. As Jennifer Scott, research director of the Weeksville Heritage Center, noted in 2011, "This was a history that was lost. . . . Our mission is to make sure that doesn't happen again." In 1989, executive director Joan Maynard told the *Congressional Record* that the Weeksville project was "not only crucial in preserving the history of Weeksville, but in helping to build a sense of continuity, self-knowledge, self-esteem and self-worth for present and future generations of Brooklyn's African-Americans." Thanks to the sustaining work of Joan Maynard, Pam Green, and all of Weeksville's

supporters, the Weeksville Heritage Center became a world-class historical site, interpreting Weeksville's story not only to African Americans in Brooklyn but to people all over the world. The Weeksville Lady
beckons us into the future.[16]

Weeksville Lady, a tintype of an unknown woman, taken ca. 1880, discovered in 1968 during the initial archaeological dig at Weeksville. Courtesy Weeksville Heritage Center.

NOTES

NOTES TO THE INTRODUCTION

1. A. M. Green, "Jottings by the Way," *Christian Recorder*, January 26, 1867.

2. *Population of the United States in 1860* (Washington, D.C., 1864), 598–604, as noted in Ira Berlin, *Slaves without Masters: The Free Negro in the Antebellum South* (New York: Vintage, 1976), 136, 176.

3. Wilson Jeremiah Moses, *The Golden Age of Black Nationalism, 1850–1975* (New York: Oxford University Press, 1988).

4. The largest known free African American community before the Civil War was Carthagena, Ohio, with six hundred residents. Mary Ann Olding, email to author, January 9, 2004. Olding has studied free black communities in Ohio for more than twenty-five years.

5. Leslie M. Alexander, *African or American? Black Identity and Political Activism in New York City, 1784–1861* (Champaign: University of Illinois Press, 2008); Ira Berlin and Leslie Harris, *Slavery in New York* (New York: New Press, 2005); Thelma Willis Foote, *Black and White Manhattan: The History of Racial Formation in Colonial New York City* (Oxford: Oxford University Press, 2004); Leslie Harris, *In the Shadow of Slavery: African Americans in New York City, 1626–1863* (Chicago: University of Chicago Press, 2002); Graham Russell Gao Hodges, *David Ruggles: A Radical Black Abolitionist and the Underground Railroad in New York City* (Chapel Hill: University of North Carolina Press, 2012); Carla Peterson, *Black Gotham: A Family History of African Americans in Nineteenth-Century New York City* (New Haven, Conn.: Yale University Press, 2011); Shane White, *"Somewhat More Independent": The End of Slavery in New York City, 1770–1810* (Athens: University of Georgia Press, 2004). For an earlier overview of African American history in Manhattan, see M. A. Harris, *A Negro History Tour of Manhattan* (New York: Greenwood, 1968).

6. Craig Wilder, *A Covenant with Color: Race and Social Power in Brooklyn* (New York: Columbia University Press, 2001); Robert Furman, *Brooklyn Heights: The Rise, Fall, and Rise of America's First Suburb* (Furman, 2011); Prithi

Kanakamedala, *In Pursuit of Freedom* (unpublished manuscript, Brooklyn Historical Society, 2012).

7. Robert J. Swan, "The Origin of Black Bedford-Stuyvesant," in Charlene Claye Van Derzee, ed., *An Introduction to the Black Contribution to the Development of Brooklyn* (Brooklyn: New Muse Community Museum of Brooklyn, 1977), as well as several manuscript studies now located at the Weeksville Heritage Society and Schomberg Library, including "Notes on the Search for Selected Residents of Weeksville" (March 18, 1971); "The Macroscopic Study of a Microscopi Community" (April 15, 1971); "Weeksville Historical Research Review—The Pieces of a Puzzle" (May 1, 1971), 6–8; "Welcome to Weeksville—An Historic Reconstruction of the Past" (ca. 1971); "Evaluation of a Prospective Research Project Concerning the Hunterfly Road House" (December 15, 1978); Roselle Henn, "Weeksville Historical Archaeological Research Project" (1980), 15; William Askins, "Test Excavations in the Basements of 1698 Bergen Street, a House Owned by the Society for the Preservation of Weeksville and Bedford-Stuyvesant History" (New York: City College of New York, 1980); Wank, Adam, Slavin Architects (WASA), "The Hunterfly Houses of Weeksville Restoration Report" (2000); Joan H. Geismar, *Weeksville Master Plan EAS: Phase IA Archaeological Assessment of the Cultural Facility Site* (Brooklyn: Philip Habib & Associates, 2001); Edward Chappell, "Draft Report, Hunterfly Road Houses, Bergen Street, Brooklyn, New York, Architectural Report" (November 2002); Neil Larson, "Assessment of the Origins of the Double House on Hunterfly Road" (April 2004); Joan H. Geismar, "Archaeology at the Hunterfly Road Houses, 1978–1982 and 2000–2003, Brooklyn, New York" (2009); Eugene Armbruster, *The Eastern District of Brooklyn* (New York: G. Quattlander, 1912), 108, 172; Eugene L. Armbruster, *Brooklyn's Eastern District* (1912; Brooklyn: privately published, 1942; 2010), 310; Mardita Hardy, "The March of Time" (Bethel A.M.E. Church Program, ca. 1930), Weeksville Heritage Society Collections; Dolores Jackson McCullough, "The Weeksville Story: An Independent Work Study Project" (City University of New York, 1971); James G. Hurley, "Annotated Bibliography on Weeksville-Carrsville and Associated Topics in Brooklyn Black History" (August 1978); David Ment and Mary Donovan, *The People of Brooklyn: A History of Two Neighborhoods. Brooklyn* (Brooklyn: Brooklyn Education & Cultural Alliance, 1980); Joan Maynard and Gwen Cottman, *Weeksville Then & Now: The Search to Discover, the Efforts to Preserve, Memories of Self in Brooklyn, New York*, 3rd ed. (Brooklyn: Society for the Preservation of Weeksville and Bedford-Stuyvesant History, 1988).

8. Henn, "Weeksville Historical Archaeological Research Report," 1981, 12–13, described the discovery of only one privy and estimated that it had been filled in no earlier than 1903.

9. We have discovered only one letter, one copy of a Weeksville newspaper, and no journal entries, account books, or manuscript church records created by

Weeksville residents before 1860. About 1970, James Hurley discovered the Thompson family papers in a private collection. He noted that "the journal of Capt. Jacob Thompson, a ship captain and resident of Weeksville, included two pay orders or receipts relating to a burial or benevolent society known as the 'Assistant Society of Weeksville' [*sic*]. Both are dated May 18, 1854, and signed by 'William Mitchel, Secretary,' but one is datelined 'Weeksville' and the other 'Carrsville.'" Although Hurley took photographs of this material, we have not been able to find these. Cited in Hurley, "Annotated Bibliography on Weeksville-Carrsville," 18–19.

10. William H. Banks, Jr., "Weeksville: Brooklyn's Hidden Treasure," *American Legacy* 3:3 (Fall 1997), 26–34; Swan, "Weeksville Historical Research Review," 6–8, and "Welcome to Weeksville," described Weeksville's early projects and listed objects retrieved from this archaeological effort.

11. "4 Cottages, Meeting House Designated as Landmarks," *Daily News Brooklyn*, August 24, 1970, reprinted in Joan Maynard, *Let's Make a Landmark* (Brooklyn: Society for the Preservation of Weeksville and Bedford-Stuyvesant History, 1988).

12. Ned Kaufman, *Race, Place, and Story: Essays on the Past and Future of Historic Preservation* (New York: Routledge, 2009).

13. Roselle Henn wrote in 1980, for example, that there was "an apparent discrepancy between the early 19th [century] dates assigned to the Hunterfly Road houses on the basis of their architectural features, and the later 19th c. dates of the artifacts associated with them," "Weeksville Historical Archaeological Research Project" (1980), 15; Askins, "Test Excavations"; WASA, "Hunterfly Houses"; Geismar, *Weeksville Master Plan EAS*; Chappell, "Draft Report, Hunterfly Road Houses"; Larson, "Assessment of the Origins." In 1980, Roselle Henn and William Askins of the City College of New York noted that the "earliest map on which they found 1702 Hunterfly Road dated to 1872." Much of the land behind the houses, they discovered, had been disturbed and refilled in the 1870s. Of the more than thirty trash pits they excavated, they found material that dated "no earlier than the last quarter of the nineteenth century." Askins reported that test excavations in the cellar of 1698 Bergen Street in 1980 revealed a bottle manufactured between 1857 and 1870, so that the house could be no older than that. Geismar, "Archaeology at the Hunterfly Road Houses," 36.

14. Henn, "Weeksville Historical Archaeological Research Project," 15; Askins, "Test Excavations"; WASA, "Hunterfly Houses"; Geismar, *Weeksville Master Plan EAS*; Chappell, "Draft Report, Hunterfly Road Houses"; Larson, "Assessment of the Origins"; Chappell, "Draft Report, Hunterfly Road Houses."

15. Many thanks to architect Paul Malo for suggesting that these buildings were most likely constructed before 1850 (consistent with architectural evidence) but moved to their current site before 1874 (as maps, assessment records, archaeological studies, and the 1863 newspaper article indicate).

NOTES TO CHAPTER 1

1. Philip Bell, "Great Anti-Colonization Meeting," *Colored American*, January 12 and 19, 1839.

2. Five European Americans bought the huge farm of John Lefferts in 1834. They sold it to Edward Copeland, who in turn sold 426 lots at auction in July 1835. On January 15, 1845, the *Brooklyn Evening Star* noted that Weeksville was "a part of Lefferts farm bought by Copland and others" (Brooklyn Historical Society, noted in James G. Hurley, "Annotated Bibliography on Weeksville-Carrsville and Associated Topics in Brooklyn Black History" (August 1978), 4). Deeds in the Kings County Clerk's Office recorded all of these transactions, including John F. Garrison and Sarah Garrison (perhaps part of the "Garrittsen" or "Gerrittsen" family) to Henry C. Thompson ("Colored Man"), May 28, 1835 (recorded August 20, 1835), block 1335, liber 52, 487. Thompson paid $2,247 for land along the Brooklyn & Jamaica Railroad. In the next few years, Thompson sold this land to the Tillmans (November 28, 1836), Simon Van Curen (June 7, 1837, liber 70, p. 533), Smiths (April 2, 1838), and others. James Weeks purchased his land from Simon Van Curen (March 26, 1838, liber 75, p. 93), Levi and Henrietta Biglow (November 1, 1839), Sarah Lefferts (January 14, 1845, recorded February 27, 1845, liber 127, p. 485), Samuel H. and Eliza Moser (May 8, 1849, recorded April 23, 1860, liber 525, p. 1), and Caesar and Isabella Weeks (May 1853, recorded June 23, 1853, liber 327, p. 340). See also Robert J. Swan, "The Origin of Black Bedford-Stuyvesant," in Charlene Claye Van Derzee, ed., *An Introduction to the Black Contribution to the Development of Brooklyn* (Brooklyn: New Muse Community Museum of Brooklyn, 1977), 73–74, 93 n. 20. Thanks to Cynthia Copeland for her work in Brooklyn city directories. For more information, see deeds researched by Judith Wellman and Lee French in 2003, now on file at Weeksville Heritage Center.

3. Swan, "Origin of Black Bedford-Stuyvesant," 73–74; Swan, "Evaluation of a Prospective Research Project Concerning the Hunterfly Road House" (December 15, 1978).

4. Samuel Cowdrey, Master of Chancery, to Francis P. Graham, July 9, 1839, recorded September 4, 1839, liber 84, p. 89, Kings County Clerk's Office. Between 1841 and his will in 1852, Graham sold off large parts of his property on blocks 1844, 1349, 1350, and 1852. See deeds researched in 2003 by Judith Wellman and Lee French, now in the archives of the Weeksville Heritage Center. See also Matthew Dripps, *Map of the City of Brooklyn, Being the Former Cities of Brooklyn and Williamsburgh and the Town of Bushwick* (New York: Matthew Dripps, 1869), plate 3; Swan, "Origin of Black Bedford-Stuyvesant," 93.

5. Only three black families lived in Bedford in 1820, along with ten free people of color who lived in households headed by European Americans and sixty-two enslaved people. Another forty-five African Americans lived in the town of Flatbush in 1820, including eight enslaved people and one free person of color in the household of John Lefferts. Robert Swan, "Land Transactions and the

Origins of Weeksville: Research Report" (Weeksville Heritage Society, April 30, 1971); U.S. census, 1820.

6. *Brooklyn Eagle*, September 18, 1898; "One Hundred and Two Years Old," *Brooklyn Eagle*, March 30, 1886.

7. Sandra Sholock Roff, "The Brooklyn African Woolman Benevolent Society Rediscovered," *Afro-Americans in New York Life and History* 10:2 (July 1986): 55–63; William Lloyd Garrison, *Thoughts on African Colonization; or, An Impartial Exhibition of the Doctrines, Principles and Purposes of the American Colonization Society, Together with the Resolutions, Addresses and Remonstrances of the Free People of Color* (Boston: Garrison and Knapp, 1832), 23; U.S. manuscript census, 1840.

8. John Lofton, *Denmark Vesey's Revolt: The Slave Plot That Lit a Fuse to Fort Sumter* (Kent, Ohio: Kent State University Press, 1964, 1983). *The Trial Record of Denmark Vesey*, introduction by John Oliver Killens (Boston: Beacon, 1970), 123–25, 142, gives Graham's testimony and sentence. Douglas R. Egerton, *He Shall Go Out Free: The Lives of Denmark Vesey* (Madison, Wis.: Madison House, 1999), 201, 231, lists Graham as a drayman and noted the name of the *Dolphin*.

9. "Married," *Colored American*, June 2, 1838, and "Died," *Colored American*, August 31, 1839; "Methodist Conference," *Liberator*, July 7, 1832; "A Much Married Minister," *Brooklyn Eagle*, January 19, 1872; "The Case of Sarah Graham," *New York Times*, February 25, 1872; Daniel A. Payne, *History of the African Methodist Episcopal Church* (Nashville, Tenn.: A.M.E. Sunday School Union, 1891), 102.

10. New York City directories, 1829–30, 1839–40, 1850, as listed in Ancestry.com.

11. "A Much Married Minister," *Brooklyn Eagle*, January 19, 1872; "The Case of Sarah Graham," *New York Times*, February 25, 1872; Francis P. Graham, deeds, Brooklyn Clerk's Office, 1839–53, copies in the Weeksville Heritage Center; *Colored American*, January 12, 1839.

12. "Crows of Crow Hill," *Brooklyn Eagle*, December 21, 1890; Eugene Armbruster, *The Eastern District of Brooklyn* (New York: G. Quattlander, 1912); Henry R. Stiles, ed., *Civil, Political, Professional and Ecclesiastical History and Commercial and Industrial Record of the County of Kings and the City of Brooklyn, N.Y. from 1683 to 1884*, vol. 2 (New York: W.W. Munsell, 1870?), 743–832a.

13. Henry Reed Stiles, *A History of the City of Brooklyn*, 3 vols. (Brooklyn, 1867–70; repr., Bowie, Md.: Heritage Books, 1993), 1:442. "Strolls Upon Old Lanes," *Brooklyn Eagle*, December 9, 1888, noted, "The Bedford Hills included, in a general way, all the territory between Atlantic avenue and the southern boundary line of the city, from Prospect Hill to east of Buffalo avenue, where the hills, as stated, did not extend south of the Parkway."

14. *Brooklyn Eagle*, July 30, 1873; H. J. S., "Miscalled 'Hunter Fly': The Course and the History of the Aander Vly Road," *Brooklyn Eagle*, October 30, 1887; Armbruster, *Eastern District*; "An American Family Grows in Brooklyn: The Lefferts Family Papers at the Brooklyn Historical Society" (Brooklyn Historical Society), www.brooklynhistory.org/exhibitions/lefferts/; "Old Brooklyn Farm Lands,"

Brooklyn Eagle, July 19, 1896; Stiles, *History of the City of Brooklyn*, 1:205–6, 441–42.

15. "American Family Grows in Brooklyn."

16. "Flatbush: A View of the Suburban Town during the Revolution," *Brooklyn Eagle*, September 15, 1887; Gertrude Lefferts Vanderbilt, "Appendix," in *The Social History of Flatbush and Manners and Customs of the Dutch Settlers in Kings County* (New York: Frederick Loeser, 1909; repr., Nabu Press, 2012), 370–85, contains an account of life in Flatbush during the Revolution by an unnamed person who was a young girl at the time. James Hurley noted the discovery of the cannonball, which was later stolen.

17. Stiles, *History of the City of Brooklyn*, 2:359; "Lefferts Historic House" (Prospect Park Alliance), www.prospectpark.org/about/history/historic_places/h_lefferts; Vanderbilt, *Social History of Flatbush*, 325.

18. "Lefferts Historic House" (Prospect Park Alliance); Stiles, "Battle of Brooklyn, August 7, 1776," in *History of the City of Brooklyn*, vol. 1.

19. Douglas R. Egerton, *Death or Liberty: African Americans and Revolutionary America* (New York: Oxford, 2009), 111, 204–6.

20. "Lefferts Historic House" (Historic House Trust of New York City), www.historichousetrust.org/item.php?i_id=19; "Lefferts Historic House" (Prospect Park Alliance); "Brooklyn's Large Estates," *Brooklyn Eagle*, June 3, 1889; www.brooklynhistory.org/exhibitions/lefferts/introduction/; "American Family Grows in Brooklyn."

21. "The Lefferts Family," *Brooklyn Eagle*, October 2, 1887, http://www.bklyn-genealogy-info.com/People/1887.leffertsfamily.html; Stiles, *History of the City of Brooklyn*, 1:175–77.

22. Swan, "Land Transactions and the Origins of Weeksville," 14.

23. "American Family Grows in Brooklyn"; Marc Linder and Lawrence S. Zacharias, *Of Cabbages and Kings County: Agriculture and the Formation of Modern Brooklyn* (Iowa City: University of Iowa Press, 1999); Alden Spooner, *Spooner's Brooklyn Directory, for the year 1822, 1822* (Brooklyn: Alden Spooner, at the Office of the Long-Island Star, 1822), Ancestry.com. In the 1820s, John Lefferts served as treasurer of the Kings County Agricultural Society.

24. U.S. census, 1820 and 1830; "Lefferts Family"; "Map of Bedford Corners, 1766–67" (Brooklyn Genealogy), www.bklyn-genealogy-info.com/Map/1766.Bedford.Corners.html.

25. U.S. census, 1810 and 1820, Ancestry.com.

26. John Barber and Henry W. Howe, *Historical Collections of the State of New York* (New York: S. Tuttle, 1842 repr., Bowie, Md.: Heritage Books, 1999), 218; Kenneth T. Jackson, Lisa Keller, and Nancy Flood, eds., *Encyclopedia of New York City*, 2nd ed. (New Haven, Conn.: Yale University Press, 2010).

27. John H. French, *Historical and Statistical Gazetteer of New York State* (New York: R.P. Smith, 1860), 365.

28. Ibid., 367.

29. *Brooklyn Eagle*, July 26, 1892.

30. *Brooklyn Eagle*, December 10, 1853; Linder and Zacharias, *Of Cabbages and Kings County*.

31. *Brooklyn Eagle*, June 3, 1889; "Old Brooklyn Farmlands," *Brooklyn Eagle*, July 19, 1896; Gertrude Lefferts Vanderbilt, *The Social History of Flatbush and Manners and Customs of the Dutch Settlers in Kings County* (New York: Frederick Loeser, 1909; repr., Nabu Press, 2012),

32. "Lefferts Family."

33. "Lefferts Historic House" (Historic House Trust of New York City); "Lefferts Historic House" (Prospect Park Alliance); "Brooklyn's Large Estates"; "American Family Grows in Brooklyn."

34. For more on Seneca Village, see Leslie Harris, *In the Shadow of Slavery: African Americans in New York City, 1626–1863* (Chicago: University of Chicago Press, 2002), 75, 266–67; Roy Rosenzweig and Elizabeth Blackmar, *The Park and the People: A History of Central Park* (Ithaca, N.Y.: Cornell University Press, 1992), 64–73; and Leslie Alexander, "The Story of Seneca Village, 1825–57," in *African or American? Black Identity and Political Activism in New York City, 1784–1861* (Champaign: University of Illinois Press, 2008), 154–73, 160.

35. Swan, "Origin of Black Bedford-Stuyvesant," 73–74.

36. Ibid., 73–74.

37. Ibid., 73–74; Swan, "Land Transactions and the Origins of Weeksville," 14, lists deed transactions. On January 15, 1845, the *Brooklyn Evening Star* noted that Weeksville was "a part of Lefferts farm bought by Copland and others" (noted in Hurley, "Annotated Bibliography on Weeksville-Carrsville," 4); Stiles, *History of the City of Brooklyn*, 2:284.

38. L75, p. 93, as noted in Swan, "Origin of Black Bedford-Stuyvesant," note 20; WASA, "Hunterfly Houses"; Cynthia Copeland, Brooklyn City Directory, 1839.

39. "How They Live," *Brooklyn Eagle*, January 14, 1883; C. R. C., "Wiping Out Crow Hill," *Brooklyn Eagle*, November 24, 1889.

40. See, e.g., *Colored American*, April 4, 1840.

41. *Colored American*, May 22, 1841.

42. *Colored American*, April 4, 1840, April 11, 1840, June 13, 1840, May 22, 1841, and August 7, 1841; *North Star*, January 25, 1850. Of the other real estate advertisements in these African American newspapers, eight were for individual houses or farms. Two were for "several valuable building lots" in Belleville, New Jersey, and one was for several hundred acres of land at the junction of Green and Fayette Counties, Ohio, advertised by J. W. Watson of Jamestown, Ohio. *Colored American*, June 15, 1839, June 13, 1840, and August 21, 1841.

43. *New York Times*, February 16, 1855.

44. "Tax Roll, 1841, 9th Ward, Brooklyn, N.Y., Vol. 9" (manuscript, Long Island Historical Society), 18–19, noted in Hurley, "Annotated Bibliography on Weeksville-Carrsville," 6; *North Star*, September 4, 1851; J. W. Colton, *Map of the Country Thirty-Three Miles around the City of New York* (New York: J. H. Colton, 1853);

Swan, "Origin of Black Bedford-Stuyvesant," 75; "The South Eastern Parkway," *Brooklyn Eagle*, October 6, 1869. Robert J. Swan suggested that Carrsville was built first, in the mid-1830s, around Richard Thompson and Samuel Anderson's land, on the border between Brooklyn and Flatbush, and Weeksville was built second, in the late 1830s, on Henry C. Thompson's land.

45. "Strolls upon Old Lines: Crow Hill and Some of Its Suggestions," *Brooklyn Eagle*, December 9, 1888. In 1888, the *Brooklyn Eagle* also described a region called Malboneville, which covered the area between Eastern Parkway and the city line and from Nostrand to New York Avenue. It described Crow Hill as extending from Brooklyn Avenue to Schenectady Avenue. C. R. C., "Wiping Out Crow Hill"; "Miss C.T. Davis, Packer '55, Recalls Schoolgirl Days," *Brooklyn Eagle*, July 29, 1919.

46. These boundaries are based partly on deed searches for all African American land owners in the Ninth Ward listed in the 1840, 1850, 1855, 1860, and 1865 censuses, which formed a distinct grouping within these blocks, partly on Robert Swan's map, "1855 Demography," in Swan, "Origin of Black Bedford-Stuyvesant," and partly on Dripps, *Map of the City of Brooklyn*, plate 3. Robert Swan's work in deeds and city directories confirmed two clusters of African American land ownership, referred to in early accounts as both Weeksville and Carrsville. The 1855 and 1865 censuses suggest at least two clusters of African American settlement.

47. Craig Wilder, *A Covenant with Color: Race and Social Power in Brooklyn* (New York: Columbia University Press, 2001), 73; Susan Zaeske, *Signatures of Citizenship: Petitioning, Antislavery, and Women's Political Identity* (Chapel Hill: University of North Carolina Press, 2003); Deborah Bingham Van Broekhoven, *The Devotion of These Women* (Amherst: University of Massachusetts Press, 2002); Paul Finkelman, "The Protection of Black Rights in Seward's New York," *Civil War History* 34:3 (September 1988): 211–34.

48. "Too Long Have Others Spoken for Us," *Freedom's Journal*, March 16, 1827.

49. *New York Mercury*, November 7, 1780, quoted in Edgar McManus, *A History of Negro Slavery in New York* (Syracuse, N.Y.: Syracuse University Press, 1966), 153.

50. McManus, *History of Negro Slavery*, 158–59.

51. Chancellor Livingston, quoted in *Journal of the Senate* (March 12, 1785), quoted in McManus, *History of Negro Slavery*, 164.

52. McManus, *History of Negro Slavery*, 168–79.

53. Ibid.; Graham Russell Hodges, *Slavery and Freedom in the Rural North: African Americans in Monmouth County, New Jersey, 1665–1865* (Madison, Wis.: Madison House, 1997) gives an excellent discussion of what life may have been like for people who lived in slavery on Long Island. "Slaves," in *Census of the State of New York for 1855* (Albany: Charles Van Benthuysen, 1857), xi.

54. McManus, *History of Negro Slavery*, 195.

55. James Oliver Horton and Lois E. Horton, *In Hope of Liberty: Culture, Community and Protest among Northern Free Blacks, 1700–1860* (New York: Oxford University Press, 1997), 197.

56. *Freedom's Journal*, March 16, 1827.

57. Patrick Rael, *Black Identity and Black Protest in the Antebellum North* (Chapel Hill: University of North Carolina Press, 2002), 216.

58. *Colored American*, March 4, 1837, quoted in Horton and Horton, *In Hope of Liberty*, 201.

59. Nathaniel Hazeltine Carter and William Leete Stone, *Reports of the Proceedings and Debates of the Convention of 1821 Assembled for the Purpose of Amending the Constitution of the State of New York* (Albany: E. and E. Hosford, 1821), 180–81, 186, 190, 198–99, 375; Philip S. Foner and George E. Walker, eds., *Proceedings of the Black State Convention, Eighteen Forty to Eighteen Sixty-Five*, vol. 1 (Philadelphia: Temple University Press, 1979).

60. *Colored American*, August 19, 1837. We cannot know more about who signed these petitions because they were all burned in the fire at the New York State Library in 1911.

61. "Grounds Owned and Occupied by Our Own People," *Frederick Douglass' Paper*, September 4, 1851.

62. *Long Island Star*, June 8 and 15, 1831, quoted in Harold X. Connolly, *A Ghetto Grows in Brooklyn* (New York: New York University Press, 1977).

63. Shane White, *"Somewhat More Independent": The End of Slavery in New York City, 1770–1810* (Athens: University of Georgia Press, 2004).

64. Robert J. Swan, "Synoptic History of Black Public Schools in Brooklyn," in Charlene Claye Van Derzee, ed., *An Introduction to the Black Contribution to the Development of Brooklyn* (Brooklyn: New Muse Community Museum of Brooklyn, 1977), 63; Roff, "Brooklyn African Woolman Benevolent Society Rediscovered."

65. Henry C. Thompson, president, John E. Jackson, secretary, "To the Public," *Long Island Star*, October 4, 1827, quoted in Robert J. Swan, "The Macroscopic Study of a Microscopic Community" (typescript, 1971).

66. Harris, *Shadow of Slavery*.

67. Howard Dodson et al., *The Black New Yorkers* (New York: John Wiley, 2000), 60; *Freedom's Journal*, July 13, 1827.

68. Linda Kerber, "Abolitionists and Amalgamators: The New York City Race Riots of 1834," *New York History* 48 (1967): 28–39; Leonard Richards, *"Gentlemen of Property and Standing": Anti-Abolition Mobs in Jacksonian America* (New York: Oxford University Press, 1970).

69. Laurence B. Goodheart, "The Chronicles of Kidnapping in New York: Resistance to the Fugitive Slave Law, 1834–1835," *Afro-Americans in New York Life and History* 8:1 (January 1984): 7–15.

70. *The First Annual Report of the New York Committee of Vigilance, for the Year 1837* (New York: Piercy & Reed, 1837); Graham Russell Gao Hodges, *David Ruggles: A Radical Black Abolitionist and the Underground Railroad in New York City* (Chapel Hill: University of North Carolina Press, 2010).

71. *First Annual Report of the New York Committee of Vigilance*, 60.

72. Ibid., 14, 75–77; Hodges, *David Ruggles*; Carol Wilson, *Freedom at Risk: The Kidnapping of Free Blacks in America, 1780–1865* (Lexington: University Press of Kentucky, 1994), 117.

73. "Report of the Select Committee on the Petition of Various Citizens to Prevent Kidnapping" (no. 341) in *Documents of the Assembly of the State of New York* (May 1, 1840); Solomon Northrup, *Twelve Years a Slave* (Auburn, N.Y.: Orton and Mulligan, 1853).

74. *African Repository* 10 (December 1834): 292; *Rights of All*, August 7, 1829, quoted in Jane H. Pease and William H. Pease, *They Who Would Be Free: Blacks' Search for Freedom, 1830–1861* (1974; repr., Champaign: University of Illinois Press, 1990), 22, 26.

75. For detailed accounts of African Americans' reaction to colonization, see Garrison, *Thoughts on African Colonization*, 23ff.

76. "Address to the Colored Citizens of Brooklyn, (N.Y.) and Its Vicinity," in Garrison, *Thoughts on African Colonization*, 27.

77. *Long Island Star*, June 8 and 15, 1831, quoted in Connolly, *Ghetto Grows in Brooklyn*; *Liberator*, August 13, 1831.

78. *Colored American*, January 12 and 19, 1839.

79. Garrison, *Thoughts on African Colonization*; *Colored American*, 1839.

80. Federal manuscript census, 1840 (Ninth Ward, Brooklyn).

81. "Tax Roll, 1841, 9th Ward, Brooklyn, N.Y., Vol. 9," Ms, Brooklyn Historical Society, noted in Hurley, "Annotated Bibliography on Weeksville-Carrsville," 6, and in Robert Swan, "Notes on the Search for Selected Residents of Weeksville" (typescript, March 18, 1971).

82. Two detailed maps, one from 1849 and one from 1869, offer conflicting evidence about when and where houses in Weeksville were constructed. In 1849, J. C. Sidney published *Sidney's Map of Twelve Miles around New York: With the Names of Property Holders*. In 1869, Matthew Dripps published his *Map of the City of Brooklyn* in the *Atlas of New York City*. Both maps indicated the sites of houses in the Weeksville area, but each map showed them in different locations. This evidence may be accurate, suggesting changes over time. It may be incorrect, simply the surveyor's best guess. Or parts of these maps may be correct and other parts not.

    Although census evidence suggests that about twenty-four families lived in the Weeksville area in 1840, Sidney's detailed map notes only fifteen houses. The arrangement of houses in the area called "Weeksville" most likely does not reflect the actual layout of these buildings, since they appear in a very different configuration in Matthew Dripps's map of 1869.

    We do not know whether any buildings existed anywhere in this area in 1839 when the farm was sold. The 1839 auction map showed only lot lines, but smaller lots at the western end of the property may have indicated, as Neil Larson has suggested, the presence of farm buildings there. (Buildings appeared in this approximate location on the 1869 map by Matthew Dripps.) The Garrittsen map noted "wood lots belonging to different owners" on Crow Hill south of the Garrittsen farm.

South of the Suydam house, where Hunterfly Road bends east, Francis P. Graham bought land in 1839. Sidney's 1849 map showed no houses on these lots, but deed evidence suggests that they certainly existed. Houses do appear on Graham's original purchase on Matthew Dripps's 1869 map, and census and deed evidence suggests that a dynamic neighborhood occupied this area by 1850.

South of Graham's land, where Hunterfly Road bends back to the south, three small houses appeared on Sidney's map, very close to the site of the current Weeksville Heritage Center houses. Later evidence from deeds, assessment records, newspaper articles, archaeological findings, and maps suggests, however, that Sidney's map was incorrect. Succeeding chapters demonstrate that no houses existed on the current site of the Weeksville Heritage Society buildings until after the Civil War.

NOTES TO CHAPTER 2

1. *Frederick Douglass' Paper*, September 4, 1851.
2. *Brooklyn Eagle*, June 27, 1873.
3. H. J. S., "Miscalled 'Hunter Fly,'" Brooklyn Eagle, October 30, 1887; "Buried Alive," *Brooklyn Eagle*, March 29, 1876; C. R. C., "Wiping Out Crow Hill," November 24, 1889.
4. Deeds: Francis P. Graham to Lydia A. E. Simmons, October 2, 1843; Lydia A. E. Simmons to Francis P. Graham, May 31, 1845.
5. U.S. census, 1850.
6. Both James LeGrant and Edward Butler were most likely Francis Graham's nephews. Graham gave lifetime income to both of them when he wrote his will in 1852, recorded in deeds, June 13, 1862, liber 576, p. 371. His mother may have been Phoebe LeGrant, who was perhaps Francis Graham's sister; *Brooklyn Eagle*, September 14, 1849. The 1855 New York State census noted that James LeGrant had moved to Weeksville seven years earliern 1845 Francis Graham purchased part of Lydia Simmons's lot, where he built (or had built) a double house at the northeast corner of Bergen Street and Rochester Avenue, which Lydia and James LeGrant shared with Edward Butler and three little girls in 1850.
7. U.S. census, 1850. Assessments showed that James LeGrant owned a house in 1850 valued at $600. No deeds exist for James LeGrant, however. It is likely that Lydia actually owned this home since she owned the land, but the assessors attributed ownership to James, as official head of household. "Picnics," *Brooklyn Eagle*, August 12, 1874.
8. *New York Age*, 1906, quoted in "Weeksville Heritage Center," Wikipedia, en.wikipedia.org/wiki/Weeksville_Heritage_Center. The 1850 U.S. census also listed two single persons named Weeks who lived in other households. Jacob Weeks, a Virginia-born laborer, was twenty-seven years old, living in a

household with two other adults and a nine-year-old girl, all with different last names. Ann E. Weeks was a one-year-old girl born in New York who lived in the same family with Edward Butler, a South Carolina-born shoemaker, and Ann E. Connor, a three-month-old baby, in a two-family house next door to Lydia and James LeGrant (from South Carolina and Washington, D.C.) and a four-year-old girl named Ann Dixon.

9. Of the 443 residents of Weeksville in 1850, 82.2 percent (366 people) were African American and only 17.8 percent (79 people) were European American. One hundred fifteen (86.5 percent) of Weeksville's 133 families were African American. In contrast, African Americans made up only 2.5 percent of the population in Brooklyn as a whole. In ten northern cities in 1850, the proportion of African Americans ranged from a low of 1.46 percent in Boston to a high of 8.85 percent in Philadelphia. Among five southern cities, the proportion ranged from a low of 16.14 percent in Louisville, Kentucky, to a high of 53.44 percent in Charleston, South Carolina. Leonard Curry, "Table A-2 Percentage of Blacks in the Populations of Fifteen Cities, 1800–1850," in *The Free Black in Urban America, 1800–1850: The Shadow of a Dream* (Chicago: University of Chicago, 1981), 246. Advertisements for lost animals document horses and cows in Weeksville in the 1860s, and newspaper articles mention dogs, goats, chickens, and geese; C. R. C., "Wiping Out Crow Hill."

10. John H. French, *Historical and Statistical Gazetteer of New York State* (New York: R.P. Smith, 1860), 370: Henry Reed Stiles, *A History of the City of Brooklyn*, 3 vols. (Brooklyn, 1867–70; repr., Bowie, Md.: Heritage Books, 1993), 2:275–59.

11. [Kings County, New York] "Religious Corporations: Sept. 18, 1785, to Dec. 16, 1875," vol. 1, Ms. Kings County Clerk, Brooklyn, copy at Weeksville Society, in James G. Hurley, "Annotated Bibliography on Weeksville-Carrsville and Associated Topics in Brooklyn Black History" (August 1978), 9; *Weeksville: Then and Now*; Long Island Historical Society, *Black Churches and Brooklyn*, Ruth Ann Stewart, curator (Exhibit Catalog, 1984); Clarence Taylor, *The Black Churches of Brooklyn* (New York: Columbia University Press, 1996); Alexander W. Wayman, *My Recollections of African M.E. Ministers, or Forty Years' Experience in the African Methodist Episcopal Church* (Philadelphia, 1881), 35, docsouth.unc.edu. The first African American church in Brooklyn was Bridge St. African Wesleyan Methodist Church, founded in 1818 by seceders from the biracial Sands Street Methodist Episcopal Church. Its first building was on High Street in 1819. It moved to 309 Bridge Street in 1854, where it remained until 1938. The second was the African Society organized at Williamsburg in 1818. This later became Varick A.M.E. Zion Church, established sometime between 1827 and 1835 at the corner of South Third and Hooper Streets. Concord Baptist was established in 1847, the same year as A.M.E. Bethel, on Concord Street near Duffield. A third denomination came in 1849 with the Siloam Presbyterian Church on lower Fulton Street, started by Rev. James N. Gloucester. In 1852, Rev. Amos N. Freeman joined Gloucester at the church's

new home at 160 Prince Street, which became an Underground Railroad site. *Journal of the Macedonia African Methodist Episcopal Church*, May 1977, cited in Richard J. Hourahan, "African Americans in Flushing, New York: 1800 to 1860," in Wini Warren, ed., *Angels of Deliverance: The Underground Railroad in Queens, Long Island, and Beyond* (Flushing, N.Y.: Queens Historical Society, 1999), 45.

12. A. W. Wayman, *Cyclopedia of African Methodism* (Baltimore: Methodist Episcopal Book Depository, 1882), 13.

13. Dolores Jackson McCullough, "The Weeksville Story: An Independent Work Study Project" (City University of New York, 1971), listed names of early stewards and trustees as found in a program from Bethel Church, ca. 1920s; manuscript census, 1850. Information on Thomas comes from Wayman, *Cyclopedia of African Methodism*, 161; U.S. census, 1850; Francis P. Graham to Nathan C. B. Thomas, deed dated 1841, Kings County Clerk's Office; 1872 city directory, Ancestry.com.

14. Daniel A. Payne, *History of the African Methodist Episcopal Church* (Nashville, Tenn.: A.M.E. Sunday School Union, 1891), 128.

15. Information on George Hogarth comes from Wayman, *Cyclopedia of African Methodism*, 80, and Payne, *History of the African Methodist Episcopal Church*, 70, 95, 102, 112, 121–25, 131, 135, 142, 148, 166, 192–93, 201–3, 219.

16. Payne, *History of the African Methodist Episcopal Church*, 192–93.

17. George Hogarth, "Condition of Our People," 1845, in Payne, *History of the African Methodist Episcopal Church*, 193.

18. Payne, *History of the African Methodist Episcopal Church*, 253, 255.

19. The 1855 New York State census listed Morel's birthplace as South Carolina. The 1860 and 1865 censuses listed it as North Carolina. There is a Pembroke Hall, whose current building was constructed in 1850 and is still standing in Edenton, North Carolina. "Junius of Cedar Hill," *North Star*, May 19, 1854; C. Peter Ripley, ed., *The Black Abolitionist Papers IV* (Chapel Hill: University of North Carolina Press, 1991), 218–19; Julie Winch, ed., *The Elite of Our People, Joseph Willson's Sketches of Black Upper-Class Life in Antebellum Philadelphia* (University Park: Pennsylvania State University Press, 2000), 135–36.

20. Written in Brooklyn, May 3, 1854, printed in *North Star*, May 19, 1854.

21. *Colored American*, May 3, 1838.

22. Julie Winch, *A Gentleman of Color: The Life of James Forten* (New York: Oxford University Press, 2002) 295, 309; *Liberator*, July 2, 1836, quoted in Winch, *Gentleman of Color*, 306; *National Enquirer and Constitutional Advocate of Universal Liberty*, November 2, 1837, quoted in Winch, *Gentleman of Color*, 309.

23. Ripley, *Black Abolitionist Papers*, 218–19.

24. Elisha Weaver, "Our Eastern Tour," *Christian Recorder*, December 14, 1861.

25. *North Star*, January 25, 1850; Deed, James Carson Brevoort and Elizabeth Dorothea Brevoort to Junius C. Morel, November 15, 1855, liber 411, p. 417 (Brooklyn Clerk's Office); NYS manuscript census, 1865.

26. Junius C. Morel, *National Enquirer*, March 11, 1837, research.udmercy.edu/digital_collections/baa/Morel_01851spe.pdf.
27. *North Star*, April 17, 1851, noted that "James C. Morel" was the Brooklyn agent for the *North Star*; Weaver, "Our Eastern Tour"; C. W., "Heads of the Colored People, No. VI," *North Star*, February 18, 1853.
28. *Frederick Douglass' Paper*, December 23, 1853.
29. *Frederick Douglass' Paper*, September 4, 1851.
30. Ripley, *Black Abolitionist Papers*, 218–19; various references to "Junius" in Accessible Archives database of African American newspapers.
31. Obituary for Caroline Morel, *Colored American*, September 22, 1838; Ripley, *Black Abolitionist Papers*, 218–19.
32. *Christian Recorder*, March 1, 1862, December 14, 1861, June 18, 1864.
33. "Religious Corporations"; Swan, "Land Transactions and the Origins of Weeksville," note 33; *Little Church on the Hill* [booklet about Berean Church's history] (n.d.); manuscript census, 1850; manuscript census, 1840; Robert J. Swan, "The Origin of Black Bedford-Stuyvesant," in Charlene Claye Van Derzee, ed., *An Introduction to the Black Contribution to the Development of Brooklyn* (Brooklyn: New Muse Community Museum of Brooklyn, 1977).
34. *Little Church on the Hill*, 14.
35. U.S. census, 1850; deeds from Samuel Howard to Simon Bundick, March 18, 1854, and Horetta Horton to Simon Bundick, October 6, 1869, Kings County Clerk's Office.
36. *Brooklyn Eagle*, May 14, 1859.
37. Leonard Black, *The Life and Sufferings of Leonard Black, a Fugitive from Slavery* (New Bedford: Benjamin Lindsey, 1847), docsouth.unc.edu/neh/black/black.html.
38. *Little Church on the Hill*; "Table of New York Churches for 1855," *American Baptist Memorial: A Statistical, Biographical, and Historical Magazine* 15 (1856): 250, Google Books; Lain's City Directory, Ancestry.com; Concord Baptist Church of Christ, 66.221.209.158/history.php; William F. Johnson, "Trouble among the Colored People at Weeksville," *Brooklyn Eagle*, April 5, 1869.
39. *Little Church on the Hill*, 11, 12, 16–18.
40. Ibid., 17–19.
41. "Anniversary of the British West India Emancipation—Celebration in Brooklyn," *Brooklyn Eagle*, August 4, 1854; *North Star*, July 30, 1864. For celebrations after the Civil War, see *Brooklyn Eagle*, August 12, 1874, August 2, 1883, August 3, 1886.
42. Junius, *Christian Recorder*, January 31, 1863.
43. Nicole Thompson-Okeowo, "Notes on Church History" (typescript, Weeksville Society, July 19, 2002), 2.
44. *Little Church on the Hill*, 13; Nicole Thomson, "Information from Brooklyn Daily Eagle Almanac."
45. Long Island Historical Society, *Black Churches and Brooklyn*.
46. Ibid.

47. Ibid.
48. Robert J. Swan, "Synoptic History of Black Public Schools in Brooklyn," in Van Derzee, *Introduction to the Black Contribution*, 63; *North Star*, April 17, 1851.
49. Carleton Mabee, "Brooklyn's Black Public Schools: Why Did Blacks Have Unusual Control Over Them?," *Journal of Long Island History* 11 (1975): 23–38; Robert J. Swan, "Did Brooklyn (N.Y.) Blacks Have Unusual Control over Their Schools? Period I: 1815–1845," *Afro-Americans in New York Life and History* (July 1983): 25–46.
50. Swan, "Synoptic History of Black Public Schools in Brooklyn," 63; *North Star*, April 17, 1851; Swan, "Did Brooklyn Blacks Have Unusual Control,?," 35–36.
51. "Brooklyn Public Schools," *New York Times*, July 19, 1855.
52. Swan, "Synoptic History of Black Public Schools in Brooklyn," 63–64.
53. *North Star*, April 17, 1851, reprinted from *Anti-Slavery Standard*.
54. James D. Bilotta, "A Quantitative Approach to Buffalo's Black Population of 1860," *Afro-Americans in New York Life and History* (July 1988): 23.
55. Numbers of literate adults come from the 1850 U.S. census and 1865 New York State census.
56. Stiles, *History of the City of Brooklyn*, 3:633; Richard Sens-Castet, "Citizens' Union Cemetery" (paper, Afro-American Studies Program, 1972, copy at Weeksville Heritage Center), 1; Carolee Inskeep, *The Graveyard Shift: A Family Historian's Guide to New York City Cemeteries* (Nashville, Tenn.: Ancestry Publishing, 1998), 40.
57. H. J. S., "Miscalled 'Hunter Fly.'"
58. Book of Conveyances, cited in Sens-Castet, "Citizens' Union Cemetery," 2–3; *Brooklyn Daily Eagle*, August 26, 1872, cited in Sens-Castet, "Citizens' Union Cemetery," 3.
59. *New York Times*, July 22, 1911.
60. Sens-Castet, "Citizens' Union Cemetery," 6–8.
61. *New York Times*, July 22, 1911.
62. Craig Steven Wilder, "The Rise and Influence of the New York African Society for Mutual Relief, 1808–1865," *Afro-Americans in New York Life and History* 22 (July 1998).
63. Ann Boylan, "Antislavery Activity among African American Women," in Jean Fagan Yellin and John C. Van Horne, eds., *Abolitionist Sisterhood: Women's Political Culture in Antebellum America* (Ithaca, N.Y.: Cornell University Press, 1994), 126, and "Women and Politics in the Era before Seneca Falls," *Journal of the Early Republic* 10:3 (Autumn 1990): 363–82; Craig Wilder, in Nina Mjagkij, ed., *Organizing Black America: An Encyclopedia of African American Associations* (New York: Taylor and Francis, 2001), 450; Daniel Perlman, "Organizations of the Free Negro in New York City, 1800–1860," *Journal of Negro History* 56 (1971): 180–97; Constitution and By-Laws of the Abyssinian Benevolent Daughters of Esther Association, of the City of New York, adopted April 19, 1839 (New York: Zuille and Leonard, 1853).

64. *Frederick Douglass' Paper*, September 4, 1851.

65. *Frederick Douglass' Paper*, September 4, 1851.

66. *Brooklyn Eagle*, June 27, 1873. These picnic grounds may have been on the block bounded by Prospect and Park Places and Patchen and Howard Avenues, an area well known to Brooklyn residents; H. J. S., "Miscalled 'Hunter Fly.'"

67. "Letter from Jamaica, L.I.," *Weekly Anglo-African*, January 21, 1860; Schomburg, noted in Hurley, "Annotated Bibliography on Weeksville-Carrsville," 2–3. 1860; *Anglo-African*, January 21, 1860; "Doubleday: Baseball and Abe Lincoln," *New York Times*, December 15, 1975, quoted an aide to baseball commissioner Bowie Kuhn, stating that one of the first recorded baseball games involving blacks was between the Weeksville Unknowns and the Union Club of Williamsburgh, "former slaves living in Brooklyn," on September 28, 1860. Weeksville won, eleven to zero. Noted in Hurley, "Annotated Bibliography on Weeksville-Carrsville," 3, copy in Weeksville Society.

68. Sean Lahman, "A Brief History of Baseball: Part I: Origins of the Game" (Baseball Archive, December 1996), http://www.baseball1.com/bb-data/e-hist-1.html; "Female Ball Players," *Brooklyn Eagle*, July 23, 1889.

69. *Weekly Anglo-African*, December 19, 1860, noted in Hurley, "Annotated Bibliography on Weeksville-Carrsville," 2–3.

70. *Brooklyn Eagle*, April 9, 1846.

71. "The Brooklyn City and Kings County Record: A Budget of General Information" (Brooklyn, 1855), 200–202, quoted in Harold X. Connolly, *A Ghetto Grows in Brooklyn* (New York: New York University Press, 1977), 13–14.

72. John J. Zuile, "Report, Committee on Education," *North Star*, April 17, 1851.

73. *North Star*, October 24, 1850.

74. Ibid.

75. Ibid.

76. Ibid.

77. Maritcha Lyons, "Memories of Yesterdays: All of Which I Saw and Part of Which I Was: An Autobiography" (unpublished manuscript, ca. 1924, Brooklyn Historical Society and Schomberg Library), 26, 46.

78. William Still, *The Underground Railroad* (Philadelphia, 1872), 186; James W. C. Pennington, *The Fugitive Blacksmith; or, Events in the History of James W.C. Pennington*, 3rd ed. (repr., New York: Greenwood, 1971); Willis Hodges, *A Free Man of Color: The Autobiography of Willis Augustus Hodges* (repr., Nashville: University of Tennessee Press, 1982); Lyons, "Memories of Yesterdays," 26.

79. *Little Church on the Hill*.

80. Bilotta, "Quantitative Approach to Buffalo's Black Population"; James Horton, "Shades of Color: The Mulatto in Three Antebellum Northern Communities," in *Free People of Color: Inside the African American Community* (Washington, D.C.: Smithsonian Institution Press, 1993), 129–30; James Oliver Horton and Lois E. Horton, "Table 6: Nativity of Boston Blacks," in *Black Bostonians: Family Life and Community Struggle in the Antebellum North* (New York: Holmes & Meier, 1979), 7.

81. Curry, Table A-6: Nativities of Adult Free Persons of Color in Fifteen Cities in 1850 (by percentage), in *Free Black in Urban America*, 249.

82. Curry, *Free Black in Urban America*, 76–78; Adelaide M. Cromwell, "The Black Presence in the West End of Boston, 1800–1864," in Donald M. Jacobs, ed., *Courage and Conscience: Black and White Abolitionists in Boston* (Bloomington, Ind.: Boston Athenaeum, Indiana University Press, 1993), 155–67; Horton and Horton, *Black Bostonians*, 5; Kenneth L. Kusmer, *A Ghetto Takes Shape: Black Cleveland, 1870–1930* (Champaign: University of Illinois Press, 1976), 31, quoted in Horton and Horton, *Black Bostonians*, 5.

83. Curry, Table A-2 Percentage of Blacks in the Populations of Fifteen Cities, 1800–1850, in *Free Black in Urban America*, 246.

84. *Brooklyn Eagle*, September 27, 1851, July 17, 1854; "Crows of Crow Hill," *Brooklyn Eagle*, December 21, 1890.

85. *Brooklyn Eagle*, May 11, 1865; *Brooklyn Eagle*, July 6, 1863.

86. "Auction Sales," *Brooklyn Eagle*, June 13, 1853.

87. Eugene Armbruster, *The Eastern District of Brooklyn* (New York: G. Quattlander, 1912); Henry R. Stiles, ed., *Civil, Political, Professional and Ecclesiastical History and Commercial and Industrial Record of the County of Kings and the City of Brooklyn, N.Y. from 1683 to 1884*, vol. 2 (New York: W.W. Munsell, ca. 1870), 743–832a; *Brooklyn Eagle*, August 10, 1850.

88. *Brooklyn Eagle*, July 25, 1850, October 25, 1852, September 23, 1862; U.S. census records, 1855, 1860, 1865.

89. W. Jeffrey Bolster, *Black Jacks: African American Seamen in the Age of Sail* (Cambridge, Mass.: Harvard University Press, 1997).

90. "Police," *Brooklyn Eagle*, August 15, 1848; "Accident," *Brooklyn Eagle*, October 10, 1859, April 13, 1865; *Brooklyn Eagle*, November 25, 1864.

91. Roy Rosenzweig and Elizabeth Blackmar, *The Park and the People: A History of Central Park* (Ithaca, N.Y.: Cornell University Press, 1992), 70.

92. Brooklyn figures come from Curry, *Free Black in Urban America*, 267, 269.

93. If we include the total population of 245 people over the age of twenty-one (women as well as men), 17.1 percent owned property.

94. *Brooklyn Eagle*, April 9, 1846; deeds; Francis P. Graham's will, recorded June 13, 1862, recorded in deeds, Brooklyn Clerk's Office, liber 576, p. 371.

95. Deeds; 1855 New York State census.

96. The *Brooklyn Eagle* reported that Graham had left the proceeds of his estate to his nephew and sister, with the estate itself going to his lawyer, N. Bergasse La Bau. "The First Wife Seeking Her Dower in the Dead Prince's Lands," *Brooklyn Eagle*, February 26, 1872.

97. Sarah Graham, Francis P. Graham's first wife, sold a lot to Elizabeth Tompkins for $500 in 1875. This may have been the site of the Graham home. *Brooklyn Eagle*, January 4, 1875.

98. The U.S. census of 1850 listed both Sarah Graham and Francis P. Graham as "married within the year."

99. Payne, *History of the African Methodist Episcopal Church*, 184.
100. Widow and Heirs of Doxie Corprew to John McMurn, July 28, 1868, liber 839, 470, Kings County Clerk's Office; "Interview with John McMurn," *Brooklyn Eagle*, July 3, 1875.
101. Francis P. Graham's will, recorded June 13, 1862, in deeds, Brooklyn Clerk's Office, liber 576, p. 371.
102. H. J. S., "Miscalled 'Hunter Fly.'"
103. *Brooklyn Eagle*, April 9, 1846; manuscript census, 1850; index to deeds for block 1850, Brooklyn Clerk's Office; Deeds, Francis P. Graham to Charles Lewis, June 18, 1841, liber 96, p. 89; Francis P. Graham to Charles Lewis, June 2, 1844; *Brooklyn Eagle*, August 22, 1851; *Brooklyn Eagle*, April 9, 1846.
104. "Francis P. Graham," *Brooklyn Eagle*, February 3, 1844; "The People vs. Francis Graham," *Brooklyn Eagle*, February 11, 1844.
105. "A Much Married Minister," *Brooklyn Eagle*, January 19, 1872. James LeGrant was convicted of stealing $4.50 from "his mother." "Colored Ladies Quarrelling," *Brooklyn Eagle*, August 22, 1851. The *Eagle* noted coyly, "If we were permitted to tell tales we would say that Mrs. Graham is the lady whose husband accused her of receiving another gent. In his absence a few days ago; but as we wish to be close-minded, we avoid making mention of the circumstance."
106. "First Wife Seeking Her Dower."
107. Francis P. Graham's will, recorded June 13, 1862, in deeds, Brooklyn Clerk's Office, liber 576, p. 371; "Much Married Minister."
108. *American Genealogical-Biographical Index (AGBI)* (Provo, Utah: Ancestry.com Operations, 1999); *Dogget's New York City Directory for 1849–50* (New York: John Doggett, 1850); "Mrs. Susan E. Tilden" (Santa Clara County Biographies, California Genealogy & History Archives), http://www.rootsweb.ancestry.com/~cagha/index.htm; *New York Times*, October 30, 1856.
109. *Brooklyn Eagle*, December 8, 1854. This article noted that Alexander Martin, city surveyor, had filed a survey map for this property on June 23, 1843. This map has not yet been found. The exact location of this five-acre plot of land is not known, nor is it clear when it was sold and to whom. "The Will Case," *Brooklyn Eagle*, March 7, 1857. In December 1854, the sheriff advertised Graham's five-acre lot (bounded by Hunterfly Road on the south and land owned by Macomber on the east and Lefferts on the west) for sale. This was not sold at that time; "First Wife Seeking Her Dower."

NOTES TO CHAPTER 3

1. Martin Delany, *The Condition, Elevation, Emigration, and Destiny of the Colored People of the United States, Politically Considered* (1852), www.gutenberg.org/files/17154/17154-h/17154-h.htm.
2. U.S. census, 1860; A. M. Green, "Jottings by the Way," *Christian Recorder*, January 26, 1867.

3. There is some confusion in the census for 1860 between household number and family number. It is possible that J. C., Sarah, and Alice Morel actually lived with a family named Whrip, whose family number is the same as the Morel family number, even though their household number is different.

4. *Christian Recorder*, October 24, 1863.

5. *Christian Recorder*, November 14, 1863.

6. Eric Burin, *Slavery and the Peculiar Solution: A History of the American Colonization Society* (Gainesville: University Press of Florida, 2008); Allan Yarema, *The American Colonization Society: An Avenue to Freedom?* (Lanham, Md.: University Press of America, 2006).

7. For a discussion of parallel debates in Manhattan over colonization, see Leslie M. Alexander, *African or American? Black Identity and Political Activism in New York City, 1784–1861* (Champaign: University of Illinois Press, 2008), 149–53.

8. *Frederick Douglass' Paper*, December 25, 1851.

9. *Frederick Douglass' Paper*, December 25, 1851.

10. The letter was dated February 9, 1852, New York, and signed by John J. Zuille (printer), Philip A. Bell, James McCune Smith (minister), Jeremiah Powers, John T. Raymond, William Burnett, William J. Wilson (principal and journalist), T. Joiner White, Robert Hamilton, G. T. Downing, Ezekiel Dias, Junius C. Morel, and Thomas Downing (restaurant owner), the "Committee of Thirteen Appointed by the People," printed in *Frederick Douglass' Paper*, February 26, 1852.

11. "A Durable Momento: Portraits by Augustus Washington, African American Daguerreotypist" (National Portrait Gallery), www.npg.si.edu/exh/awash/awhart.htm.

12. Quoted in Jane Rhodes, *Mary Ann Shadd Cary: The Black Press and Protest in the Nineteenth Century* (Bloomington: Indiana University Press, 1999), 44; Helen Rappaport, "Mary Ann Shadd Cary," *Encyclopedia of Women Social Reformers* 1 (2001): 137–38.

13. *Provincial Freeman*, May 6, 1854.

14. *Provincial Freeman*, July 15, 1854.

15. "J.N.S.," *Provincial Freeman*, January 27, 1855.

16. Mary Jane Robinson, reprinted for the *Anti-Slavery Standard* in the *Provincial Freeman*, January 13, 1855. Thanks to Bryan and Shannon Prince of Buxton, Ontario, for first sharing this letter.

17. *Provincial Freeman*, January 13, 1855.

18. Manuscript census, 1850, transcribed by Theresa Ventura.

19. *Christian Recorder*, October 17, 1863.

20. For more on the African Civilization Society, see Joel A. Schor, *Henry Highland Garnet: A Voice of Black Radicalism in the Nineteenth Century* (Westport, Conn.: Greenwood, 1977), 150–74; Richard K. MacMaster, "Henry Highland Garnet and the African Civilization Society," *Journal of Presbyterian History* 48 (1970):

95–112; Carol Faulkner, "'A Proper Recognition of Our Manhood': The African Civilization Society and the Freedmen's Aid Movement," *Afro-Americans in York Life and History* 24:1 (2000).

21. James McCune Smith, "Henry Highland Garnet," in *Henry Highland Garnet, A Memorial Discourse* (Washington, D.C.: 1865); Henry Highland Garnet, "The Past and the Present Condition, and the Destiny, of the Colored Race," ed. Paul Royster (speech delivered January 10, 1848), DigitalCommons at the University of Nebraska–Lincoln.

22. "Henry Highland Garnet," in William J. Simmons, *Men of Mark: Eminent, Progressive, and Rising* (Cleveland, Ohio: George Rewell, 1887), 656–61. For more on Henry Highland Garnet, see Earl Ofari Hutchinson, *Let Your Motto Be Resistance: The Life and Thought of Henry Highland Garnet* (Boston: Beacon, 1972); Schor, *Henry Highland Garnet*; "Henry Highland Garnet," in Jack Rummel, *African-American Social Leaders and Activists* (Info Based Publishing, 2003), 79–80.

23. Simmons, *Men of Mark*, 1007–9.

24. Delany, *Condition, Elevation, Emigration, and Destiny*.

25. Ibid.

26. Simmons, *Men of Mark*.

27. "Meeting of the Friends of African Civilization in Brooklyn, April 8th, 1861," Constitution of the African Civilization Society (New Haven, Conn.: Thomas J. Stafford, 1861), 9, http://archive.org/details/constitutionofafooafri.

28. "Special Meeting of the African Civilization Society, November 4th, 1861" (New Haven, Conn.: Thomas J. Stafford, 1861), 2, http://archive.org/details/constitutionofafooafri.

29. *Christian Recorder*, May 30, 1863.

30. Ibid.

31. *Christian Recorder*, October 24, 1863.

32. Ibid.

33. *Christian Recorder*, January 2, 1864.

34. Ibid.

35. "Weeksville in Commotion Again," *Brooklyn Eagle*, March 26, 1869; *Christian Recorder*, January 9, 1864; Green, "Jottings by the Way."

36. Junius, *Christian Recorder*, June 30, 1864.

37. *Christian Recorder*, October 24, 1863.

38. Simmons, *Men of Mark*, 866–71; *Christian Recorder*, December 14, 1861, June 18, 1864; "Cain, Richard H. (1825–1887)," www.blackpast.org/?q=aah/cain-richard-h-1825-1887; Bruce A. Ragsdale and Joel D. Tresse, *Black Americans in Congress 1870–1989* (Washington, D.C.: U.S. Government Printing Office, 1990).

39. Kenneth L. Roff, "Brooklyn's Reaction to Black Suffrage in 1860," *Afro-Americans in New York Life and History* 2:1 (January 1978): 29.

40. Ibid., 36.

41. Junius, *Christian Recorder*, January 31, 1863.

42. Harry Bradshaw Matthews, *Voices from the Front Line: New York's African American Statesmen of the Underground Railroad Freedom Trail and the United States Colored Troops Organized in the Empire State, 1863–1865* (Oneonta, N.Y.: Hartwick College, 2000), 5–6; "Junius," *Christian Recorder*, July 30, 1864.

43. *Harper's Weekly*, February 13, 1864, 98.

44. "Junius," *Christian Recorder*, May 23, 1863.

45. "Brooklyn," *New York Sun*, [July 1963].

46. "Junius," *Christian Recorder*, July 25, 1863.

47. Ibid.; Barnet Schecter, *The Devil's Own Work: The Civil War Draft Riots and the Fight to Reconstruct America* (New York: Walker & Company, 2005) is the most recent detailed account of the draft riots.

48. "Junius," *Christian Recorder*, August 15, 1863.

49. Ibid.

50. Wm. W. Wickes and R. P. Buck, "Brooklyn, September 11, 1863, Report of the Committee of Merchants for the Relief of Colored People, Suffering from the Late Riots in the City of New York, July 1863" (New York: George A. Whitehorne, 1863).

51. C. R. C., "Wiping Out Crow Hill," *Brooklyn Eagle*, November 24, 1889; Adina Back and Francis Morrone, *Flatbush Neighborhood History Guide* (Brooklyn: Brooklyn Historical Society, 2008), 35.

52. Wickes and Buck, "Brooklyn, September 11, 1863, Report of the Committee of Merchants."

53. "Junius," *Christian Recorder*, September 12, 1863.

54. Simmons, *Men of Mark*, 1007.

55. Matthews, *Voices from the Front Line*, 6, 136; Janet B. Hewett, ed., *The Roster of Union Soldiers, 1861–1865: United States Colored Troops, M589-1–M589-98*, 2 vols. (Wilmington, N.C.: Broadfoot, 1997), noted three listings for Alfred Cornish, serving in the Fifty-Fourth, Seventh, and Fifty-Eighth Infantry units. Thanks to Harry Bradshaw Matthews for sharing his personal copy of this index with me.

56. "Junius," *Christian Recorder*, August 22, 1863; *New York Tribune*, August 3, 1863, quoted in Iver Bernstein, *The New York City Draft Riots: Their Significance for American Society and Politics in the Age of the Civil War* (New York: Oxford University Press, 1990), 66.

57. Harry Bradshaw Matthews, *Honoring New York's Forgotten Soldiers: African Americans of the Civil War* (Oneonta, N.Y.: Hartwick College, 1998), 3; Matthews, *Voices from the Front Line*, 129.

58. "Junius," *Christian Recorder*, December 12, 1863.

59. *Harper's Weekly*, March 19, 1864, 178.

60. Union League Club, Banquet, 56, cited in Bernstein, *New York City Draft Riots*, 67.

61. Matthews, *Voices from the Front Line*, 7–8, 112, 129, 136. Ages are estimates from those recorded in the 1865 New York State manuscript census.

62. Ibid., 6; "Junius," *Christian Recorder*, August 22, 1863; New York State manuscript census, 1865; Matthews, *Voices from the Front Line*, 5–6.

63. New York State manuscript census, 1865; *Dictionary of American Naval Fighting Ships*, www.history.navy.mil/danfs/g5/glaucus.htm.

64. The 1865 census noted army service of these Weeksville residents: James Weeks's naval service is documented in S. E. Koestline to Robert J. Swan, April 28, 1971, copy in Weeksville Heritage Center; the 1910 census noted Cornish's service in the army. This is probably an undercount of the actual number of Weeksville residents who had served in the Civil War, since many Weeksville enlistees most likely moved elsewhere after the war.

65. Ira Berlin, Joseph P. Reidy, and Leslie S. Rowland, eds., *Freedom's Soldiers: The Black Military Experience in the Civil War* (Cambridge: Cambridge University Press, 1998), 20.

66. David W. Blight, *Frederick Douglass' Civil War: Keeping Faith in Jubilee* (Baton Rouge: Louisiana State University Press, 1991), 147.

67. *Christian Recorder*, December 12, 1863. "When it is remembered that this society is composed of such men as Revs. D. Payne, Rev. H. H. Garnet, H. M. Wilson, R. H. Cain, Geo. W. Levere, Amos G. Beman, B. W. Wilkins, John Cary, D. W. Vandevere, John Peterson, Esq., J. C. Morrel, R. Delancy, M.D., Peter S. Porter, and many others, and endorsed by such friends of the colored race as Rev. Dr. S. H. Tyng, Rev. Dr. Potts, Rev. Dr. Bellows, and many of our tried friends,—directed by such leading minds as are presented,—men who are at the head of large and flourishing congregations of colored people—surely it commends itself to the confidence of all friends of the cause of liberty throughout the country."

68. Thomas H. C. Hinton, Washington, D.C., April 9, 1864, printed in the *Christian Recorder*, April 16, 1864. For more on Maria W. Stewart, see Marilyn Richardson, *Maria W. Stewart: America's First Black Woman Political Writer: Essays and Speeches* (Bloomington: Indiana University Press, 1987) and Eleanor Flexner, "Maria W. Miller Stewart," in Edward T. James, Janet Wilson James, and Paul S. Boyer, eds., *Notable American Women*, vol. 3 (Cambridge, Mass.: Belknap, 1971), 377–78.

69. Flexner, "Maria W. Stewart"; Richardson, *Maria W. Stewart*.

70. *Christian Recorder*, December 12, 1863.

71. *Freedman's Torchlight*, reprinted in *Freedmen's Schools and Textbooks*, vol. 3 (New York: AMS Press, 1980).

72. Ronald E. Butchart, "'We Best Can Instruct Our Own People': New York African Americans in the Freedmen's Schools, 1861–1875," *Afro-Americans in New York Life and History* 12:1 (January 1988): 27–49.

73. *Freedman's Torchlight*, reprinted in *Freedmen's Schools and Textbooks*, vol. 3 (New York: AMS Press, 1980); Green, "Jottings by the Way."

74. "The Troubles in Weeksville," *Brooklyn Eagle*, March 10, 1869; "The Colored Clergymen," *Brooklyn Eagle*, November 15, 1870; Deed, J. Carson Brevoort to George V. Brown, receiver of the African Civilization Society, June 1871, liber

1004, p. 503; Deed, George V. Brown, receiver of the African Civilization Society to John Flamer, July 1, 1871, liber 1004, p. 505. The *Brooklyn Eagle* accused managers of the African Civilization Society and the Howard Orphan Asylum of "The Weeksville Attempt at Bribery," *Brooklyn Eagle*, January 25, 1871.

75. "Henry Highland Garnet," in Simmons, *Men of Mark*, 660. Garnet's 1843 speech is available in Deirdre Mullane, ed., *Crossing the Danger Water: Three Hundred Years of African-American Writing* (New York: Doubleday, 1993); Darlene Clark Hine, *Black Women in America* (New York: Oxford University Press, 2005).

76. Simmons, *Men of Mark*, 620, docsouth.unc.edu/neh/simmons/ill42.html; *New York Age*, July 4, 1892; Carter G. Woodson, *The History of the Negro Church* (Washington, D.C.: Associated Publishers, ca. 1921), 243, docsouth.unc.edu/church/woodson/ill243.html; A. W. Pegues, *Our Baptist Ministers and Schools* (Springfield, Mass.: Willey and Company, 1892), 375–80, repeated material that originally appeared in Simmons, *Men of Mark*.

77. On November 7, 1871, the *Brooklyn Eagle* referred to "the National Monitor (of Weeksville)." Simmons, *Men of Mark*, 620; "The Colored People," *Brooklyn Eagle*, November 28, 1886.

78. U.S. census, 1880; "The Colored People.".

79. *The Cushite; or, The Children of Ham (the Negro Race) as Seen by the Ancient Historians and Poets* (1887; repr., New York: African Islamic, 1988); *The Cushite; or, The Descendants of Ham: As Found in the Sacred Scriptures and in the Writings of Ancient Historians and Poets from Noah to the Christian Era* (Springfield, Mass.: Willey and Company, 1893); Rufus L. Perry, "The Scriptures," in Edward M. Brawley, ed., *The Negro Baptist Pulpit: A Collection of Sermons and Papers on Baptist Doctrine and Missionary and Educational Work, by Colored Baptist Ministers* (Philadelphia: American Baptist Publication Society, 1890), 28–38. Thanks to the American Baptist Historical Society for their help.

80. "Rufus L. Perry, D.D., Ph.D.," *New York Age*, July 4, 1891; Simmons, *Men of Mark*, 620; "The Colored People."

81. Various issues of the *Brooklyn Eagle*; "Rufus L. Perry, D.D., Ph.D.," *New York Age*, July 4, 1891; Harold X. Connolly, *A Ghetto Grows in Brooklyn* (New York: New York University Press, 1977), 25; Simmons, *Men of Mark*, 620; Rufus L. Perry, Jr., *Man: Viewed from Science and the Talmud* (Brooklyn: R. Hamilton, 1916).

82. New York State census, 1865; "Philo," *Christian Recorder*, January 9, 1864.

83. New York State manuscript census, 1865.

84. W. Jeffrey Bolster, *Black Jacks: African American Seamen in the Age of Sail* (Cambridge, Mass.: Harvard University Press, 1997).

NOTES TO CHAPTER 4

1. "The Troubles in Weeksville," *Brooklyn Eagle*, March 10, 1869.

2. Hugh Davis, *"We Will Be Satisfied with Nothing Less": The African American Struggle for Equal Rights in the North during Reconstruction* (Ithaca, N.Y.: Cornell University Press, 2011), xiii, 2.

3. "Troubles in Weeksville."

4. "Index of the Register of Deaths in the City of Brooklyn, 1848–66," quoted in Dolores Jackson McCullough, "The Weeksville Story: An Independent Work Study Project" (City University of New York, 1971), 25; *Brooklyn Union Argus*, June 10, 1879, Ancestry.com; *Brooklyn Eagle*, November 8, 1871, noted Nathan Thomas's age.

5. "More Trouble, War in the Crow Hill Baptist Church," *Brooklyn Eagle*, July 22, 1874; "Crow Hill, The Berean Baptist Church in a Flurry of Excitement," *Brooklyn Eagle*, July 29, 1874; *Brooklyn Union Argus*, June 10, 1879, archiver. rootsweb.ancestry.com/th/read/NYBROOKLYN/2002-12/1041354576, reported on Bundick's will; Wilhelmena Rhodes Kelly, *Crown Heights and Weeksville* (Charleston, S.C.: Arcadia, 2009), 18.

6. U.S. census, 1880.

7. *Brooklyn Eagle*, December 31, 1902.

8. "What Will They Do with Their Hogs," *Brooklyn Eagle*, March 2, 1874, December 18, 1875, August 13, 1880, December 8, 1893, November 14, 1902.

9. *Brooklyn Eagle*, March 20, 1874, December 21, 1875; "Buried Alive," *Brooklyn Eagle*, March 29, 1876; "New Buildings," *Brooklyn Eagle*, September 24, 1884, December 19, 1884, December 18, 1885, September 20, 1889, November 23, 1893, November 3, 1896;

10. "National League," *Liberator*, December 23, 1864; "Appeal," *Christian Recorder*, December 24, 1864; "Richard Harvey Cain," History, Art, and Archives, U.S. House of Representatives, http://history.house.gov/People/Detail/10470.

11. J. H., "Letter from Albany, New York," *Christian Recorder*, April 1, 1865; "An Appeal: National Equal Rights Bureau," *Christian Recorder*, April 15, 1865.

12. "The Colored Voters and Booth, Roberts and Boggs," *Brooklyn Eagle*, November 2, 1865.

13. Davis, *"We Will Be Satisfied with Nothing Less,"* chap. 2, quote on "idealism and pragmatism," 63.

14. "Politics in Weeksville," *Brooklyn Eagle*, May 17, 1870.

15. *Brooklyn Eagle*, December 23, 1870, October 21, 1874, October 12, 1875; 1870 and 1880 U.S. census and city directories, 1870–77, as listed in Ancestry.com.

16. *New York Globe*, September 27, 1884.

17. "How They Live," *Brooklyn Eagle*, January 14, 1883.

18. Ibid.

19. Martha S. Jones, *All Bound Up Together: The Woman Question in African American Public Culture, 1830–1900* (Chapel Hill: University of North Carolina Press, 2007) outlined this development nationally for the nineteenth century. Deborah Gray White, *Too Heavy a Load: Black Women in Defense of Themselves, 1894–1994* (New York: Norton, 1999) discussed the story in the late nineteenth and early twentieth centuries.

20. Linda K. Kerber, *Women of the Republic: Intellect and Ideology in Revolutionary America* (Chapel Hill: University of North Carolina Press, 1980);

Linda K. Kerber, "The Republican Mother: Women and the Enlighten-ment—An American Perspective," in *Toward an Intellectual History of Women: Essays by Linda K. Kerber* (Chapel Hill: University of North Carolina Press, 1997).

21. Martin Delany, *The Condition, Elevation, Emigration, and Destiny of the Colored People of the United States, Politically Considered* (1852), www.gutenberg.org/files/17154/17154-h/17154-h.htm.

22. Carol Faulkner, "'A Proper Recognition of Our Manhood': The African Civilization Society and the Freedmen's Aid Movement," *Afro-Americans in York Life and History* 24:1 (2000).

23. R. H. Cain, *Christian Recorder*, January 7, 1865, quoted in ibid.

24. Jones, *All Bound Up Together*, 3; Maria W. Stewart, "Religion and the Pure Principles of Morality" (1833), reprinted in Marilyn Richardson, ed., *Maria W. Stewart: America's First Black Woman Political Writer: Essays and Speeches* (Bloomington: Indiana University Press, 1987), 28–42; Jarena Lee, "Life and Religious Experience of Jarena Lee, a Coloured Lady," in *Sisters of the Spirit: Three Black Women's Autobiographies of the Nineteenth Century*, ed. William L. Andrews (Bloomington: Indiana University Press, 1986), 25–48.

25. Jones, *All Bound Up Together*, 59–61.

26. Ibid., 102–4.

27. Ibid.

28. For a discussion of debates over school integration, see Davis, *"We Will Be Satisfied with Nothing Less,"* chap. 3.

29. *Brooklyn Eagle*, February 24, 1869; Carleton Mabee, *Black Education in New York State from Colonial to Modern Times* (Syracuse, N.Y.: Syracuse University Press, 1979), 86. Mabee noted that white and black children also attended school together in Rochester about the same time. In Syracuse, Edmonia Highgate graduated from a Syracuse public high school in the 1850s.

30. *Brooklyn Eagle*, March 3, 1869; Mabee, *Black Education*, 86.

31. *Brooklyn Eagle*, February 24, 1869; *Brooklyn City Directory* (1872), Ancestry.com.

32. *Brooklyn Eagle*, February 24, 1869, March 3, 1869, April 5, 1869.

33. *Brooklyn Eagle*, February 24, 1869.

34. Ibid.

35. Ibid.

36. Board of Education, "Troubles in Colored School No. 2," *Brooklyn Eagle*, March 3, 1869; "Weeksville in Commotion Again," *Brooklyn Eagle*, March 26, 1869.

37. Mary Ann G. Brown, "A History of the Colored Schools in Brooklyn during the 1800's" (typescript, Medgar Evers College, n.d.), 11, copy at the Weeksville Society.

38. "Trouble among the Darkies," *Brooklyn Eagle*, February 8, 1865. The paper published Bundick's entire letter, *"verbatim et literatum,"* they assured their readers. The letter was full of misspellings, and given the *Eagle*'s generally unsympathetic attitude toward African Americans, it is difficult to know how accurate this

transcript is. *National Monitor*, quoted in "Colored Public School," *Brooklyn Eagle*, July 28, 1873.

39. *New York Freeman*, September 25, 1886.

40. *New York Age*, August 8, 1891, October 10, 1891.

41. Mabee, *Black Education*, 201, 208, 211.

42. "The Color Line in the Public Schools," *Brooklyn Eagle*, June 11, 1883; "The Color Line," *Brooklyn Eagle*, June 21, 1883; "Color Line: Causing a Stir in the Eastern District," *Brooklyn Eagle*, February 25, 1884; "School Board and the Color Line," *Brooklyn Eagle*, March 20, 1890.

43. Carla Peterson, *Black Gotham: A Family History of African Americans in Nineteenth-Century New York City* (New Haven, Conn.: Yale University Press, 2011), 2–4 and elsewhere. Peterson's book focuses on the family surrounding Philip White and his father-in-law Philip Guignon. Rufus L. Perry, "Colored People Protest," *Brooklyn Eagle*, April 30, 1892; Mabee, *Black Education*, 224.

44. *New York Age*, August 8, 1891.

45. Albert S. Broussard, *African-American Odyssey: The Stewarts, 1853–1963* (Lawrence, Kansas: University Press of Kansas, 1998), 56.

46. Ibid., 64.

47. Various issues of the *Brooklyn Eagle*; Harold X. Connolly, *A Ghetto Grows in Brooklyn* (New York: New York University Press, 1977), 24; *New York Globe*, January 6, 1883; *New York Age*, July 27, 1889.

48. Mabee, *Black Education*, 152.

49. *New York Age*, October 25, 1890. The *New York Age* was the successor to the *New York Freeman*.

50. "Brooklyn School Matters," *New York Age*, October 10, 1891; "Brooklyn's New School Building," *New York Age*, October 24, 1891. For a history of the board's action in relation to this school, see "Mixed Schools," *Brooklyn Eagle*, May 4, 1892.

51. Mabee, *Black Education*, 221–22.

52. "Mixed Schools."

53. Mabee, *Black Education*, 223.

54. "Stewart's Little Plan," *Brooklyn Eagle*, August 16, 1892.

55. "Sims' Change of Heart," *Brooklyn Eagle*, March 6, 1893.

56. "The Gossip of the Town," *Brooklyn Eagle*, December 2, 1892; "To Consolidate Two Schools," *Brooklyn Eagle*, December 3, 1892.

57. "Last of the Color Line," *Brooklyn Eagle*, March 8, 1893.

58. Ibid.

59. "Public School No. 83," *Brooklyn Eagle*, June 19, 1893.

60. Mabee, *Black Education*, 225.

61. Ibid., 116.

62. Maritcha Lyons, "Memories of Yesterday, All of Which I Saw and Part of Which I Was: An Autobiography" (typescript, Schomberg Library, New York Public Library, ca. 1924), 29ff.

63. New York State census, 1892; U.S. census, 1900, 1910, 1920, Ancestry.com; Advertising card, "A. Lyons, Jr., Dealer in Teas, Coffees, and Spices, 51 St. Felix Street, Brooklyn, New York, All Orders Promptly Attended To," Schomberg Library, New York Public Library.

64. Lyons, "Memories of Yesterday"; Jessie Carney Smith, *Notable Black American Women* (Detroit, Mich.: Gale, 1996), 417–20, Google Books; Tonya Bolden, *Maritcha: A Nineteenth-Century American Girl* (New York: Harry N. Abrams, 2005); "Death of Albro Lyons," *New York Age*, January 9, 1896.

65. *New York* Age, January 2, 1929; *Brooklyn and Long Island News*, February 6, 1929.

66. Quoted in Jones, *All Bound Up Together*, 156. Jones discusses women's rights in black churches, 151–71.

67. *Brooklyn Eagle*, May 5, 1886, November 28, 1886, December 4, 1889, January 8, 1890, March 14, 1890, May 14, 1890, November 5, 1890.

68. "Brooklyn Literary Union," *Brooklyn Eagle*, May 8, 1890; "Brooklyn Literary Union," *Brooklyn Eagle*, September 8, 1886; "It Was Women's Night," *Brooklyn Eagle*, November 16, 1892.

69. C. R. C., "Wiping Out Crow Hill," *Brooklyn Eagle*, November 24, 1889.

70. For photos of many of these, see Kelly, *Crown Heights and Weeksville*.

71. "Howard Orphan Asylum," *New York Freeman*, November 14, 1891; "The Colored Clergymen," *Brooklyn Eagle*, November 15, 1870; "The Weeksville Attempt at Bribery," *Brooklyn Eagle*, January 25, 1871.

72. "Howard Orphan Asylum"; Gunja SenGupta, *From Slavery to Poverty* (New York: New York University Press, 2009), uses archival records from the Howard Orphanage and Industrial School to tell its story from a variety of perspectives, including those of children themselves, after this institution's move out of Weeksville.

73. U.S. manuscript census, 1870.

74. Ibid.

75. Carleton Mabee, "Charity in Travail: Two Orphan Asylums for Blacks," *New York History* 55 (1979): 55–77. For more on William F. Johnson, see ibid., 64–66; "Weeksville in Commotion Again."

76. "Little Colored Orphans," *New York Times*, July 22, 1894.

77. Mabee, "Charity in Travail," 64–65.

78. Ibid. Names of officers in the *New York Freeman*, May 29, 1886, October 11, 1890. For more on the New York City Asylum, see William Seraile, *Angels of Mercy: White Women and the History of New York's Colored Orphan Asylum* (New York: Fordham University Press, 2011).

79. "Brooklyn Notes," *New York Globe*, April 14, 1883, June 30, 1883, October 13, 1883, August 16, 1884.

80. *New York Globe*, October 18, 1884.

81. *New York Freeman*, May 29, 1886, July 14, 1886, September 19, 1891; "Little Colored Orphans."

82. *New York Freeman*, January 4, 1890, October 11, 1890.

83. *New York Globe*, August 16, 1884.

84. *New York Globe*, October 11, 1884; *New York Freeman*, November 24, 1888, July 13, 1889, July 27, 1889.

85. *New York Freeman*, July 27, 1889.

86. *Howard, Hand Book* (1899), quoted in Mabee, "Charity in Travail," 71; *New York Age*, February 25, 1909.

87. Phillips Verner Bradford and Harvey Blume, *Ota Benga: The Pygmy in the Zoo* (New York: St. Martin's, 1992).

88. *Brooklyn Daily Eagle*, March 19, 1911, quoted in Mabee, "Charity in Travail," 71; Howard, *Annual Report* (1910), 11–12, quoted in Mabee, "Charity in Travail," 72; "Howard Orphan Asylum"; "African American Medical Pioneers: Mary Eliza Mahoney," in *American Experience: Partners of the Heart*, http://www.pbs.org/wgbh/amex/partners/early/e_pioneers_mahoney.html.

89. Booker T. Washington to L. H. Wood, November 18, 1913, Wood Papers, quoted in Mabee, "Charity in Travail," 63. Thanks to Victoria Huver for helping to compile these names from articles in the *New York Globe* and *New York Age*.

90. *New York Age*, May 18, 1911.

91. "Zion's Home for the Aged," *Brooklyn Eagle*, April 30, 1875; "Home for the Aged," *Brooklyn Eagle*, June 29, 1877; "Little to Eat," *Brooklyn Eagle*, February 6, 1890.

92. "In Aid of the Zion Home," *Brooklyn Home*, June 2, 1887.

93. "Little to Eat."

94. Ibid.; "Can't Be Found," *Brooklyn Eagle*, February 7, 1890; "Affairs of Zion's Home," *Brooklyn Eagle*, February 9, 1890; "Zion Home," *Brooklyn Eagle*, February 23, 1890; "Trouble in Zion Home," *Brooklyn Eagle*, June 7, 1890.

95. Sue Buck, "A Brief History of the International Order of the King's Daughters and Sons" (International Order of the King's Daughters and Sons), www.iokds.org/history.html.

96. "For the Zion Home," *Brooklyn Eagle*, Mary 14, 1890; "Zion Home for the Aged," *Brooklyn Eagle*, December 12, 1890; "Women's Work in Behalf of Poor and Aged Negroes," *Brooklyn Eagle*, December 16, 1890.

97. "For Aged Colored People," *Brooklyn Eagle*, April 13, 1891; "For Aged Colored People," *Brooklyn Eagle*, April 18, 1891; "The Zion Home," *Brooklyn Eagle*, April 24, 1891.

98. "Brethren," *Brooklyn Eagle*, June 21, 1876; *New York Age*, April 25, 1891.

99. Joan Maynard and Gwen Cottman, *Weeksville Then & Now* (Brooklyn: Society for the Preservation of Weeksville and Bedford-Stuyvesant History, 1983), 23. Leslie L. Alexander, "Susan Smith McKinney, M.D., 1847–1918," *Journal of the National Medical Association* 67:2 (March 1975): 173–75, reported that Susan Smith was born "at the corner of Fulton Street and Buffalo Avenue in Brooklyn, New York. This area, now called Weeksville, was then a farm extending south from Fulton Street." Thanks to Judith Burgess-Abiodun for sharing her knowledge of Susan Smith McKinney-Steward.

100. For examples of some of these fund-raisers, see "In Aid of the Colored People's Home," *Brooklyn Eagle*, May 17, 1891; "For Aged Colored People" *Brooklyn Eagle*, June 5, 1891; "For Aged Colored People," *Brooklyn Eagle*, June 4, 1893; "Some Happy Old Folks," *Brooklyn Eagle*, November 5, 1893; "Autumn Donation Visit," *Brooklyn Eagle*, October 28, 1895; "Colored People's Home: Thanksgiving Donation Visit Arranged for Next Tuesday," *Brooklyn Eagle*, November 22, 1896; "For Aged Colored People: 'Hamlet & Co.' to Be Given at the Academy of Music," *Brooklyn Eagle*, April 23, 1897; "Colored People's New Home," *Brooklyn Eagle*, January 23, 1900.

101. "Colored People's New Home."

102. "Aunt Jane's 103rd Birthday," *Brooklyn Eagle*, May 8, 1896; "To Build a New Home for Old Colored People," *Brooklyn Eagle*, June 25, 1899; "Home for Colored People," *Brooklyn Eagle*, April 8, 1902.

103. "Born a Slave, Died Aged 94," *Brooklyn Eagle*, April 25, 1895.

104. "For Aged Colored People," *Brooklyn Eagle*, May 7, 1897; "For Aged Colored People," *Brooklyn Eagle*, January 25, 1900.

105. "To Build a New Home for Old Colored People."

106. "Aged Colored People's Home," *Brooklyn Eagle*, January 26, 1900.

107. "Lecture for Colored Home," *Brooklyn Eagle*, April 13, 1902; "Picnic for Home for the Aged," *Brooklyn Eagle*, July 3, 1902; "Fair for Colored Home," *Brooklyn Eagle*, November 23, 1902.

NOTES TO CHAPTER 5

1. "Crow Hill," *Brooklyn Eagle*, August 14, 1873; "Strolls upon Old Lines: Crow Hill and Some of Its Suggestions," *Brooklyn Eagle*, December 9, 1888.

2. H. J. S., "Miscalled 'Hunter Fly,'" *Brooklyn Eagle*, October 30, 1887; "Crow Hill," *Brooklyn Eagle*, July 29, 1874.

3. "The South Eastern Parkway," *Brooklyn Eagle*, October 6, 1869; *Brooklyn Eagle*, July 11, 1857, December 23, 1868.

4. Since Weeksville was not a separate census district, its population can be estimated only from the census (which does not list addresses before 1880) by counting people within the general boundaries of the cluster of African American families. As European Americans settled within these boundaries after 1850, it became more and more difficult to define the edges of the village, so these population figures are only rough estimates. In addition, two distinct areas are revealed in both the 1855 and 1865 census records (although not the 1850 and 1860 censuses). It is not clear whether that is a function of the route the census takers took, or whether it reveals the continuing presence of two parts of the settlement—the early Weeksville and Carrsville/Crow Hill. I have not counted the European American residents listed in the census in the pages between the two clusters of African American families in 1855 and 1865. *Census of the State of New York for 1867* (Albany: Charles Van Benthuysen, 1867).

5. "Crow Hill," *Brooklyn Eagle*, August 14, 1873; *Census of the State of New York for 1867*; *Twelfth Census of the United States: Population, Part II* (Washington, D.C.: Bureau of the Census, 1902); manuscript census, 1870.

6. "Crow Hill," *Brooklyn Eagle*, August 14, 1873; *Brooklyn Eagle*, July 30, 1873.

7. "South Eastern Parkway."

8. "Common Council," *Brooklyn Eagle*, February 21, 1867, June 23, 1868, May 1, 1869, August 14, 1873, August 18, 1873, December 30, 1874.

9. "Crow Hill," *Brooklyn Eagle*, August 14, 1873; "Strolls upon Old Lines"; "Sanborn Insurance Map," 1888; "Child Killed by a Cave In," *Brooklyn Eagle*, May 24, 1896.

10. "Crow Hill," *Brooklyn Eagle*, August 14, 1873.

11. "How They Live," *Brooklyn Eagle*, January 14, 1883.

12. Ibid.; *Brooklyn Eagle*, August 11, 1883.

13. "How They Live."

14. Ibid.

15. Ibid.

16. Quoted in Lynda Rose Day, *Making a Way to Freedom: A History of African Americans on Long Island* (Toronto: Empire State Books 1997), 74.

17. Ira Berlin, "Structure of the Free Negro Caste," *Journal of Social History* 9:3 (Spring 1976): 301. In the South, the situation was quite different, as Ira Berlin noted. There, free African Americans put their energies into economic advancement rather than into political action. In an exhaustive study, Loren Schweninger documented free black property ownership in the South and concluded that "in the fifteen southern states and the District of Columbia, approximately one of five free black heads of family owned at least some real property (total number 9,640) in 1860, while slightly more than two out of five whites did so. By 1870, approximately 11,000 Negroes had acquired at least $1,000 in real and/or personal holdings and another 157,000 (according to the sample) had managed to move out of the propertyless group. A total of 43,268 had become landowners. By 1910, a generation and a half after freedom, this had risen more than tenfold, with 426,449 Negroes in the South owning their own farms or homes (out of approximately 1,741,019 families) and others owning various tracts of rural land and undeveloped city lots." Loren Schweninger, *Black Property Owners in the South, 1790–1915* (Champaign: University of Illinois Press, 1990), 45; Jane H. Pease and William H. Pease, *They Who Would Be Free: Blacks' Search for Freedom, 1830–1861* (1974; repr., Champaign: University of Illinois Press, 1990), 299, 298.

18. Graham Russell Hodges, *Slavery and Freedom in the Rural North: African Americans in Monmouth County, New Jersey, 1665–1865* (Madison, Wis.: Madison House, 1997), 189, 191.

19. U.S. census, 1870.

20. Francis P. Graham's will, recorded in deeds, June 13, 1862, Brooklyn Clerk's Office, liber 576, p. 371; U.S. census, 1870; city directories, Ancestry.com.

21. Widow and Heirs of Doxie Corprew to John McMurn, July 28, 1868, liber 839, p. 470; Ancestry.com reported details about McMurn from IRS tax assessments, 1862–1918, city directories, 1870, 1874–75, and 1879–81; naturalization records, August 4, 1876; death records, 1880 federal census. "Interview with John McMurn," *Brooklyn Eagle*, July 3, 1875.

22. Lydia LeGrant, assessment records, in New York City Department of Records, Municipal Archives; U.S. census, 1880.

23. Designated as New York City landmarks, June 23, 1970, and July 21, 1970. "New York Preservation Archive Project," http://www.nypap.org/content/hunterfly-road-houses; Neil Larson, "Assessment of the Origins of the Double House on Hunterfly Road" (April 2004).

24. There were several Samuel Garrittsens who owned land in this area. One (August 8, 1763–September 11, 1799) married Elsie Lefferts Garrittsen (March 11, 1761–July 23, 1841), who would have been seventy-eight years old when this land was sold in 1839. A second Samuel Garrittsen (August 9, 1750–November 7, 1822) married Altea Rider in 1770 and inherited the Garrittsen tide mill. His grandson Samuel Garrittsen (1800–September 20, 1876) inherited the tide mill. It is not known which Samuel Garrittsen owned the land in what became Weeksville. "Gerrittsen's Mill" (Brooklyn Genealogy), www.bklyn-genealogy-info.com/Town/dutch/gerrit.html. Larson, "Assessment of the Origins," 5–7, argued that these were built as tenant houses.

25. "Real Estate," *Brooklyn Eagle*, February 22, 1845; "Sale of Brooklyn Real Estate," *Brooklyn Eagle*, May 15, 1863; *Reports from the Court of Claims Submitted to the House of Representatives (Cases Decided in the United State Court of Claims*, 3 vols. (Washington, D.C.: James B. Steedman, 1858), 1:21, Google Books; Edward Pessen, *Riches, Class, and Power : America before the Civil War* (New Brunswick, N.J.: Transaction Books, 1989), 51; Michael Egan, *Natural Protest: Essays on the History of American Environmentalism* (New York: Taylor and Francis, 2009), 43, 60; Jacob Judd, "Brooklyn's Health and Sanitation, 1834–55," *Long Island History* 7:1 (1967). From the 1840s until Bouton's death in 1862, the *Brooklyn Eagle* contains many references to Bouton's tax assessments and real estate dealings.

26. Population data from 1840 and 1850 federal manuscript censuses. Stephen Lash and Betty Ezequelle Associates for the New York City Landmarks Preservation Commission, "National Register Nomination. Houses on Hunterfly Road. 1698, 1700, 1702–1704, 1706–1708" (1972); Roselle Henn, "The Weeksville Historical Archaeological Research Project: A Progress Report and Proposal for Further Research" (New York: City College of New York, 1981), 14; Larson, "Assessment of the Origins," a report prepared on the basis of a charrette conducted at Weeksville in December 2003, with Neil Larson of Neil Larson Associates, Bernard Herman from the University of Delaware, Myron Stachiw from Roger Williams University in Rhode Island, and Tom Paske, from Westfield, Massachusetts, who had worked on the original restoration of Weeksville in the early

1980s. In addition, Clement Scantlebury, site supervisor for Weeksville, another original member of the restoration team, was also present, along with Kathleen LaFrank and Mark Peckham from the New York State Office of Parks, Recreation, and Historic Preservation.

27. Robert Swan, "Evaluation of a Prospective Research Project Concerning the Hunterfly Road House" (December 15, 1978), 5–8.

28. In 1980, Roselle Henn and William Askins of the City College of New York noted that the "earliest map on which they found 1702 Hunterfly Road dated to 1872." Much of the land behind the houses, they discovered, had been disturbed and filled in the 1870s. Of the more than thirty trash pits they excavated, they found material that dated "no earlier than the last quarter of the nineteenth century." William Askins reported that test excavations in the cellar of 1698 Bergen Street in 1980 revealed a bottle manufactured between 1857 and 1870, so that the house could be no older than that. William Askins, "Test Excavations in the Basements of 1698 Bergen Street, a House Owned by the Society for the Preservation of Weeksville and Bedford-Stuyvesant History" (New York: City College of New York, 1980); Wank, Adam, Slavin Architects (WASA), "The Hunterfly Houses of Weeksville Restoration Report" (2000); Joan H. Geismar, *Weeksville Master Plan EAS: Phase IA Archaeological Assessment of the Cultural Facility Site* (Brooklyn: Philip Habib & Associates, 2001), 13–17; Joan H. Geismar, "Archaeology at the Hunterfly Road Houses, 1978–1982 and 2000–2003, Brooklyn, New York" (2009), abstract.

29. "Sale of Brooklyn Real Estate."

30. *Brooklyn Eagle*, December 23, 1868, July 30, 1873.

31. Naturalization records, city directories, census records, and death records for Ferdinand F. Volckening and Gustav Volckening, as noted in Ancestry.com. *Brooklyn Eagle*, September 4, 1873.

32. These lots were marked on a "Map of the Property of the Late Samuel Bouton in the Ninth Ward of the City of Brooklyn Dated Brooklyn April 28, 1863," as noted in the deed. This map has never been found. Deed, John W. Hunter and Henry W. Conklin, executors of Samuel Bouton, to Ferdinand W. Volckening, May 14, 1863, liber ?, p. 350. Neil Larson, "Assessment of the Origins," 13, described Volckening's lots carefully: "In the deed, the parcel was defined as Lot 19 in Block 185, reflecting that the overlay of city plan had become official in eastern Brooklyn. This was an odd, irregular lot at the easterly end of the block with 75 ft. frontage on Wyckoff Street and mere 7½ ft. frontage on Bergen Street with Hunterfly Road cutting across its easterly side, for which Volckening paid $445. The deed described six lots. Three lots identified as nos. 41, 42 and 43 were 2500 sq. ft. in area, each with 25-foot frontages on Wyckoff Street. Lots nos. 2, 3 and 4 had been partitioned in the remaining Idaho-shaped space on the north side of the lot with frontages on Hunterfly Road, and the deed conveyed the portion of the road in front of the lots to the centerline to the grantee for access to them." *Brooklyn Eagle*, October 8, 1874.

33. Maps give inconsistent information about the number and location of houses actually located on Volckening's property at various times. The Hopkins map in 1880, the earliest map after the Dripps map of 1869, showed three houses in this cluster. That same year, G. W. Bromley's insurance map showed only two houses here. Bromley seems to have left off this map at least two houses known to be standing in the neighborhood just north of Hunterfly Road, however, so the accuracy of his map is questionable. The Robinson map of 1886 showed five buildings (including four houses and what may have been an outbuilding behind what is now 1702–04). The 1888 Sanborn map also showed five houses (including a small one behind what is now 1706–08). The Bromley map of 1893 continued to show five structures (most likely four houses and an outbuilding behind 1702–04). What is now 1706–08 may have been numbered 1237 St. Marks Avenue. WASA, "Master Plan" (2001); G. M. Hopkins, *Detailed Estate and Old Farm Line Atlas of the City of Brooklyn*, 6 vols. (New York: G.M. Hopkins, 1880), vol. 1, plate P; *Atlas of the Entire City of Brooklyn* (New York: G. W. Bromley, 1880), Plate 33.

34. Edward Chappell, "Draft Report, Hunterfly Road Houses, Bergen Street, Brooklyn, New York, Architectural Report" (November 2002); Deed, Augustus and Albertina Schelling to Ferdinand F. Volckening, December 18, 1883, liber ?, p. 341, noted in "Map of the Property of the Late Samuel Bouton in the Ninth Ward of the City of Brooklyn Dated Brooklyn April 28, 1863, as surveyed by Silas Ludlow, City Surveyor" (map not found).

35. Larson, "Assessment of the Origins"; *Brooklyn Eagle*, May 28, 1873.

36. Francis P. Graham's will, recorded June 13, 1862, in deeds, Brooklyn Clerk's Office, liber 576, p. 371. Francis Graham made out his will on February 3, 1852, and died a year later.

37. Deeds, N. Bergasse La Bau and Mary A. La Bau to Daniel H. McDonnell, June 13, 1862, liber 576, p. 384; James and Jane Moody to Patrick Heney, August 20, 1860, liber 535, p. 328; Widow and Heirs of Doxie Corprew to John McMurn, July 28, 1868, liber 839, p. 470; Nathan C. B. Thomas and Henrietta M. Thomas to Jane Smith, November 7, 1868, liber 855, p. 480; Widow of Francis P. Graham to David R. Brown, February 18, 1871, liber 983, p. 153; Widow of Francis P. Graham to John and Mary McGrand, July 1, 1871, liber 1004, p. 396; Widow of Francis P. Graham to Patrick Heney, September 1, 1871, liber 1012, p. 487; Widow of Francis P. Graham to Caroline R. Ritter, November 13, 1871, liber 1022, p. 285; Sarah Graham to John Flamer, October 23, 1872, liber 1073, p. 76.

38. James and Jane Moody to Patrick Heney, August 20, 1860, liber 535, p. 328; Widow and Heirs of Doxie Corprew to John McMurn, July 28, 1868, liber 839, p. 470; Nathan C. B. Thomas and Henrietta M. Thomas to Jane Smith, November 7, 1868, liber 855, p. 480; Widow of Francis P. Graham to David R. Brown, February 18, 1871, liber 983, p. 153; Widow of Francis P. Graham to John and Mary McGrand, July 1, 1871, liber 1004, p. 396; Widow of Francis P. Graham to Patrick Heney, September 1, 1871, liber 1012, p. 487; Widow of Francis P. Graham to

Caroline R. Ritter, November 13, 1871, liber 1022, p. 285; Sarah Graham to John Flamer, October 23, 1872, liber 1073, p. 76. *Brooklyn Eagle*, 1887; Sanborn Map, 1888.

39. *Brooklyn Eagle*, March 11, 1871. Property auctioned was described as "north-erly by woodland now of the heirs of Samuel Garrison, deceased, Leffert Lefferts and Michael Stryker, in several courses, thirty chains, forty-four and one-half links; easterly by woodland of Robert DeBevoise, one chain eighty-two links; southerly by woodland of said Robert DeBevoise, in several courses, twenty-nine chains, eightyoeight links, and westerly by woodland of Johnson Leake, containing four acres, three roods, four perches and sixteen one-hundredths of a perch, including a road running across the same, near the westerly end thereof, called the Hunter Fly road. Dated February 16, 1871." These names are listed on the Perris map of 1855 as owning woodlots east of Hunterfly Road.

40. "A Much Married Minister," *Brooklyn Eagle*, January 19, 1872; "The Case of Sarah Graham, Widow of Prince Graham," *New York Times*, February 25, 1872; "The First Wife Seeking Her Dower in the Dead Prince's Lands," *Brooklyn Eagle*, February 26, 1872; Sarah Graham to John Flamer, October 23, 1872, liber 1073, p. 76.

41. "Setting Up an Estate," *Brooklyn Eagle*, December 29, 1877.

42. For a 1923 photo of one of these houses, see Wilhelmina Kelly, *Bedford-Stuyvesant* (Arcadia Press), reprinted courtesy of New-York Historical Society in chapter 2. H. J. S., "Miscalled 'Hunter Fly.'" Problems with the validity of the deed to this property continued until 1911. On April 12, 1865, before final documents for selling the property to the Mount Pleasant Cemetery Association were complete, real estate investor Paul Pontau (Pontou) died, leaving his share in the cemetery property, one-tenth of the total, to his wife Nannette as executrix. All ten private owners, including Nanette Pontau, deeded the property to the Mount Pleasant Cemetery Association when it was officially incorporated on May 30, 1865. Nannette Pontau, however, failed to add the word "executrix" after her signature. When the property was sold again in 1870, Nannette Pontau had remarried and moved to South Carolina. Problems with her status as executrix confused the title until 1911, when the New York State legislature passed a special act to clear up conflicting demands. "Fifty Year Cloud of Titles Cleared," *New York Times*, July 22, 1911.

43. Census records, 1850, 1855; Francis P. Graham to Lydia A. E. Simmons, October 2, 1843; Lydia A. E. Simmons to Francis P. Graham, May 31, 1845.

44. Census records, 1850 and 1855; deeds for Graham's property.

45. Thanks to Ed Chappell, "Draft Report, Hunterfly Road Houses," for these measurements and for a discussion of when the rear wings were added.

46. Frederick Law Olmsted, *The Cotton Kingdom* (New York: Mason Brothers, 1861), 237–38, http://books.google.com/ebooks/reader?id=E-_cIo218rkC&printsec=frontcover&output=reader&pg=GBS.PA237.

47. Chappell, "Draft Report, Hunterfly Road Houses."

48. Olmsted, *Cotton Kingdom*.

49. U.S. census, 1870. Tracing probable Hunterfly Road residents from the 1870 census back and forth through city directories, Joan Geismar located possible residents of the current Hunterfly Road houses as early as 1865–67. This essay suggests, however, that these families actually lived farther south on Hunterfly Road, near the corner of Buffalo Avenue and Wyckoff Street. Geismar, *Weeksville Master Plan EAS*, 15–16; Geismar, "Archaeology at the Hunterfly Road Houses," 3, 7–10; NYS manuscript census, 1865. No one in this neighborhood was listed in this census. It is possible that the census taker simply skipped this whole area.

50. "Weeksville," *Brooklyn Eagle*, July 30, 1873. See H. J. S., "Miscalled 'Hunter Fly,'" for a discussion of Suydam's Pond.

51. City directories and U.S. manuscript census records, 1870 and 1880, Ancestry. com. "Declaration for Pension," May 23, 1912, by Alfred Cornish, 1698 Bergen Street, Brooklyn, National Archives and Records Service. Thanks to Patrick Schroeder for locating this.

NOTES TO CHAPTER 6

1. "Strolls upon Old Lines: Crow Hill and Some of Its Suggestions," *Brooklyn Eagle*, December 9, 1888.

2. "Real Estate. Growth of Brooklyn During the Last Ten Years," *Brooklyn Eagle*, February 27, 1884.

3. "Remarkable and Rapid Growth of East New York," *Brooklyn Eagle*, March 25, 1894.

4. "Lefferts Real Estate Auction, June 2, 1887," "An American Family Grows in Brooklyn: Developing Brooklyn" (Brooklyn Historical Society), www.brooklyn-history.org/exhibitions/lefferts/developing-brooklyn.

5. "Strolls upon Old Lines."

6. H. J. S., "Miscalled 'Hunter Fly,'" *Brooklyn Eagle*, October 30, 1887; U.S. census, 1880. It is tempting to assume that H. J. S. meant to say that four old houses "two of which are quite old," stood "northwest" instead of "northeast" of the corner of Buffalo and St. Marks. If so, these would have been the houses currently owned by the Weeksville Heritage Center.

7. H. J. S., "Miscalled 'Hunter Fly'"; U.S. census, 1880.

8. Matthew Dripps, *Map of the City of Brooklyn, Being the Former Cities of Brooklyn and Williamsburgh and the Town of Bushwick* (New York: Matthew Dripps, 1869); U.S. census, 1870.

9. H. J. S., "Miscalled 'Hunter Fly.'" The 1880 census for Hunterfly Road is confusing. The families listed on Hunterfly Road live farther north, close to Atlantic Avenue. More work needs to be done with this census to determine whether or not census records exist for the houses under consideration here. It is possible that earthmoving created such a disturbance in the area that the census taker ignored this neighborhood.

10. H. J. S., "Miscalled 'Hunter Fly.'"

11. "Strolls upon Old Lines."

12. C. R. C., "Wiping Out Crow Hill," *Brooklyn Eagle*, November 24, 1889; "Brooklyn Landmarks," *Brooklyn Eagle*, July 30, 1893.

13. "The Last of New York's Picturesque Squatters," *New York Herald*, September 29, 1912; "'Bob' Mitchell Means to Hold on to His Property," *Brooklyn Standard Union*, June 26, 1910.

14. "To Scare 'Night Doctors,'" *Brooklyn Eagle*, November 22, 1893.

15. Certificate no. 517313, Pension Records for Alfred Cornish, National Archives and Records Administration (found by Patrick Schroeder); U.S. manuscript census, 1900.

16. Because of the order in which the census taker listed these families, it is difficult to correlate them with the specific residences on Hunterfly Road. Although the seven families match the seven known rental properties, the census taker did not indicate which of these were in double-family houses and which in single-family dwellings. It is possible that the Johnson family, at 1 Hunterfly Road, lived in the current 1700 Bergen Street; the Burke and Holtz families, at 3 and 5 Hunterfly Road, lived at what is now 1702–04 Bergen Street; and the Mitchell and Bilelah families, at 7 and 9 Hunterfly Road, lived at what is now 1706–08 Bergen Street.

17. U.S. census, 1910; Joan H. Geismar, *Weeksville Master Plan EAS: Phase IA Archaeological Assessment of the Cultural Facility Site* (Brooklyn: Philip Habib & Associates, 2001), 17. As Roselle Henn has suggested in her research in the 1905 census and in city directories surrounding this census year, Alfred and Frances Cornish lived at 1698 Bergen Street from 1901 to 1907.

18. U.S. manuscript census, 1910. Photocopies for this census were very difficult to read, and some of the ages for the Johnson family may be off by a year or two.

19. Certificate no. 517313, Pension Records for Alfred Cornish.

20. Joan Maynard and Gwen Cottman, *Weeksville Then and Now* (Brooklyn: Society for the Preservation of Weeksville and Bedford-Stuyvesant History, 1983); Erin Donnelly, "The Social Role of Museums: A Look at the Society for the Preservation of Weeksville and Bedford-Stuyvesant History" (master's thesis, New York University, March 2003).

NOTES TO CHAPTER 7

1. "The newly completed Kingsborough Houses in Bedford-Stuyvesant, Brooklyn, circa 1941, showing the backyards of tenements much like the ones replaced by the housing project," neg. C-42, photo 02.005.010 (New York City Housing Authority, LaGuardia and Wagner Archives, LaGuardia Community College); "Kingsborough House, NYCHA Housing Developments" (New York City Housing Authority), http://www.nyc.gov/html/nycha/html/developments/bklynkingsboro.shtml.

2. New York City Housing Authority.

3. Wolfgang Saxon, "Joseph Haynes, 66, Found Old Black Settlement," *New York Times*, March 16, 1997; interview with James Hurley by Judith Wellman, November 13, 2012; notes from Weeksville Heritage Center on an interview with James Hurley and Dolores McCullough for StoryCorps, December 11, 2006; Marilyn Daley, "3 Uncover Forgotten History of the Negro," *New York Times*, May 27, 1968, in Weeksville Heritage Center; Joan Maynard and Gwen Cottman, *Weeksville Then and Now* (Brooklyn: Society for the Preservation of Weeksville and Bedford-Stuyvesant History, 1983) and Erin Donnelly, "The Social Role of Museums: A Look at the Society for the Preservation of Weeksville and Bedford-Stuyvesant History" (master's thesis, New York University, March 2003). James Hurley and Joseph Haynes remained close friends until Haynes's death in 1997. "He was such a wonderful guy," remembered Hurley. "He was like a guardian angel."

4. Hurley, interview by Wellman,; interview with James Hurley by Dolores McCullough for StoryCorps, December 11, 2006. Jim Hurley noted that many of these artifacts, including the Revolutionary-era cannonball, were later stolen.

5. Hurley, interview by Wellman; video of Barbara Jackson teaching children at P.S. 243, courtesy of Weeksville Heritage Center.

6. Hurley, interview by Wellman; Hurley, interview by McCullough.

7. Hurley, interview by Wellman.

8. "Weeksville Buys," *New York Times*, June 24, 1973; Douglas Martin, "Joan Maynard Dies at 77," *New York Times*, January 24, 2006.

9. Li/Saltzman Architects, http://www.lisaltzman.com/architecture/adaptive-use/2011/06/21/weeksville/.

10. Douglas Martin, "About New York: In Black History, Reconstruction Is Also a Struggle," *New York Times*, February 9, 1991; conversations with Joan Maynard and Clement Scantlebury, 2005.

11. Nathan Tempey, "Pamela Green, Executive Director of the Weeksville Heritage Center," *New York Times*, February 15, 2011; Nicole M. Christian, "In Brooklyn, Group Hopes to Save Freed Slaves' Homes," *Chicago Tribune*, November 11, 2001.

12. Nicole M. Christian, "In Brooklyn, Group Hopes to Save Freed Slaves' Homes," *New York Times*, October 29, 2001; *Chicago Tribune*, November 11, 2001; Kevin Plumberg, "Let's Make a Landmark—Bed Stuy's Weeksville Becomes a Tourist Attraction," *Brooklyn Rail*, October 1, 2003, http://brooklynrail.org/2003/10/local/lets-make-a-landmark-bed-stuys-weeksville-becomes-a-tourist-attraction; Anthony Ramirez, "Haven for Blacks in Civil War Riots Now Safeguards History," *New York Times*, June 5, 2005; Judith Wellman, Neil Larson, et al., "African American Life in Weeksville, New York, 1835–1910" (manuscript, Weeksville Heritage Center), with formal National Register nomination of the Hunterfly Road Historic District, based on this report, by Kathleen LaFrank, New York State Office of Parks, Recreation, and Historic Preservation, accepted by National Register on March 22, 2006.

13. Weeksville Press Release, "Mayor Bloomberg Announces Groundbreaking for New Education and Cultural Arts Building at Weeksville Heritage Center," June 4, 2008.

14. Sewall Chan, "Honoring Brooklyn's Role in Ending Slavery," *New York Times*, August 13, 2007; John Strausbaugh, "On the Trail of Brooklyn's Underground Railroad," *New York Times*, October 12, 2007; Linda Villarosa, "New Play Reveals Brooklyn's Slave-Owning Past," *New York Times*, April 26, 2012; Prithi Kanakamedala, "In Pursuit of Freedom" (manuscript, Brooklyn Historical Society).

15. Akira Barclay, "Weeksville Heritage Center Celebrates Brooklyn's Black History at 'Save the Memories of Self' Awards Benefit," *Black Gives Back: Chronicling African American Philanthropy* (June 27, 2013), http://www.blackgivesback.com/2013/06/weeksville-heritage-center-celebrates.html#.UpNuUY3EOeY; Akira Barclay, "Weeksville Visionaries Preserve the Legacy of Historic Site in Brooklyn," *Black Gives Back: Chronicling African American Philanthropy* (April 5, 2012), http://www.blackgivesback.com/2012/04/weeksville-visionaries-preserve-legacy.html#.UpNueY3EOeY; John Morris Dixon, "Weeksville Heritage Center," *Architect*, October 17, 2013; "Invitation to Weeksville Heritage Center Ribbon Cutting Ceremony" (December 11, 2013, Weeksville Heritage Center flyer).

16. Alexis Okeowo, "In Fast-Gentrifying Bed-Stuy, a Celebration of Early Black Settlers," *New York Times*, September 29, 2011; quote from Joan Maynard in Hon. Major R. Owens, in the House of Representatives, "Weeksville Preservation Project," *Congressional Record*, February 22, 1989, http://thomas.loc.gov/cgi-bin/query/z?r101:E22FE9-381.

INDEX

Abraham, James H., 122

Abrams, Hana S., 83

Abrams, Thomas, 122

Abyssinian Benevolent Daughters of Esther Association, 3, 52, 73, 74

Africa, 2, 4, 43, 44, 45, 50, 52, 55, 56, 86, 89, 91, 106, 107, 109, 110

African American newspapers, 7, 8, 31, 38, 60

African Civilization Society, 3, 4, 52, 61, 96, 100, 106, 107, 108, 109, 110, 111, 112, 113, 114, 125–27, 129, 131, 132, 135, 138, 142, 145, 149, 156, 167, 174, 237, 238

African Methodist Episcopal (A.M.E.) Church, 16, 17, 45, 50, 54, 55, 56, 61, 65, 105, 146, 177, 224

African Methodist Episcopal Zion Church, 105, 177

African Union Society, 68

African Wesleyan Methodist Church, 52, 53

African Woolman Benevolent Society, 14, 41, 67, 73

Africanus, Edward C., 53, 54, 56

agricultural industry, farm laborers, 21, 26, 83; garden produce, 24, 26; vegetables, 24, 26, 87

Albany, 17, 39, 40, 84, 95, 138, 141, 118, *after* 136 (Map 8), 197, 203

Alberti, George F., 56

Alexander, Leslie, 5, 29

Allen, John Q., 152

Almond, H., 150

American Anti-Slavery Society, 34, 59

American Colonization Society, 14, 44, 45, 61, 100, 106, 110; Anti-Colonization Meeting, 17, 46. *See also* colonization movement

American Moral Reform Society, 59

American Revolution (Revolutionary War): Long Island, 11, 18, 20–23, 28, 35, 36, 40, 78, 230; cannonball, 21, 230, 246n16

Anderson, Cornelius, 83

Anderson, Celinda and Matilda, 126

Anderson, Frank, 122

Anderson, John, 121

Anderson, Samuel, 1, 13–15, 29, 30, 47, *after* 136 (Map 6)

Anti-slavery: debates, 35; petitions, 34, 39, 40, 141

Automobile, 226–27

architectural evidence, 9, 10, 193, 194, 195, 201, 243n13, 243n15

archaeological research, 8, 243n13

archaeological work, 6, 8, 233; archaeological digs, 10, 197, 198; at New York City Community College, 8, 231

ABOUT THE AUTHOR

Judith Wellman, Professor Emerita from the State University of New York at Oswego, and Director of Historical New York Research Associates, specializes in historic sites relating to African Americans, women's rights, and the Underground Railroad. She lives in an 1830s house built by an African American miller on the banks of a mill pond, surrounded by good neighbors, friendly cats, one bossy but sweet dog, and unruly but delightful gardens.